MW00461843

◆ ◆ ◆

"This book—like its subject, the story of Taliesin—is multilayered, magical, and potent."
—Penny Billington, author of *The Path of Druidry* and editor of *Touchstone*

"If you are captivated by the exploration of Welsh and Celtic myth, Kristoffer Hughes's in-depth, scholarly work belongs on your bookshelf."
—Ellen Dugan, author of *Practical Protection Magick* and *Witches Tarot*

"In this book, Kris Hughes takes up his druid's staff and guides us through the winding paths of the tale of Taliesin with insight, learning, and inspiration so that we too may drink the magical brew in the cauldron of Cerridwen and emerge transformed."
—Anna Franklin, author of *The Sacred Circle Tarot*

"The story of Cerridwen and Taliesin can be heard from the bones of Britain itself. Kris acts as your guide through this seminal tale of the Island of the Mighty, a tale you won't just read, but will become a part of, with each turning of the page. Highly recommended."
—Damh the Bard, Pendragon of the Order of Bards, Ovates and Druids

from the

Cauldron Born

Photo © I. Gibbs

About the Author

Kristoffer Hughes (Wales) is chief of the Anglesey Druid Order, a Mount Haemus scholar, and a member of the Order of Bards, Ovates and Druids. He is a teacher, writer, workshop leader, and guest speaker at Pagan conferences, camps, and festivals throughout the United Kingdom and Europe. Hughes has also contributed to Welsh and English television and radio. Videos, soundbytes, and contact information for the author can be found here:

WWW.ANGLESEYDRUIDORDER.CO.UK

Kristoffer Hughes

from the

Cauldron
Born

Exploring the Magic
of Welsh Legend & Lore

Llewellyn Publications
Woodbury, Minnesota

From the Cauldron Born: Exploring the Magic of Welsh Legend & Lore © 2012 by Kristoffer Hughes. All rights reserved. No part of this book may be used or reproduced in any manner whatsoever, including Internet usage, without written permission from Llewellyn Publications, except in the case of brief quotations embodied in critical articles and reviews.

FIRST EDITION
Second Printing, 2014

Author photo by I. Gibbs
Book design by Rebecca Zins
Cover design by Adrienne Zimiga
Cover illustration by John Blumen
(cauldron: aldegonde/Shutterstock.com;
landscape: gillmar/Shutterstock.com)
Interior illustration from *Celtic Designs CD-ROM and Book* (Dover Publications, 1997)

Llewellyn Publications is a registered trademark of Llewellyn Worldwide Ltd.

Library of Congress Cataloging-in-Publication Data
Hughes, Kristoffer, 1971–
   From the cauldron born : exploring the magic of Welsh legend & lore / Kristoffer Hughes.—1st ed.
      p. cm.
   Includes bibliographical references (p.   ) and index.
   ISBN 978-0-7387-3349-4
   1. Wales—Religion. 2. Taliesin. 3. Mythology, Celtic. 4. Folklore—Wales. I. Title.
   BL980.G7H84 2012
   299′.166—dc23
                                    2012029849

Llewellyn Worldwide Ltd. does not participate in, endorse, or have any authority or responsibility concerning private business transactions between our authors and the public.
   All mail addressed to the author is forwarded, but the publisher cannot, unless specifically instructed by the author, give out an address or phone number.
   Any Internet references contained in this work are current at publication time, but the publisher cannot guarantee that a specific location will continue to be maintained. Please refer to the publisher's website for links to authors' websites and other sources.

Llewellyn Publications
A Division of Llewellyn Worldwide Ltd.
2143 Wooddale Drive
Woodbury, MN 55125-2989
www.llewellyn.com
Printed in the United States of America

This book is dedicated to my mum, Gillian: 100,000 words
cannot express my gratitude or love. This book exists because of you.
Diolch am cyr fy nghalon, am y bywyd y rhoddest ti i fi,
Dwi'n dy garu di mwy na gall eiriau ddisgrifio.
C

Contents

Acknowledgments

My initial thanks go to Damh the Bard and Cerri Lee for asking me to speak about this subject at one of their camps. Subsequently I got to spend a weekend with Cerri and the Cauldron Ladies at the banks of Lake Tegid, where we immersed ourselves in the tale. Your enthusiasm, passion, devotion, and commitment to this material served as the inspiration for this book, and I thank you all so much for including me in your magic.

Chris Hickman has been a gift from the gods, with tips and advice and being quick to respond when a mad author on the verge of losing the plot screams for help from the shadows! Thank you for your words, wisdom, insights, and help. Thanks to Sue Hickman and her steadfast friendship and help; you may be quiet, but you still pack a punch. Barrie and Kristal Jenks have been the most steadfast of friends, and their encouragement and belief moves me deeply; thank you for everything you do and also for running to the rescue—Barrie's ability to conjure rescue methods are quite astonishing. Michelle Axe also came to my aid with tips and advice, with her broom ever at the ready; thank you for your wisdom and enthusiasm. Ian Gibbs has been a rock throughout the entire project, particularly when the fronds of my sanity wore thin and my confidence failed. Having Cerridwen and her clan constantly around the house is quite a challenge for even the most adept magician, and he has taken it all in stride; thank you. To Mark Doody, who is the finest Muggle I have ever had the pleasure to know: although this stuff is practically French to you, you have never wavered in your belief in me; thank you for your constant encouragement and for being my friend. Thanks to Chris Hurst for her invaluable inspiration in relation to the shadow; your words and insights are a joy to behold.

Angela Grant, my contact into the dusty world of libraries and Celtic studies, has been a font of wisdom and knowledge. Thank you for humouring me and answering what must, at times, have been the most frustrating of queries. You have been a gift from the gods.

My sincerest thanks to the hard-working, attentive, and patient team at Llewellyn Publications who have welcomed me into the family with open arms. Thank you for everything that you do; I am indebted to you all.

Last, but by no means least, my thanks and gratitude to the witch goddess and the prophet Taliesin, whose material and legend bring to my life the most joy and meaning.

Introduction

The purpose of this book is to share my own personal connection and experience of the most mysterious, profound, and transformative tale to arise from Celtic Wales. It concerns the adventures of an innocent young boy who is transformed into an all-seeing prophet by a witch's magic, and the mysteries therein. The subjects of the tale—namely, Cerridwen, Gwion Bach, and Taliesin—have had a profound impact on my life and my spiritual explorations. I aim to share some of my discoveries with you here. Enough has been said academically concerning this tale, and this book will differ from the traditional scholarly explorations. Linguistic and cultural significance and developments of the Celtic tales are of great interest to me, but I write this book from a deep, soul-filled love of the allegories and of the practical application of the mysteries and their ability to enlighten the spirit and inspire the heart. I have attempted to bridge the gap between the world of academia and the realm of the visionary to present a work that is based on sources both scholarly and of the spirit.

Here I will examine the historical significance of the tale and how it fits into the landscape of Wales. I do this to provide a background to the story in the hope that the reader may sense its place and feel its homeland through these words. Previous works on the subject have included references and explorations of cognate material from the Irish mythological sagas and other European sources. This present work does not make reference to other cycles of myth to substantiate the material at hand or to provide references for related themes. I have attempted, as much as possible, to explore it entirely within the Welsh Celtic system. My intention is not to dismiss the neighbouring mythologies—on the contrary, they are of deep value to those lands and traditions—alas, my connection to them is limited, and I fear that any dissection or comparison would be superficial on my part.

The initial concept for this book followed a vision and an intense working with the archetypes of the tale of Cerridwen and Taliesin. After years of devotion to these archetypes, I realised that there is no single book that deals entirely with the subject matter and examines its content. There are several books that deal with the tale to a lesser extent or refer to the archetypes within it, but as yet there is very little in one edition that deals entirely with the themes of this magical, ancient tale. After years of moaning that there was nothing available that I could reach and delve into, all contained between two soft paperbacks, I concluded that the only option left to me was to write it myself! The resulting effort you now hold in your hands—or, in our ever-increasing technological age, gazes at you from the screen of an electronic device.

This book is split in to three sections. In the first part, you will find a general exploration of the tale—where it came from, how it arose, how it survived, and in what way it is relevant to our lives today. The second section contains three versions of the tales, two of which are traditional and translated from the manuscripts that have survived the ages, and one written entirely by me. The third section contains a dissection of the individual characters/archetypes and components of the tale—what they represent, how they engage with the mysteries, and how we ourselves interact with them. Finally, a year-long ritual will be presented to you for your own perusal, providing you with an opportunity to explore the allegories in a more practical, transformative manner over a year and a day. Subsequent rites are also included.

Land of My Fathers

The Celtic nations are abundant with tales of magic, transformation, and deep mystery. They sing of ages past and of an older, deeper magic; they are infuriatingly difficult to understand yet delightfully beautiful and simple. As a consequence, the tales and legends can seem nonsensical and contradictory, but fear not: there are tools and methods for exploring them in such a way that opens the spirit to their understanding. The legends and tales of these lands weave a magic that stitches and captures mystery and connection; they are capable of reaching through the mists of time to affect the here and now.

My attraction to Paganism was, I feel, inevitable, but being raised in a predominantly Christian society wasn't an encouraging or a nurturing environment to enable a child to explore the Pagan mysteries. I was drawn to mystery from an early age and perhaps was always a little different from my peers. Christianity seemed the only course of action, yet somehow it did not convey to my spirit the sense of deep awe, wonder, and excitement my being would encounter when confronted with the gods of my land, the old tales and the various archetypes that sing from pages and lips. I wanted to be a part of that, but alas—no textbook or handbook, no tome of instruction existed to inform me of what to do, how to do it, or where to explore something that at that time I could not adequately articulate. What could be done? Fortunately, the old gods and archetypes of the land and of the people were there; I needed only to trust, to let go of the hows, wheres, and what ifs and launch myself into the exploration of what had always tweaked the harp strings of my heart and the fronds of my spirit.

I quickly discovered that I was not alone in my quandary; at the time, so many others around me were struggling to make sense of a need that arose from the shadows of their spirits. With no teachers and very few books on the subject, we had only the remnants of mystery hidden within our native tales and legends. Years of tumultuous growth and the ever-present storm of early adolescence acted as a distraction from the searching, yet something remained constant—some deep urge to know more, to sense more, to connect to something, whatever that something was. In actuality, I needn't have feared or worried, for in time that connection would happen of its own accord. I firmly believe that it was there all the while, waiting to be discovered—to be unlocked from the confusion of adolescence. The spirits of the land of my fathers would arise to guide me.

Growing Pains

It was the prophet Taliesin that came to me, that ever-present spirit of my people's connection to the land and to the mystery of being. I recall a time when I suffered terribly with sinusitis; around the age of thirteen, the condition would begin as a dull throbbing between my eyes, rising to an intense scream that caused my eyes to stream with tears, my lungs to gasp with pain. I would writhe on the bed, unable to focus, lost in the storm of agony. I would see things that were not necessarily there—creatures would run about the walls, and teary eyes would avert themselves from the terror that would consume me if I focused upon them. And then, one pain-filled afternoon, I observed a person sitting at the bottom of the bed. It watched me closely, this peculiar androgynous individual, a subtle smile upon its face; it seemed neither man nor woman, adult nor child, but something betwixt and between.

I was crying, wanting my grandmother and the magical quality that grandmas have to make things seem altogether better. I vaguely recall asking the person for its name; whether I vocalised the query or not I forget, but in response its smile broadened, and from between its eyes, in the very spot where my pain was at its most intense, a spark arose. I can see it still, a tiny bright blue spark, almost like the pilot light of a gas burner. The light consumed the skin on its forehead and somehow fell in on itself, as if penetrating the cranium; like a fire of no earthly source, blue lights leaped and danced around the abyss that appeared in its head. The creature smiled ever greatly, a reassuring smile that all was okay, that I was not to fear. In a flash the light erupted from its forehead and beamed into the room, blinding me momentarily, and yet through the dazzle I could still see the serene countenance of its facial features. Its mouth opened, and I heard the words "You know who I am; I am Taliesin," the words echoing in my pain-filled head, not received through my auditory senses but somehow arriving in my mind. The chemical messengers from the pain relief in my system suddenly got to work; the harsh edge of pain subsided, and I felt sleepy and comforted, my eyes heavy, and the light at the bottom of the bed faded. There was nobody

there; only the whirring of the washing machine downstairs tickled my consciousness. I dreamed of a cauldron, of animals and fish, of an intimidating
lady in grey with a basket full of plants and berries.

My descent into the painful world of sinusitis would last two or three
days; recovery was always rapid, the sudden release from the pressure in
those strange empty spaces within our skulls. The vision of the person at
the bottom of the bed simply sank into the recesses of my mind; I gave it
little thought until a couple weeks later, when I discovered an illustrated
copy of the *Tale of Taliesin* under the bed. I had always loved this book, the
black-and-white line drawings evoking a magic from the pages; I must have
been reading it just before I was debilitated by pain. Years later, the haunting
qualities of that vision or hallucination would inspire me to seek the mystery between the words of Taliesin's tale, to uncover the hidden meaning in
the themes and the mystery that it attempts to convey. I would turn twenty
years old by the time the tales would affect me again, having gone through
the turmoils of adolescence and waiting for the hormonal maelstrom to settle. I was inspired to seek out the archetypes and mysteries that my ancestors
had secreted in the seemingly innocent tales and legends of my people.

In one of my favourite secondhand bookshops in the coastal town of
Caergybi on the island of Anglesey, I discovered a book by the Celtic scholar
John Morris-Jones. It wasn't necessarily something I would have been at all
interested in, but something within it tickled my curiosity, so I parted with
a pound or two and took it home. A certain quote from it caused my heart
to quicken:

> Quite enough has been said to show that these poems and tales,
> which were mist and mystery to those who would look at them
> through glass, become clear when focused at from a distance, and
> the mists and most of the mystery vanishes.[1]

Somehow things *did* become clearer; a sense of direction and clarity
descended upon me, and I read and reread that paragraph over and over
again. Finally I realised that these tales and legends were never meant to be

---

1   Morris-Jones, *Taliesin*, 253.

read, for one would only end up scratching one's head in bafflement; they were to be experienced, to be immersed within. What were initially created to be conveyed and transmitted from the lips of the bards had become stagnant in the written form, reliquaries of dry ink on parchment. That this act preserved the magic cannot be disputed, but it also acted as a curse, for once something is written, it cannot easily be changed without criticism or objection; it becomes an article for evisceration, a mystery of linguistics and the beauty of language and its development and evolution. Yet the key to their understanding lies not in the words but in the spaces between them, in the blank lines and the potential void betwixt the sentences of ink. I had to proceed with no instruction other than the inherent need to explore and connect with the mysteries that my ancestors had bequeathed. And so I began with the tale of Taliesin and the magical cauldron of inspiration and transformation that lies at the heart of the Celtic Pagan and Druidic traditions.

◆ ◆ ◆

Ultimately, this is a personal journey; while it is my journey, over the years I have noted that my experience shares a commonality with others who have sought out the mysteries. My development and exploration of the Celtic material ultimately led me to becoming the head of the Anglesey Druid Order and a student of the Order of Bards, Ovates and Druids, whose community encourages the sharing of mystery. As a result I embarked upon this journey of putting fingers to laptop to share with you, the reader, my journey into the cauldron of the witch goddess Cerridwen. I do this in the hope that some of these words or the description of my own journey will inspire you to seek out the magic of the cauldron and invoke the radiant brow by igniting the fire in your head—a fire of wonder, of magic, of inspiration, of awe and music and poetry.

But I'm Not Welsh!

Does it haunt you at night, wondering how one connects with an archetype from the other side of the planet? Not an uncommon ailment, I can assure you; but fear not, it is not grounded in anything concrete and should not affect your ability to connect to the mystery of the tales. The Welsh people of the Middle Ages served to preserve these tales; the truth of the matter is that they are significantly older than the political delineation of the nation of Wales. They are not entirely the property of the Welsh but belong to the islands of Britain and to anyone who connects to them, regardless of one's position on the planet. The tales arose from the landscape of Britain and were relevant to the inhabitants of these lands then as they are now, but the mysteries contained within them cannot be confined to location. The origins of the tales' creation may well be locality-specific, but the mysteries they contain are soul-specific—they apply to anyone, anywhere, and any seeker who wishes to reach into the cauldron of the great witch goddess and discover its secrets may do so.

Whether you are on the south coast of Britain, sitting in the sunshine of Los Angeles, or stomping through the snows of northern Sweden, the magic within the tales of the Celtic people does apply; they are relevant. The themes within them can be superimposed onto your own landscape.

Connecting

There is no right or wrong way to connect to the themes within this tale, but what you can be assured of is that it is a journey that will profoundly affect your life and connect you to an ancient mystery that provides tried and tested keys to the spirit. Its primary function is to connect the querent by means of the cauldron to the most sacred and all-encompassing spirit of Celtica, Awen. This awe-inspiring flowing spirit beats at the heart of the Celtic tradition; it sings a song that was old when the world was new, and it brings body and soul into ecstatic rapture. Inexorably connected, the cauldron and Awen entice you into mystery.

You hold a book in your hand that is an account of connection; it is based in the real world of one person in particular: me. My intention for writing this book was to offer a guide, a lending hand, that can brush aside some of the confusing aspects and misconceptions that we may have established in relation to these tales. Nearly two decades of working with the mysteries of Cerridwen's cauldron have gone into this book; hopefully that will stand you in good stead to explore the mysteries for yourself.

We can be guided to a certain understanding of the tales, led by the hand of those who do know and have swum with the mysteries. However, the voyage of exploration and ultimately initiation is by its very nature a solitary, individual journey. Some humans can be fickle; some will want to be led, to be told, to have it served on a plate. Alas, that method is ineffective—we must approach the cauldron of inspiration ourselves, boil the broth ourselves, be burnt and subsequently ingest the divine drops of Awen ourselves—no one can do it for us.

The cauldrons of Celtic mythology will not boil the food of a coward; the same applies for the cauldron at the centre of this book. A degree of bravery, of stamina, is required to approach the cauldrons of Celtica; they are not to be messed with but should be handled with integrity, foresight, and good intention. To stagger up to the cauldron with much bravado and cast all and sundry into it would be foolhardy; it may boil too quickly, and what may rise from its steam may be a little more than we bargained for. So approach cautiously, having prepared well for the journey ahead, with reverence and respect for the antiquity and heritage of the cauldron and what it stands for.

How to Use This Book

This book is primarily a guide—a friendly hand that takes you on a journey to approach the cauldron. Its primary purpose is to inform and provide insight into the deep magic of the Celtic mysteries. It also serves to educate. Begin by reading the entire book from cover to cover to ensure that you are deeply familiar with the tale—its archetypes, components, and their meaning. You will find various exercises throughout the book; some are contemplative, whilst others require a physical ritual, journey, or action. There is a crossover aspect to the archetypes where one may share attributes with another; this is quite normal and essential to the unfolding act of transformation. However, as a consequence, you will find that the interpretation of one character may affect another, and that some themes may be repeated to a small extent. I have attempted to separate the archetypes as much as is humanly possible; this is a difficult task, for they are not entirely meant to be studied alone. The interplay between the characters and components is essential to the tale, and the crossover point between one character's influence and another's is not always clear.

As you use this book, bear in mind the limitations of the written word; after all, this tale was a product of the oral tradition. This book is not intended to be an academic tome; its purpose is largely visionary. As you use it, I suggest that you utilise your own subtle senses, and meditate on the themes as you encounter them. Take time to digest the information, and above all, don't just take my word for it—encounter the witch goddess and the prophet yourself, for that is my ultimate intention: to introduce you to the heart of Celtic magic.

A Practical Note

I suggest that during the course of your journey through this book and into the themes it contains that you create a space in honour of it. By all means use your current altar, a half-empty shelf on a bookcase, or a little corner of your living room.

This journey is steeped in ancestry and ancestral wisdom; therefore, have photographs of loved ones who have died and pictures or illustrations indicative of your lineage and ancestry. These could be anything from a photo of a mountain range in Wales to a symbol of the red dragon or an old map—anything that connects you to your heritage. In the centre of your space and occupying pride of place should be a cauldron; size is not important, neither is its material—it could be a real cauldron, a trinket, an old brass ornament, or one from a magical store adorned with symbols of the Craft. Spend some time finding the right things.

At the back of your space, behind the cauldron, place three candles or nightlight holders. An incense burner or joss stick holder should also be present. Take your time, and create a space that feels and looks good.

Now that your space has been built, we can resume the journey. A ceremony of dedication will be found at the end of part 1.

A Note on Pronunciation and Text

Welsh is a tricky language to learn and requires acrobatics of the tongue. However, do not be daunted by the strange words that follow; they are not as difficult as you may think. They merely require you to abandon the normal patterns of your current language. By this, your mouth will need to move consciously and with an awareness of the words you utter. The Welsh language is lyrical; every letter of every word is important and must be pronounced fully and with due attention. With this in mind, every Welsh word that appears in this book will have a phonetic pronunciation to accompany it and can be found in the glossary at the back of this book. A concise pronunciation guide will be presented at the end of the book for your perusal.

Various texts and manuscripts have been consulted in the writing of this book; all references are provided within the main body of the text as footnotes and within the selected bibliography.

◆ ◆ ◆

I write this book in honour of my ancestors, in honour of the cauldron and the great witch who devoted herself to its creation. I write it in honour of the prophet and the great poet Taliesin, who inspires my life and is a vital component of my spiritual adventure. I write in the hope that the bright light of inspiration will shine from your brow, and that in return you too will honour and keep the magic of our Celtic ancestors alive and well.

I challenge you to explore and devote a period of your life to the study and exploration of the iconography and magic of the prophet, the witch, and the cauldron. I hope that by writing this book I may provide you with certain tools to facilitate your journey into the magic and mystery that lie within this remarkable and life-changing tale.

So come, let us make haste and light the fire that will burn beneath our cauldron as we venture into the heart of Celtic magic.

Kristoffer Hughes
Isle of Anglesey, Wales
NOVEMBER 2011

The Cauldron Born

◆ ◆ ◆

My song arises from the cauldron of Cerridwen,
Unrestrained is my tongue, a repository for inspiration.

Taliesin

◆ ◆ ◆

Prior to any exploration of the themes and mysteries contained within the myth of Cerridwen and Taliesin, it is pertinent to explore the background of the story. Therefore, this section will focus mainly on a general overview and introduction to the tale and its history. The landscape that gave birth to the tale will also feature here, providing images and details of a place that instigated a myth of this nature. I will explore its relevance to the Pagan traditions of today and provide an explanation of how it survived the ages and how it was to finally settle in written form. The conclusion, I hope, will provide you with a vivid account and understanding of the colourful history of the tale and an appreciation of it as a living entity in its own right.

What Is the Story?

Retellings of the tale, both traditional and modern, will follow in part 2, but to begin with, indulge me in a little exploration of exactly what the story is, where it came from, and how it has survived the ages. I always think a little imaginary journey is an effective means of grasping something that you may not be familiar with as yet, and even if you are well versed in the tale, it will act as a little refresher to the imagination. So I shall begin by taking you on a little sojourn into the story to provide you with a visualised image of its contents before we begin to explore it.

Imagine yourself as a raven. The rays of the midday sun shine on the immaculate, deep blackness of your feathers; the deep, croaking *prruk-prruk-prruk* sound of your song rises from your lungs to echo about the valley below.

A vast lake stretches beneath you, the sun's rays tickling its mirrorlike surface, hardly rippled by the gentle breeze that swims down the mountains on either side. On the southern banks of the lake, smoke arises from a well-tended fire, over which sits the largest cauldron ever seen. As you swoop down, you note the contents of the cauldron; steam bursts from the bubbles that form on the surface of the boiling liquid. Nearby a young boy coughs loudly and rubs at his stinging, smoke-filled eyes. He pokes at the fire as if rebuking it for sending its smoke in his direction. He climbs the steps nearby and, with a spoon far too big for him to realistically handle, resumes his endless stirring of the great cauldron. Watching him is a man of astounding ugliness; so ugly, in fact, that you recoil in midflight. Yet to soothe the shock you note a maiden sitting gracefully, weaving flowers as beautiful as she is. She notices you and gazes up, her beauty rising to meet you, caressing your spirit like a warm blanket on a cold winter's night.

You spiral, catch a thermal, and rise naturally into the blue sky, allowing the spirits of air to take you at their will. The sylphs carry you to the northern banks of the lake until movement below causes you to leave the embrace of warm air and descend quickly and efficiently to the creaking branch of an old oak. Below you, a woman gazes up and sends a greeting to you; you respond with your usual harsh yet beautiful cackle. The woman has presence; she is imbued with something that you do not understand, yet you feel it—it is an old power of some kind, older than the valleys and lakes, older than the yews in the gardens of the dead.

She carries on her arm a basket woven of the finest willow; it is full to capacity with a selection of plants, flowers, barks, seeds, and fruit. She bends down to greet a meadowsweet flower and calls to it by name; she sings a song to it that you do not understand, yet its beauty compels you to descend to a lower branch to take a closer look. The woman looks up, her song unbroken, and looks directly into your right eye and winks at you. A smile breaks over her face as she reaches down with immense grace and gentleness and plucks the flower from its stem. Still singing, she casts it into her basket. Her bare feet hardly make a sound as she leaves the little grove of trees and heads for the cauldron.

The contents of her basket are cast into the shimmering, bubbling belly of the cauldron—each item in turn is lifted and honoured as she sings to it and, with a gentle throw, casts each one into the liquid. She smiles, she sings, the boy stirs, the cauldron bubbles.

◆ ◆ ◆

And so we set the scene for the exploration of our little tale. It concerns an epic journey of a woman intent on bestowing qualities of virtue and intelligence, wisdom and decorum on her son, who, alas, was born with an ugliness so great that neither she, nor anyone else for that matter, could cast a gaze upon him without being repulsed—an unfortunate turn of events for a mother whose fruits were not what she expected. But being well versed in the art and craft of magic, she assured herself that all would be well, a solution could be found. What follows is a roller-coaster ride into a full-blown journey of initiation and transformation concerning an innocent from a nearby village who succumbs to the unusual request of a powerful woman to stir her cauldron for an entire year and a day.

If your imaginary journey as a raven were to continue, it would eventually witness a great cracking of the cauldron, the boiling mixture condensing rapidly and exploding. Unfortunately its untimely expulsion causes three blessed drops to land on the callused thumb of the innocent stirrer. He sucks his thumb and is instantaneously bestowed with the wisdom and sciences of all the worlds. He knows the future, the past, and (of course) the present, and he knows the fury rising in the basket bearer as she witnesses the calamity. The young lad has stolen the magic intended for her son; she is scorned, and her fury erupts. A chase ensues; in the guise of various animals, the humans lose their shape, adopting another, running, swimming, flying, eating! As a consequence of all this running about, swooping through the air, and stuffing her face full of corn, the woman finds herself with child. And as the sun and moon dance their perpetual parade, you as the raven witness the birth of a child whose brow radiates with such a light that you cannot look at it for fear of being dazzled.

In a Nutshell...

If you were to retell this story in its most basic form, it would, I guess, take you about five to ten minutes, yet those short minutes would be filled with immensely powerful magic and mystery.

The tale can be summarized and broken down into small, bite-sized pieces. And in that proverbial nutshell we have the following components:

- a witch / wise woman / mother
- a simmering cauldron
- an ugly son and a beautiful daughter
- a husband
- an innocent young boy
- a blind man
- three divine drops of liquid
- a shapeshifting chase
- consumption followed by conception
- birth
- a child of great beauty, power, and wisdom

Our story concerns a woman who can be perceived as a witch, a sorceress, an herbalist, and a goddess. Her son, the motive for her relentless foraging and spellcasting, is the ugly one called Morfran Afagddu, meaning "utter darkness." Her daughter, Creirfyw, the fair one, is the shining light of beauty in our story. Then we have Gwion Bach, the stirrer, who is the main protagonist; Morda, the blind man employed to keep the fire lit; and a husband called Tegid Foel, after whom the current lake in the town of Bala is named. Finally we meet Taliesin, he with the radiant brow, the embodiment of the substance brewed within the vessel of the witch goddess Cerridwen. This nonhuman character, the enigmatic cauldron, is the heart of mystery; it is all-powerful yet deadly, transformative, destructive, and inspiring. It sits in a central position within the tale, affecting everything that surrounds it.

The Power of Myth

The Celtic tales arise from a time when the islands of Britain had not been segregated into neat little parcels, perfectly delineated by borders and invisible boundaries. The old tales and legends were alive and thriving during a time when there was no such thing as England and Wales; such concepts had yet to be invented. As a consequence, the tales continue to sing of a misty period in time—before the Romans came, long before the Saxons and Normans invaded—when we all shared the same language and relished in a common mythology based on the land and the relationship the tribe had with it.

Mythologies act as keys to the lucid awakening of the spirit; cultures the world over share a surprising commonality within their mythologies. In the British Isles, the similarities between the British and Irish myths are obvious: they share similar themes and contain identical traits and archetypes that have common attributions with their opposite cultural counterparts. Within these myths, it was generally accepted that a mere mortal—a simple human being—by a series of transformations, challenges, and initiations, could become the epitome and embodiment of wisdom and magic.

According to the great mythologist Joseph Campbell, mythology is "an organization of images metaphoric of experience, action, and fulfilment of the human spirit in the field of a given culture at a given time."[2]

Culture is fluid, moving constantly, like a stream—streams that become rivers, rivers that flow into deep lakes of communities, becoming rivers again, flowing and feeding the land and the people. Culture and cultural expression have been given the capacity to move beyond physical boundaries as our world shrinks, as people become closer owing to the advancements of our technologies. To journey back to the time of the Iron Age, before the advancement of Rome and its empire, we would discover that what was culturally specific to the tribes of the Ordovician people of my lands would not necessarily have been reflected on the American continent. Mythologies arose that were specific to the land and the interaction the tribe had with it, but that changed—what would have been an eight-day walk from one region

---

2   Campbell, *The Inner Reaches of Outer Space*, xxiii.

to another now takes less than an hour. The spanning of oceans that would have taken weeks of peril and risk can now be leapt in a matter of hours. As our society advanced, so cultural expressions advanced, developed, and became applicable to new times and new people, until they found themselves being recited and whispered to folk on the other side of the globe.

The tribe is now spread across the continents, but they carry within them the wisdom of their ancestors; after all, we are the sum totality of all that has been before us—nothing is lost; forgotten for a time, perhaps, but never lost. Today that fulfilment of the human spirit by means of mythological, magical transformation is applicable wherever these tales are told. They are made appropriate to new locations, singing of a connection that the tribe has with a new land. The cultural expression and influences of the old Celtic peoples can be seen far and wide, from the banks of the sacred river Severn, where the goddess Sabrina whispers her magic to the land, to the tumultuous waters of the rushing, spring-embracing Saco River in Maine. At the banks of these rivers, within sacred groves the world over, one can visualise the priests of today offering their libations and gifts solemnly to the gods of the ancient Celtic world, made relevant to the current age. The gods still breathe; they are alive for as long as we keep them alive.

In my musings and flights of fancy, I often wonder if there was a day when the gods did actually walk the earth. My imagination soars, permitted by the imagery given to us by amazing storytellers to see a time when humans and fey, mortals and gods walked side by side. Mythologies developed from this concept and demonstrate a time and place where we walked shoulder to shoulder with those who exist just beyond the breath, hidden to mortal eyes by the veils of cynicism, disbelief, and apathy. Surviving to this day in the oral narrative tradition of these lands is the belief that the gods and the fey, the fair folk, were shielded from our human eyes by the very fact that we distanced ourselves from the land. A veil was drawn across our cynical eyes, preventing us the sight that inspired our myths, our history of the heart and spirit.

There is no smoke without fire, and the fires that burnt so brightly in these lands so many centuries ago continue to burn. The native mythologies arose out of a need, but unlike the revealed orthodox religions, they did not arise out of a need to understand death and to be assured of the survival of the apparent identity beyond it. They arose to exemplify that life is the current embodiment of mystery—that truth exists in living, not in the fear of dying and the hope that we may survive it. The revealed religions teach a system of continuity, where the immortal human spirit retains its current, ever-changing identity and carries it onto the next world. By retaining this aspect of the identity, the spirit can then be rewarded or punished in a manner that would instill joy or terror. But the form of effective reward or punishment is entirely dependent on the fact that we do retain our apparent identities, without which the reward or punishment would be ineffective. This mythology arose into a structured dogma, one that offers comfort to the faithful and fear to the sinners.

When we examine some of the Celtic myths and poetry, we find within them recurring themes that speak of various states being experienced by the initiate simultaneously. Taliesin himself talks of having been myriad things before attaining his current form: "I have been a multitude of shapes before I assumed this form; I was a drop of rain in the air, I was the brightest of stars…"[3]

The mysteries within the Celtic mythologies speak of a constant, permanent state of being that preceded this life, is woven into this life, and simply continues on its merry course after this experience comes to its natural end. This life is simply one chapter in the book of the universe. The mysteries of Celtica do not teach an abandonment of living but instead inspire us to a state of lucid living. Within this state of lucidity we become aware of the fine threads that connect us to nature, to an understanding that we are an integral aspect of this world and of the spiritual realms, not something that is separate from it or in some state of perpetual suffering.

The mythologies of the Celtic people continue to inspire and to teach, reaching into the twenty-first century like fingertips of wisdom that rise from the depths of the cauldron. It can be said that a culture does not retain

---

3   From the poem "Kat Godeu" in the Book of Taliesin.

what has no significance to it—if something does not apply, then get rid of it; if something is of no use, then abandon it. The tales and myths of our Celtic ancestors have survived because they are relevant; they are not simply antiquities of language preserved for their beauty and rhythm. They are as relevant today as they were yesterday and a thousand years ago, for they speak to the spirit—they acknowledge that spirit and body are as one, sharing the same space, living in the richness of life, relishing in experience. They are relevant, for they contain truths pertinent to culture; they are comprised of keys, culturally specific keys that demonstrate our ancestors' understanding of mystery and spirit. It is us, the practitioners of the old ways in the new world, who continue to make these tales significant, relevant, and applicable.

The Landscape of Myth

At this point, a description is in order of the physical locality where our tale is set to provide you with an image of the beauty, ruggedness, and wildness of Cerridwen's landscape. Technology will enable you to observe the landscape by means of Internet satellite imagery if you so wish, transporting you via cyberspace to images that may be used in your meditations and journey work. To achieve this, simply type the names Bala or Llanuwchllyn into a search engine, and just like magic it will appear before your very eyes.

The location of the tale of Cerridwen and her cauldron is firmly placed in what is now the Snowdonia National Park. In a valley carved from ice a mile high, the melting waters and rain-soaked mountains created a four-mile-long lake. Our early ancestors settled at either end of the lake. Today to the northeast sits the town of Bala, whose name refers to the estuary created by a sacred river dedicated and named after the goddess Ayrwen (Dee). She was a goddess of war and battle, invoked to bestow courage and bravery, victory and triumph. Her waters run into the lake at one end and flow out of the opposite, her qualities and attributions swimming, for a while, with the sacred waters of Cerridwen. At the opposite end of the lake, nestled into the narrowing valley, is the charming village of Llanuwchllyn, meaning "the parish above the lake." Betwixt and between these two points sprawl the waters of Lake Bala, known locally as Llyn Tegid (the Lake of Tegid).

To stand on the shores of the lake, home of Cerridwen and her family, what strikes one initially is the silence, the stillness—too much of a stillness for it not to have been filled to capacity just a second before one arrived. There is heaviness to the air, not in an oppressive manner but rather reflecting the weight of magic and wisdom that imbues the place. It is a place where dragons sleep, where magic feels imminent; it sings of floods, of witches and goddesses, of prophets and kings. Lake Tegid's tree-lined shores sing in unison with the magic that rises from the dark depths of the pristine waters. The majestic mountains of the Snowdonia range peer into the mirrorlike surface, casting long reflections of land and sky. Standing on the shores of the lake, one can appreciate why such a myth would have arisen from such an inspiring and naturally beautiful location. Some of the old texts claim that Cerridwen and her family lived on an island in the middle of the lake; today no island is present, perhaps having sunk to the depths in an age-long past. During clement weather the area is stunning, especially when basked in sunshine, allowing one to be immersed in an atmosphere of enchantment and infinite possibilities whilst contemplating the mysteries under the tree-dappled light of our nearest star. The grass is soft and welcoming, tickling bare feet that step in awe at the beauty of the place, each footfall sensing the pulsing stories that radiate from the ground, through trunk and branch, to reach the clouds captured by mountain peaks.

The nose is enticed by the aroma of the abundant herbs and wildflowers that festoon the lakeshore—alchemilla, meadowsweet, coltsfoot, honeysuckle, and bramble, to name but a handful—ample ingredients for the brewing of an Awen-filled potion. Fingers can caress the coolness of water, embrace the moss- and lichen-encrusted trunks and branches of a plethora of tree species. The eyes may gaze at the reflections in the mirrorlike surface of the lake and watch the fish that glide gracefully beneath the water's surface, creatures that sing their own song of connection to a place.

But perhaps most remarkable is the fact that this place actually exists—it is not a location from a far-flung fairy tale or a country submerged beneath the waves. It is real and tangible, a place one can visit and be in direct contact with powerful archetypes firmly rooted in tradition and location. It provides a unique opportunity for soul-filled connection. Not only is one able to read and hear these tales, to experience them in that place between the worlds, but the physical body can journey to it. Standing thigh-deep in the sacred waters of Cerridwen provides a tool for connection like no other. To then warm the body by a fire on her shores, lost in the rapture of being in the moment, the mind's eye can see the simmering cauldron atop its flames, its belly caressed by the heat. Given this opportunity to physically be present, the body and mind are permitted to leap free from the confines of everyday society. We become enraptured by the magic of something so old, so mysterious, that the mind can break free from the density of the cranium and lose itself in the blissfulness of being at one with mystery and the life-changing magic that results from such immersion.

Location is important for rites of pilgrimage, to enhance the meditative tools required for spirit journeys to distant lands, but no physical journey is required or expected to sense, connect, and be inspired by this tale and others like it. For the tale has become more than the totality of its location; it has reached out into the world for centuries past as bards, minstrels, and storytellers took it to distant corners of the land. Eventually the tale would travel even further to each corner of the planet—moving, transforming, inspiring.

Surviving the Ages

Against all the odds, against all enemies, somehow or another, these tales did survive and make it right through to the current century. Several factors ensured their survival, and when evaluated as a whole they present something immensely magical. To understand and appreciate what the tales endured, it is necessary to gain a little background knowledge into the forces that strived to keep them alive. I will briefly touch on three vital aspects that secured the survival of Celtica's tales, these being:

- the Narrative Spirit
- the bards
- the monasteries

The bards and monasteries represent the human, physical machinery that kept the tales alive. However, the first aspect of survival is fluid—it has no face to speak of, no actual physical presence; it exists in the breath, in the air, in the wind that blows across the mountains. The tales arose from the depths of the human ability to imagine, to see beyond the visible world and into realms of potentiality and magic. The tales, legends, stories, and lore of the Celtic people did not exist in a vacuum; rather, they were and continue to be nurtured and nourished by the community in which they exist and thrive. Without the community to colour the material and perpetuate them, they would simply cease to exist and vanish into obscurity. Thankfully a deep, ancient relationship developed between the spirit behind the tales and the people to whom they were relevant. This is what is known as the Narrative Spirit. It is the living, inspiring, Awen-filled creative force that prevented stagnation and thus perpetuated the tales. It is the magic behind the words that fall from lips and rise from dusty parchment.

Consequently, the Narrative Spirit facilitated the continuation of the tales from the golden age of our Celtic ancestors to the present day. Being a living tradition, it adapted to change with remarkable aplomb; the situations and functions of the tales changed with each passing century, coloured by society at the time, yet the actual fundamental content of them remained more or less unchanged. They retained their magic even when confronted with so much change. Had they existed simply in the literal sense, they would have surely perished; it is the Narrative Spirit flowing through the words of the storyteller, bard, and poet that ensured survival of the tradition. It is this living entity that gives voice to the next category of survival mechanism.

The Bards

Contrary to popular belief, bards are not redundant relics of an ancient past; they continue to perpetuate their craft to this day, having done so from the height of the Celtic golden age. Etymologically, the word *bard* is of Celtic origin, possibly originating in Gaul, and retains the same sound throughout the six primary Celtic lands. The current Welsh language defines bard (Welsh *bardd*) as a transmitter of tradition and Awen, an individual trained in the old traditions of storytelling and the dissemination of tribal wisdom. In Wales they were specifically trained in the old tongue and were primarily members of the bardic orders. Their task was to memorise countless tales, prose, poetry, and songs, and to retain this information and knowledge and then transmit it via the narrative tradition to the people. They were simultaneously servants of society, tradition, the gods, and the spirit of culture and heritage. Within the Welsh language another meaning for the word bard is *daroganwr*, meaning "prophet," and it is true that much of the old poetry of the Celtic bards contains prophecies, some of which have been realised and others which speak of things yet to come. A bard is not simply a teller of tales; like the many skins and layers of an onion, their role is also multilayered and steeped in tradition, mystery, and magic.

In the Welsh bardic tradition, the role of the storyteller was given the title of *cyfarwydd*, a word that further emphasises the mysterious, magical quality of the bardic schools or orders. Literally translated, the term means "the familiar learned one." However, the University of Wales's *Dictionary of the Welsh Language* also stipulates that the cyfarwydd were also skilled in magic.[4] Think for a moment about the meaning of the word *magic*; you will have built assumptions of what it means, how it is understood, how you have used it and worked with it. To many it is the subtle craft of conjuration, spellcasting, ritualised forms of invocation, and the creation of change in accordance to the might of the will. Whatever your interpretation of magic is, there is another older, powerful form of it that exists in the proclamation of the bard. The words the cyfarwydd utter do not exist in a vacuum; they

---

4   Bevan, *Geiriadur Prifysgol Cymru (A Dictionary of the Welsh Language)*, 685.

are multi-intentional and arise from an ethereal spiritual connection to a lineage of ancestry. Each generation of cyfarwydd practised, rehearsed, and connected to the magic of the bardic mysteries in a manner applicable to the time. By use of that magic, the bards and the cyfarwydd ensured the survival of the material by use of visionary methods that were and continue to radiate from the cauldron of inspiration. In the bardic sense, there is another form of magic that differs from the conventional, a magic that lies beneath the undeniable power of words and suggests an older, primal origin of magic that connects us to the origin of the spirit and the nature of the universe.

The role of the bard, the cyfarwydd in Wales, was to lead the people and through that leadership to inspire, enabling the audience to see beyond the purely physical, to utilise Awen to give meaning to what was meaningless, to make possible what was impossible. The bards vividly made the unseen worlds visible, sparking the imagination to explore worlds separated from ours by only a gossamer strand of silken thread. They would entertain— bringing about laughter and satire in a world devoid of multimedia technology whilst simultaneously teaching the mysteries and spirit-laden truths that hid within their words to those who had ears to hear. This they achieved by proxy of the connection they had to the source material, a bridge of heritage and tradition reaching back through the mists of time to the great cauldron.

The threads of structure that bridge the present to the past have not changed; they continue to serve the mysteries of the old ways and do so by means of the bards of today. These are our writers, singers, poets, musicians, and artists. The traditions of the British Isles have long been accused of having no continuity—that any form of apostolic succession to the old world of druids and priests has long been severed, but have they? Perhaps it is simply a matter of misdirected perception. However tenuous the links to the past are, they arguably exist and provide a doorway that links us to the wisdom of the bards of old. The chain of continuity may not be as apparent as a book or dogma or some other physical means of record or instruction, but the chain exists in the power of words and the ability of those words to move the body and spirit to closer proximity.

Bards bring about life; they cause things to exist that previously were un-manifest. The bards ensured the continuation of the spoken word and the power that inherently lies within it, and the bards of today perpetuate this tradition.

The Rise of the Monasteries

The other vital aspect in the chain of survival was the monastic estab-lishments of medieval Wales. The obvious dichotomy here is the sudden mixture of Pagan material with the new Christian religion, and one could sincerely ask the question of why this material was kept and preserved in monasteries with their more than obvious references to the old religion! We may never get to the bottom of this dilemma, but several theories have been put forth over the years. What is imperative to accept and understand is that whatever animosity existed between the Christian and Pagan traditions, these were somehow reconciled, and the power of the church was utilised to preserve the material at hand, perhaps unwittingly. It has been suggested that some members of the monastic institutions were also secret members of the ancient bardic traditions and were placed in prime positions to docu-ment the narrative tradition, knowing that times were changing. The world was evolving in a literal sense, and it was vital that the material of the old bardic schools evolved with it; being a living tradition, it simply adapted by means of its practitioners to fit in with the times.

This concept is reiterated by one of Wales's most eminent and respected Celtic scholars, Marged Haycock, from the University of Wales, who is quoted as saying:

> It was imperative that the concept of Taliesin moved along in Chris-tian terms too, absorbing the latest elements of learning as well as retaining the keys to the mysteries of the Cynfyd (the old world and old ways), ensuring its continuous survival.[5]

The above statement clearly demonstrates the remarkable achievements of the bards to ensure the survival of the tradition, but they did so in an even

---

5   Haycock, "Preiddeu Annwn," 58.

more remarkable manner. It seems that Christian references were placed, sometimes totally out of sync with the style of poetry, where blatant references to the old ways existed within the narrative tradition. Written in the language of the people of Britain over a considerable number of centuries, these manuscripts were initially scribed and then rewritten several times over countless years. With their contradictory mixture of pro-clerical and anti-clerical themes and the blatant references to a pantheon of non-Christian gods, I would imagine that the common inventory scribe of the Middle Ages, having little knowledge of the old language, must have been baffled by the material. But Latinised words pertinent to the Christian tradition would have leaped out at him from the parchments, perhaps convincing the scribes and monasteries to value the texts and deem them worthy of keeping.

Seemingly the mysteries were concealed for their own protection, preserved for future generations remarkably by utilising the power of the church. And right there, in an institution that opposed the old ways, the mysteries were intentionally eviscerated into riddles that would require cross-references and intertextual skills to reform them. They were concealed by simply designating them as pointless, quaint folk tales that contained pertinent references to Christianity to prevent their destruction. The scribe in my musings is a secret member of the bardic tradition; he has within him the prophetic Narrative Spirit and sacrifices his entire life to the preservation of mystery.

The Celtic material has suffered heavy criticism throughout the centuries and perhaps more so in recent years. Even within Paganism itself there has been a blatant attack upon the material by those who have little understanding of it or its validity. Those who devalue the material do so by claiming that the medieval manuscripts do not pertain to a period before the coming of Christianity. This serves to demonstrate ignorance of the source material and the historical contexts of the manuscripts. It also does not take into consideration the amount of times the material has been translated and copied.

Interestingly, in her statement, Marged Haycock confirms that the material, although superimposed with Christian references, has within it vital keys to the mysteries of what is called the *Cynfyd*, literally translated as the "old world" or "previous world." It is the term "key" that is the vital component of her statement, for that is precisely what we find within the old tales: powerful keys that unlock doors to untold mystery and magic. The keys are still here; they exist for those who feel the calling of the Narrative Spirit to explore and decipher—to seek out the various locks and find the keys that fit them.

For most, the immense achievements and struggles of our ancestors who were in possession of the Narrative Spirit go unnoticed. By honouring and acknowledging the struggles of our ancestors, we begin to hear clearly the message of Awen contained within the cauldron of potentiality. Combined with the efforts of countless individuals who lived, breathed, and died to ensure a continuation of the mysteries, they served to save the past for the people of the future. A faceless individual in the distant future became their inspiration; if we ignore the calling of the cauldron and dismiss the efforts of our ancestors, they will have struggled in vain. Our responsibility to maintain survival, to become current guardians of the knowledge to ensure their continuation, causes us to have the ability to respond in a manner that honours the past and looks to the future, where body and spirit combine to enrich an apathetic world where the spirit is neglected.

From Mouth to Parchment

The tale of Cerridwen and Taliesin in its written format is relatively late, the copies that survive having been penned at some point during the middle half of the sixteenth century. It is generally accepted that the surviving manuscripts were copied from an earlier source that has subsequently vanished. Several manuscripts exist today that record the Cerridwen and Taliesin material; the designation of YT (*Ystoria Taliesin: The Story of Taliesin*) or HT (*Hanes Taliesin: The History of Taliesin*) are used interchangeably when referring to this specific tale. The majority of the manuscripts that include the tale are now stored as treasures in the vaults of the National Library of Wales in the western university town of Aberystwyth, in the county of Ceredigion.

The tale itself is presented in two defined parts or sections, the style and themes of which are very different in nature. The majority of folk familiar with the tale are mostly acquainted with the first section, whose themes are far more mysterious than the second. The themes seem to appear entirely allegorical and pertain to individuals of supernatural erudition and prowess who have the powers of shapeshifting and transformation. The symbology of the first section deals with obvious magical processes and describes an initiatory journey bestowed upon a seemingly innocent individual. However, the second half of the tale, in stark contrast, deals with semi-historical subjects and the rituals and customs of medieval courts. Several poems attributed to the mouth of the semi-historical Taliesin also appear in the second section, some of which are immensely beautiful and profound in the description of his origination. The poetry reveals his connection to a primal source of wisdom and magic, where he is in possession of the prophetic, all-knowing spirit of Awen. Except for an exploration of some of the poetry in the second part of the tale that is pertinent to an understanding of the nature of Taliesin the prophet, this book will focus almost entirely on the first half of the tale.

All in all, around eleven manuscripts contain the tale of Cerridwen and Taliesin to a lesser or greater extent. Some focus on both aspects of the tale, whilst others focus mainly on the first section. A further twenty-four manuscripts contain some of the poetry, which is to be found in the second section, along with references to the cauldron and the birth of Taliesin. The most extensive record of the tale is to be found in a body of work called Chronicle of the History of the World (designated within the National Library as MS NLW 5276D) by the antiquarian Elis Gruffudd, written during the sixteenth century.

It is more than likely that the forty or so manuscripts that have reached the present from the sixteenth century onwards only represent a small body of record. Several other manuscripts probably exist in private libraries and collections that have not successfully been rescued by the National Library.

◆ ◆ ◆

The survival of the native tales of Celtica is dependent on several factors, as I have explored above. Having examined the attributes that ensured their continuation and the magic of the Narrative Spirit, we are more able to perceive the powers that secured their survival. For something to retain its applicability and authenticity, it requires something other than human effort—a sublime quality must exist to guarantee survival. Without relationship, without connection, there is no drive; a task is doomed to fail. One can only speculate as to the amount of time that has passed since the tales were first told in the oral tradition, long before they were penned onto parchment; perhaps over two thousand years or more have subsequently gone by, yet the tales persist. This fact alone demonstrates their relevance; they survive because they are a living tradition.

EXERCISE

What does it mean to connect to something that isn't physical—that cannot be quantified or even articulated in the logical, rational manner that society imposes on us? How can we express a connection to something ethereally fluid? What does it feel to be the totality of time and generation and heritage?

Without thinking about them too much, ask yourself these simple questions:

- Who am I?
- Where did I come from?
- Why am I here?
- What am I?

These are questions that may have arisen in the mind of Taliesin, had he not already been in possession of the answers. The questions all relate to a common word in the English language: "I." We say it almost without thinking: "I have a head, I have a mouth, I have a mind, I have a soul." Very rarely do we ponder to think who that "I" is and what it is referring to. Our identities change in accordance to our environments and the people we encounter, and again based on the depth of relationship we have with them.

Without thinking too much about the answers—just let them fall out and onto your notepad—ask yourself:

- Who am I to my mother?
- Who am I to my brother/sister?
- Who am I to my children?
- Who am I to my best friend?
- Who am I to that guy at work whom I rarely speak to but greet every day?
- Who am I to my community?
- Who am I to me?

You will find that you are myriad personalities to myriad people; of course it is difficult to accurately know who you are to anybody at all, which demonstrates the fluidity of a person. We assume we know who we are in the world, but do we? Our assumptions are based on an ever-changing apparent identity, one that is altered and influenced by life. That is the person who interacts with the world, but the spirit doesn't change—it remains a constant, it is the permanent identity. It is the "I." It relishes in the experience of the human persona interacting with the world, a complex mass of contradictions, emotions, motivations, and influences. The ever-present "I" is the silent observer within; it is what connects the body and the mind to all that has ever been, to the constant flow and dance of the universe. But the damned cranium—that hard, bony cap around our brains—can sometimes get in the way; however, when we equate that chunk of bone with the cauldron, our perception begins to change.

Contemplate the Following:

Close your eyes and imagine the material forming your head to be composed of black cast iron—solid, unmoving, and impenetrable. The very top of your head, the crown, is open and forms the mouth of the cauldron now envisioned as your entire head. You don't have to be all mystical and spooky; you don't have to see it in full 3D animation. Just imagine it. It can be as elegant, enchanting, or silly as you wish; let all imaginings be yours, in your style, your way.

As the steam rises from the cauldron, become aware of the depth within it—your brain is in there somewhere; you can neither feel it nor sense it, it's just there doing its thing. Is your mind in there too? If so, where? Is it in your brain or a part of your brain? Is it a part of the cauldron? The cauldron, however, has no bottom—it is like Dr. Who's fantastic TARDIS, infinitely bigger on the inside!

Leave the cauldron where it is; imagine that behind each shoulder stand your mum and dad. Your mum is on the left, your dad on the right. Behind your mum stand her parents; the same on your dad's side. Behind their parents stand your great-grandparents; behind those, each subsequent generation, forming a triangle of individuals so vast that the limited range of the human mind simply cannot fathom it. Your visualisation will quickly be unable to conceptualise all those people. Why?

Your human mind will attempt to base each image of every individual imbued with the apparent quality you perceived within them as a result of relationship. The further back you go, the less apparent the relationship—*apparent* being the keyword! You have no actual experience of these people, so your visualisation of them becomes somewhat cloudy; they appear as faceless, ethereal beings with no names, no sense of place, but does that negate their existence and connection to you? No, not at all; they are an essential part of your makeup, they were necessary to you being in the world, and you are the sum total of them all.

Allow your consciousness to drift with the steam that rises from the cauldron, which is still acting as your head. Imagine a floating sensation as your consciousness lifts into the air; imagine looking down from that steam and observing your human body standing at the pinnacle of a vast triangle of people reaching back to the origin of the species—the triangle loses its human lineage and falls onto four legs in animal form. It loses legs and hair and becomes cells, cells in a primordial sea on a planet that makes a system, a sun which shines in totality of suns before it, stars that shine in a great triangle reaching back into the darkness at the beginning of the physical universe. Imagine it all.

Now quickly descend back into the cauldron—which is still the head of your human form—slap a lid onto it, and the cauldron vanishes, leaving your human head quite intact. The inside of your head remains in the darkness that it has always inhabited, the same darkness that caused the universe to spring into light. You carry within you the very spark of existence, and you are connected to the beginning of the universe. You are the universe; you are its sum totality.

EXERCISE: SACRED SPACE

Arrange yourself before the space that you created during the introduction.

Take a breath with the sky above you.

Take a breath with the land that supports you.

Take a breath with the seas that surround you.

Strike a match and breathe deeply as you invoke the image of a powerful witch goddess; allow her form to assume naturally, without force. Reach forward as you exhale slowly and light the candle on the left. Watch as the flame takes hold; introduce yourself to Cerridwen and state your intentions upon this journey.

As above, light another match, breathe deeply, and invoke the image of a person whose forehead dazzles with a radiant light. Touch the flame to the wick of the candle on the right. Introduce yourself to this image and state your intention.

Again, light another match. With a deep breath, imagine three rays of light emanating from above your sacred space, each ray illuminating each candle. As you exhale, light the central wick. Say out loud three times:

Awen I sing, from the deep I bring it.

Gaze into the depth of your cauldron and allow your eyes to defocus. It has no bottom; its belly reaches into the vastness of the universe. Allow your mind to wander into it and dissolve into the rapture of Awen.

When you are ready, become aware of your surroundings and return to the here and now.

Using your own words of gratitude, honour the ancestors for preserving the tales.

PART 2

One Tale of Old, Thrice Retold

◆ ◆ ◆

My first words spoke of the cauldron,
It is kindled by the breath of nine maidens.
It is rimmed darkly and embellished with pearls.
It will not boil the food of a coward.

Taliesin

◆ ◆ ◆

In order to present a cross section of the tale in its various forms, I have chosen to explore two manuscripts from the sixteenth century, namely Elis Gruffudd's Chronicle of the History of the World (NLW MS 5276D) and John Jones of Gellilyfdy's Peniarth MS 111. Both manuscripts are preserved at the National Library of Wales.

The differing manuscripts serve to demonstrate the fluid, ever-changing nature of the tales and how they morphed themselves into landscape and communities, responding to local figures, politics, and news of the day. They are also demonstrative of the different personalities who recorded them. Only five hundred years or so have passed since some of the manuscripts were written—at least the ones that we are aware of. We may never know to what extent they were recorded prior to that time, but many scholars believe that the themes are far older than initially perceived and may well have been originally recorded onto parchment as early as the ninth century.[6] The manuscripts differ in various forms, but they all retain the fundamental principles or themes of the tale, differing only in certain particulars such as time of year, personal names, and so forth.

What is apparent upon examination of the manuscripts is the emotional connection the writers had to the tale. Seemingly, Elis Gruffudd feels no great passion and simply copies the tale from a subsequently vanished text and whatever oral sources were available to him. He comments within the main body of the text that the themes are against faith and piety; they seem to contradict his own belief system. However, the work of John Jones is quite the contrary: it expresses the tale with passion and an appreciation for

---

6   Ford, *Ystoria Taliesin*, and Williams, *Chwedl Taliesin*.

the mystery, and may well imply that he took the oral tradition as his direct source for the penning of the tale.

Another fragment of the tale is recorded in the work of Llewellyn Sion, a late sixteenth-century bard. However, some controversy surrounds the Llewellyn Sion version, as many initially believed that this poet was an invention of the great Celtic genius Iolo Morganwg, who was responsible for the penning of hundreds of manuscripts pertaining to ancient British Celtic customs and traditions. In recent years it has been discovered that Llewellyn Sion did exist and was not, as many initially thought, a pure invention of Iolo Morganwg.[7] The fragment recorded by Sion and the subsequent controversy make any evisceration difficult and could potentially confuse and compound an amateur student of the mysteries; needless to say, this text, attributed the number NLW 13075b, is kept at the National Library of Wales. I mention this text only in passing to demonstrate the complex nature of the various manuscripts and the manner by which controversy arose over the centuries.

We may never know to what extent the writers of the past were involved with the intentional preservation of the mysteries, but we can deduce that the tales were important enough to be rendered worthy of scribing. In dark, dusty cells, the scribes scratched away with quill and ink, each one immersed in the tales to a greater or lesser extent, each one serving the old ways, whether intentionally or not.

One must remember that society in Wales at the time of recording was highly Christianised, and the celebration of the old ways would have been scorned. In fact, during the fifteenth and sixteenth centuries, the practical application of the themes within the tales would have been punishable by death, as they were more akin to Witchcraft, as perceived by the church, than anything traditional. The authors were subject to a society greatly different from our own. With this in mind, it is easier to understand the differences within the tales and how some themes appear in one script and not in another. We have to take into consideration the nature of the individual scribing them onto parchment. They will have had their own ulterior

---

7   Ford, *A Fragment of the Hanes Taliesin by Llywelyn Sion.*

motives, their own agendas and beliefs, and, in some instances, such as Elis Gruffudd, prejudices. However, superseding the opinions and prejudices of the authors was a drive or a need to preserve; whether the motive was one of curiosity, national literary pride, or of intentional preservation of mystery, we may never know.

Thankfully we have been left a rich legacy of literature that reflects the Pagan past of the Celtic people, but that is simply one facet, one aspect, of the legacy. We have also inherited their passion and drive to appreciate myth and legend as history of the heart and as tools of transformation. It is vitally important to refrain from total literalism; there is no joy there, and it can serve to become inappropriate dogma or doctrine that has the potential to become steadfast and unmoving. The Pagan traditions are not beyond the same fates that befell the revealed religions, where allegory was and is taken as fact, something written by man through the spirit of their god. Within Paganism it must be appreciated that the written form of these tales, however vital to their preservation, is not indicative of stagnant, unchanging mythologies. The written word is not the be-all and end-all of the tales but rather is a portal to their understanding, and this understanding works on two levels. On the one hand, we have the academic passion some have for the evolution and development of the Celtic languages and the manner by which the tales reflect known history and historical figures. On the other hand, we have the visionary, deeply intuitive application of the tales where they serve to combine body and spirit in a manner that is steeped in magic. The two should work together, hand in hand, spirit to spirit; to unbalance either would be foolhardy.

The visionary application of the tales should take the scribal form into consideration, and any effective magician must have an awareness of their origin and to what extent they have been studied. Magicians are practical folk; they see two worlds that dance together harmoniously, and for this to be a dance of integrity, a magician should be learned in the development of the written form as well as being capable of perceiving and utilising the spiritual aspect of the tales. The same can be applied to the purely academic study of the material, and in recent years a change of attitude has been present within academia with the rise of an appreciation that the tales are thematically representative of the Pagan past and its gods. In other words, the spiritual expression of the tales should have an understanding of the academic, and the academic an appreciation and acceptance of the visionary. The two can work and coexist side by side, harmoniously and with integrity. We should never fall into the illusion that what is written is marked in stone; it is not. It is simply one method of connection. The spirit is also more than capable of accessing the mysteries—what lies betwixt and between the words of dry ink—and integrating them into everyday living in a manner that is simultaneously conducive to their continuous preservation and individually transformative.

In addition to the traditional translations of two sixteenth-century authors, I will add my own rendition of the tale, presented in a vivid narrative, representative of twenty-first-century storytelling. I do this to demonstrate that the tales are adaptable, non-stagnant, and applicable to the here and now. One could even present the tale as happening today, using modern symbols to represent the allegories of the original.

An important facet in the tale's retelling by a magical practitioner or bard is the connection he or she has to the mysteries, for it is this connection that is primarily transmitted through the tale—it is this spirit that entices and invokes the spirit of another. Without this connection, without the experience of the initiatory qualities hidden in the heart of allegory, the tale is just a story; connection is vital to effective transmission. To become a priest of the old gods and their mysteries, one must first experience transformation, and this tale provides the keys to access the magic that transforms the profane into the sublime. You will hopefully note and sense the different connection the two authors I have utilised for translation had to the tale, and feel the quality of that connection reaching out to you from over five hundred years of history.

And so we move on to the telling of the tale. I suggest that the manner by which you read the following be different from the ordinary task of reading.

They are written in a manner that is strange and unfamiliar to the modern eye. We have been programmed in ways of grammar and the effective use of language in its written form; these tales do not conform to those rules and may therefore seem oddly structured and peculiar. The sentences are brief; they focus primarily on the fundamental themes and do not engage in verbosity or the vivid invoking of imagination by in-depth descriptions. They simply serve to get the story across efficiently and effectively, in a manner that is easy to remember and recall.

Read the following traditional translations sequentially, and then reread them out loud. Close the book and rerun the tale in your mind, recalling the imagery it presents; you will find that you will easily remember the tale with very little difficulty. Now tell the tale out loud; it doesn't matter if there is anyone there to listen to you or not, just tell it as you see it in your imagination. This simple task alone is sufficient to instigate a connection to the tale. By using imagination, speech, imagery, and words, you utilise several methods of communicating with the story, forming a connection to it that is beyond the simple task of reading.

I reiterate that only the first half of the tale is pertinent to this book. Although I touch briefly upon the second, it is not relevant to the exploration of the mysteries; as stated previously, the two parts are considerably different in nature and purpose.

The following version was translated by me from the text of Elis Gruffudd's Chronicle of the History of the World. This is the oldest known written record of the first half of the tale. The first line of the tale is significant, for Elis informs us that the tale was widespread in Wales, and its telling was current among the people of that time. This tells us that the tale itself was still a relevant aspect of the popular imagination and was in continuous use—it was not an ancient relic but an essential part of the bard's repertoire. Elis is drawing from two relevant sources here: the written format that he is copying and the narrative tradition that he is listening to within the folkloric consciousness. Although we are not informed of who the people actually are, we can assume that he is referring to the bards of the day and the common family storytellers. The medievalist Will Parker suggests that the relevance of written and oral sources sought by Elis reflected a legacy of the School of Taliesin, a repository for the Narrative Spirit and covert initiates of the mysteries.[8]

The Tale of Gwion Bach
(NLW MS 5276D)

The following is the story of Gwion Bach that is most prevalent in Wales.

In the days of Arthur, a nobleman lived in the land that today is called Penllyn. His name was Tegid Foel, and his homestead according to the story was a body of water known today as Llyn Tegid. And the story says that he also had a wife and to her was given the name Cerridwen, and she, so says the tale, was learned in the three crafts, which are known as magic, witchcraft, and divination. Also, the tale says that Tegid and Cerridwen had a son whose looks, shape, and form were terribly ugly. They named him Morfran, meaning "sea crow," but owing to his ugliness they eventually called him Afagddu, "utter darkness."

Because of their son's wretchedness, his mother became very sad in her heart, for there was no obvious means by which her son would win acceptance amongst the learned men of the day unless he beheld qualities markedly different from his looks. And so to deal with this matter, she turned her thoughts towards her craft to see how best she could make him in possession of the Prophetic Spirit and a great storyteller of the world to come.

After much labouring she discovered that there was such a way of bestowing upon him such knowledge by using the powers of the herbs of the earth and the effort of a human. This was what she must do: gather certain herbs and plants of the earth upon certain days and hours, and to cast them all into a cauldron of water, and then to arrange the cauldron upon a fire. This had to be warmed continuously in order to boil the cauldron night and day for as long as a year and a day. Within this allotted time she would see that three drops of all the multitude of herbs would spring forth, and upon whichever

---

8 Parker, *The Four Branches of the Mabinogi*, 98.

man they would fall, she would see that he would be all-knowing in all arts and full of the Prophetic Spirit. She would also see that the remaining liquid of the herbs, except for the three drops which came before, shall be the most powerful poison there could be in the world, and this shall cause the cauldron to shatter and spill its poison upon the earth.

Now, this story is against reason and contrary to faith and piety. But the body of the story tells how she did collect great numbers of herbs of the earth, these which she put into the cauldron of water and placed upon a fire. The story says that she took an old blind man to stir the cauldron and to tend it, but it says nothing of his name any more than it tells us who the author of the tale is. But it does tell us the name of the boy who led the old man: Gwion Bach, he who Cerridwen set the task to stoke the fire beneath the cauldron. In this manner, each kept to his task, tending the fire and stirring the cauldron, whilst Cerridwen kept it full of water and herbs until the end of a year and a day.

At that time Cerridwen took her son, Morfran, and placed him close to the cauldron to receive the drops when their hour of readiness arrived for them to leap out of the cauldron. In that time Cerridwen set her haunches down to rest; in that time she happened to sleep, and during that time the three amazing drops leapt from the cauldron, these which fell on Gwion Bach, who had pushed Morfran out of the way. And at that, the cauldron let out a scream and, owing to the poison, it shattered. At that Cerridwen awoke from her slumber and was enraged to see Gwion, who was filled with knowledge. Gwion in his wisdom sensed her temper was poisonous and that she intended to destroy him totally as soon as she discovered how he had deprived her son of the remarkable drops. At this he took to his feet and fled. Cerridwen, upon recovering from her madness, enquired of her son and thus discovered how Gwion had driven him away from that place she had stationed him. On knowing this she ran from the house like a madman in pursuit of Gwion Bach, and it is said that she saw him run in the shape of a hare. Because of this she turned herself into a black greyhound bitch and followed him here and there. After a lengthy pursuit, Gwion tired and became a salmon in water; Cerridwen gave chase in the form of an otter bitch. In pursuit, the chase took to air, Gwion as a bird and she as a hawk. After a long pursuit in many shapes, she chased him so hard he was forced to enter a barn where a great tower of winnowed wheat stood. And in this manner he became a grain of wheat. Cerridwen, unrelented, turned herself into a black tufted (or crested) hen, and as the tale tells, she pecked and swallowed Gwion into her belly.

And there she carried him for nine months, when after which time she delivered him forth. When she looked upon that child who entered the world, she did not have within her heart the ability to do him physical harm nor permit any other in her sight to harm him. In the end, she had made a coracle, or skin-belly, which would fit around the babe entirely; this she cast into the lake—some say that it was a river, whilst other books says she put him to sea. He was found a long time afterwards, as this present work will show in good course.[9]

At this point, the writer pursues further histories of the British Isles, returning later in the body of his work, to the second half of the tale, which finds Taliesin caught in the salmon weir of Gwyddno Garanhir on the eve of Calan Gaeaf (Samhain); more on this a little later.

◆ ◆ ◆

The following version was translated by me from the text of John Jones of Gellilyfdy. As mentioned previously, I have maintained sentence length, style, punctuation, and so on as much as possible to maintain their original nuances.

Hanes Taliesin
(PENIARTH MS III)

In ages past, a nobleman who was named Tegid Foel lived in the middle of Lake Tegid with his betrothed wife, who was named Karidwen [sic], and from that wife was born a son who was named Morfran the son of Tegid,

---

9   From NLW MS 5276D and with reference to Ford, *Ystoria Taliesin*, 65–67.

and also a daughter named Creirfyw, and the fairest maiden in all the world was she, but Morfran was of such ugliness that he was named Afagddu ("utter darkness"). Karidwen took to thinking that it would be unlikely for him to be amidst the noble because of his ugliness unless there was upon him some skill or honourable knowledge, which were attributes of Arthur and his Round Table.

So she took to the crafts of the book of the Pheryllt to boil a cauldron of Awen and knowledge to impart upon her son so that he would be dignified of character for his knowledge and acquaintance of the world.

And so she took to boil the cauldron, and once begun, the boiling could not be halted until a year and a day had passed and three blessed drops from the Prophetic Spirit be found therein. She employed a young boy called Gwion Bach from LlanFair yn Caer Einion in Powys to tend the cauldron, and a blind man named Morda to tend the fire beneath it, and she entrusted them to not allow the boiling to cease until a year and a day had passed. And she by means of books of astronomy and by the hours and movements of the planets did gather the beneficial herbs of all kinds. And as Cerridwen was resting from her profits near the end of the year and a day, three drops of liquid accidentally leapt from the cauldron onto the thumb of Gwion Bach; lest he be burnt, he thrust the digit into his mouth, and as soon as those drops entered his being Gwion knew all that was and all that would be, and he knew also of Karidwen's fury to come, for great was his knowledge, and in fear of her he took towards his own land and the cauldron broke in two pieces; the water within was now poison except for the three blessed drops. The liquid poisoned the horses of Gwyddno Garanhir who drank from the estuary whose waters were contaminated by the cauldron, and because of that the estuary has forever been named Gwenwynfeirch Gwyddno ("the estuary of Gwyddno's poisoned horses").

And with that Karidwen came forth and saw that her labours over a year and a day were lost. In her fury she hit Morda until his remaining eye became loose in its socket and shouted at him for being stupid to lose the contents of the cauldron. This is true, he told Karidwen, but it was Gwion Bach, not I, who ingested the liquid. Knowing this, Gwion took forth in the shape of a hare and Karidwen took speed in the shape of a greyhound bitch towards the river Ayrfen; he jumped into the river and became a fish and she also took to the water in the shape of an otter bitch, but he took to the sky in the shape of a bird and she took chase in the form of a hawk; she chased him without mercy. Gwion feared he would be caught and killed, and below him he spied a pile of winnowed wheat, and to it he took in the shape of a single grain. Relentlessly Karidwen took the form of a black crested hen, and with her feet she scratched at the pile until she came upon that single grain; promptly she swallowed him. And, according to the story, for nine months she was with child, and pity befell her: she could not bring her heart to kill the child who was born so fair, so instead she dressed him within a skin-belly coracle and set him to sail on the twenty-ninth day of April.[10]

◆ ◆ ◆

Pertinent to an understanding of the continuation of the Taliesin story, it is worthy to note that he is said to have floated in his coracle for approximately forty years (depending on the manuscript at hand), from the time of Arthur to the beginning of Maelgwn's time. It is said that a wealthy gentleman by the name of Gwyddno Garanhir living near the fort of Deganwy in North Wales had a son by the name of Elffin, who was in service at the court of King Maelgwn of Gwynedd. The old texts state that Gwyddno had a salmon weir in which was caught an abundance of salmon every Halloween or Beltane, depending on which text you read. This discrepancy of seasons has caused some confusion in the academic world for decades, but for the purposes of an exploration of mystery, they are easily reconciled. Both Halloween/Samhain (or Calan Gaeaf in the native tongue) and Beltane (also known as Calan Mai) are liminal periods—they are the pivotal points in time when one season gives birth to another. At Beltane spring gives way to summer, and at Samhain we see the first stirrings of the birth of winter. Within the tale, the river and the salmon weir, at the point where it meets the sea, is a place of liminality that presents the newborn Taliesin to the world.

---

10   Peniarth MS 111 and with reference to Ford, *Ystoria Taliesin*, 133–35.

It is written that when Gwyddno Garanhir's son Elffin and his people arrived at the weir, they were disappointed to not find any salmon; normally over one hundred pounds' worth of fish would be found. Instead they discovered a coracle. Elffin took a knife and cut the skin of the coracle, revealing a radiant human forehead. Upon seeing this, Elffin declared, "Behold the radiant brow," i.e., Taliesin.

It was assumed from that point on that this was the spirit of Gwion Bach imbued with the sacred drops of Awen, having been in the womb of the witch-goddess Cerridwen and then reborn in the form of Taliesin the prophet. Elffin and his family took the child under their wing, who immediately, despite his infancy, began to sing in praise of Elffin. The remainder of the tale concerns the roles of courtiers and princes at the royal court of King Maelgwn of Gwynedd. The second half of the tale is worthy of reading but lacks the magical, transformative qualities of the first half. However, it does contain some lines of poetry that allude to the origin of Taliesin and express his supernatural qualities; these will be taken into consideration and examined in the section devoted entirely to Taliesin and his mysteries.

For the purposes of this book, only an introduction to the themes of the second half is required for an understanding of Taliesin's development. I would suggest that you read a copy of the tale in both parts, though, for some of the second half's poetry is indeed rather wonderful. I will explore some themes from the poetry in relation to the first half of the story, and also poetry contained within a further manuscript called the Book of Taliesin, throughout part 3 of this book.

As to the tale itself, the above translations are by no means exhaustive; they are simply the oldest in written form. As previously mentioned, several other manuscripts contain aspects of the story from which a more vivid account can be created whilst retaining the allegories within the tale. I include below a partially novelised version of the tale in an attempt to imbue within your imagination a sense of colour, time, tension, and locale. As suggested earlier, I recommend that once you are familiar with the tale, you retell it in your own words in accordance to your experience with its themes and mysteries whilst simultaneously retaining its fundamental message of magic.

The Tale of the Prophet, the Witch, and the Cauldron

Once upon a time there lived a nobleman called Tegid Foel, so named because not a single hair grew upon his head. His home stood upon the shores of a great lake near the ancient town of Bala in North Wales. Tegid was betrothed to a powerful and wise witch by the name of Cerridwen, a woman both feared and revered for her powers and her abilities to enchant or curse.

The couple were blessed by the fairest of daughters, perhaps the most beautiful maiden to have ever lived, and she was aptly named Creirfyw, meaning "the finest." The heads of all men would turn as she passed by, the sparkle in their eyes betraying the lust they harboured for her deliciousness.

But a curse must have been placed upon Cerridwen's womb, for her son—named Morfran, meaning "sea crow"—was, alas, the ugliest man to have ever lived. His ugliness was such that his mother, in despair, renamed him Afagddu, meaning "utter darkness." But, as any mother, she loved and adored her child and wished nothing but greatness for him. But Afagddu was shunned by the community, for his countenance was of such ugliness that most found his appearance abhorrent and would serve to avoid him at all cost. In desperation, Cerridwen fathomed that if he was wise, he would gain the respect of the community and be amongst the learned folk, that somehow his ugliness would be compensated by the abilities of his mind. The nobility would adore him and see beyond his countenance and learn to love him as his family did.

Cerridwen—being a wise, powerful magician learned in the three sacred arts of magic, witchcraft, and divination—prepared a plan that would free her son of his appalling countenance. And in her wisdom she contemplated her dilemma and consulted the sacred book of the Pheryllt, the great, ancient magicians who were watchers from the otherworld. These magicians, the keepers of magic and science, once lived in a magical fort in the mountains of Snowdonia but had vanished into the west. Within a surviving grimoire she discovered a spell to brew a magical substance that, when ingested, would impart all the wisdom and knowledge of all the worlds upon the recipient. The brew of Awen—the divine, flowing spirit of inspiration—would take time, devotion, and care in its creation. Such was Cerridwen's determination, she set out to collect the herbs and materials required. The land about the lake was abundant in herbs and plants of magical qualities, and she took to her task with optimism and a smile, confident that her son would soon be free of the chains that bound him.

She had a great cauldron made of the finest cast iron, the likes of which had never been seen. The cauldron was set upon a roaring fire that would burn for a year and a day; night and day the flames would lick the cauldron's belly, warming the brew. She employed a blind man called Morda to stoke the fire and keep its hunger for wood at bay, and Gwion Bach to stir its contents.

For the duration of a year and a day Cerridwen worked relentlessly, gathering the sacred herbs and fungi from the banks of the blessed lake. Into the great cauldron they were cast, its magic rising with every ingredient, its song emanating from the depths and origination of the universe. As the appointed time arrived, Cerridwen in her exhaustion took to slumber beneath the trees; her work was done, and time would now dictate the readiness of the brew.

But whilst she slept the brew boiled with great rapidity, and cracks appeared about the cauldron's belly. Gwion Bach approached the cauldron curiously, at which point the brew in its fury expelled three sacred drops. Alas, the boiling liquid hastily descended onto the edge of Gwion Bach's thumb. Its heat seared the flesh, and instinctively he raised it to his mouth, plunging the scalded flesh onto the coolness of his tongue. The cauldron, as if anticipating the coming events, sighed heavily; birds became silent, the waves of the great lake fell motionless, and the world held its breath.

In an instant Gwion's eyes turned black; all the wisdom, knowledge, and sciences of all the worlds both seen and unseen rushed into his being. The whites of his eyes vanished beneath the power of such knowledge, the dark pits of his eyes transforming into pools of nothingness that yet contained the potential for all things to spring into being. The cauldron's sigh rose into that of a scream; its cracks became chasms, and in a mighty explosion it ruptured, sending shards of cast iron and boiling liquid into the four corners of the world. Its remaining liquid, now more poisonous than the berries of all the yews in all the world, flowed silently into the watercourse; horses and cattle along the river's banks died so quickly that their eyes remained open, their corpses silent sentinels of the transformative and destructive powers of the cauldron.

Gwion, imbued with universal wisdom, knew the outcome of this event and felt Cerridwen's eyes spring open at the calamity. When she saw what had befallen her labours, a deep fury rose within her. Her eyes observed the calamity that befell her cauldron, and she saw in the eyes of Gwion Bach that Awen was bestowed upon him. Like a dragon arising from the deepest chasms of the earth, her fury erupted.

Gwion Bach took to the hills, and with Awen within him he found that his shape could be changed. As a hare he bounded over hill and down dale. Cerridwen gave chase, her form changing to that of a greyhound. The chase continued until Gwion as a hare felt his legs heavy under the strain; a river before him compelled him to enter its waters, and as a salmon he swam through the depths. Cerridwen relentlessly followed, diving as a greyhound to transform as an otter bitch. Through the world of water she pursued him, her fury rising ever greater.

Gwion as a salmon looked to the surface and leaped from the water's hold; as a wren he took to the skies, and she, as a hawk, pursued. The realms of air held the chase as the wren flew from the claws of the hawk. Beneath him, on farmland, he observed a heap of wheat and dived into its mass, instantly transforming into a single grain. But Cerridwen would not surrender her chase. As a black tufted hen she began to peck at the grain, swallowing each one in turn until none remained. The chase was over, her fury satiated in the knowledge that Gwion Bach had been destroyed in the fires of her belly.

But Awen is above all such things, and as a consequence Cerridwen found herself to be with child, whose kicking was a constant reminder of her plight, her fury, and her anger. Her son would remain ugly, and Gwion Bach would live! She vowed to kill the child upon birth and drown it in the waters of her sacred lake.

The appointed day arrived, and her contractions grew strong; as her waters broke, her screams echoed through the valley. The child slithered from her womb, and her fury rose yet again. She reached for the babe in readiness to kill it, but its countenance struck her heart. The child's beauty tore her spirit into a million pieces; his eyes stared at her, and within them she could see all the magic of all the worlds. She found not a vestige of loathing for the child. It would live. She would send the child through the realms of water and into the laps of the gods as they saw fit.

Into a leather coracle she placed the child and set the vessel upon the sacred waters of Lake Bala. Away it sailed and for forty years travelled the width of Wales until caught in the weir of Gwyddno Garanhir. Instead of salmon on that fateful Samhain eve, Gwyddno's son Elffin found a child within the coracle. Upon unveiling the child from the depths of the leather and raising the babe aloft, a light shone from its brow, a blinding light of inspiration. "Behold, the child has a radiant brow!" he proclaimed. "Let him henceforth be known as Taliesin, he with the radiant brow!"

◆ ◆ ◆

The three examples above will serve to demonstrate the subtle differences within the tale yet simultaneously maintain the fundamental magic and mystery at its heart. Regardless of the motives of the scribe or narrator, the tale expresses a unique life of its own. Its power and ability to survive seems to transcend simple human endeavours and feels magical, as if it exists within its own right, as if it can almost take care of itself. However, one cannot deny the power of the bards' storytelling and the part it has played in the survival of this extraordinary tale.

Consider for a moment the momentous trials, tribulations, and adversity this tale and others have been subject to over the centuries. Admire, if you can, the sheer determination of the Narrative Spirit and the endeavours of the people who risked their lives to ensure its preservation. Cast your mind back if you are fortunate enough to remember the uprising of the Pagan traditions in the mid-1950s and onwards. Gerald Gardner, Doreen Valiente, and Ross Nichols reintroduced the magic that these tales contained and made them available to everyday, modern Pagans, who devoured them as myths appropriate to the new traditions of Paganism. These tales survive, and that fact in itself speaks volumes in relation to their value as mythologies worthy of preservation and dissemination.

Now that you have seen three versions of this tale, and hopefully will have read and re-read them, you will find that the fundamental components of the tale that pertain to its mystery will have been retained by your mind. You may not at this stage have any further understanding of the allegories contained therein, but rest assured: by some power or force beyond the words themselves, their subtle ability to inspire and awaken the spirit will be working away at your subconscious. I suggest that, having immersed yourself in the tale to a lesser or greater intent, you begin to express it creatively, developing a relationship with it as you progress. Your only limit here is imagination; use whatever medium suits you. The key factor here is to develop, to familiarise yourself with the themes of the tale and with the magic that bubbles from the depth of the cauldron to tickle the imagination and tease the spirit into lucidity.

The Power of Imagination

The sheer potentiality of our species is reliant on our ability to imagine. When we tap into this magical cauldron of imagery and potential, we access a realm of possibilities beyond our wildest dreams. There is no doubt that our powers of imagination have moulded and changed the world we inhabit; it is the power of this human ability that has built civilisations and created cities and towns, technology and machinery. We came about this ability by sharing stories; initially they would have been recollections of victories in hunting, of the first spark of fire that changed the human world. Eventually they morphed and transformed into allegories and metaphors, some of which served the realm of the spirit. The tale at hand belongs to this category.

Imperative to connection, one must be fully immersed in the tale; it must be made alive within you. This task is easier than one would initially imagine. If you are working with the tale in a solitary sense, imagine yourself as the characters within it; do this prior to reading the next section of this book. Before you are influenced by the interpretations that follow, journey, by means of your imagination, into the world of the tale, where you begin to see through the characters' eyes and hear through their ears.

Many people struggle with the task of visualisation; others struggle to meditate or journey into the inner reaches of the mind, but ask someone to imagine something and generally they are able to do so. All that is required to begin the journey of connection is your imagination. Do not be daunted or plagued by doubts or feel insecure that you may not be doing something properly; your way is the right way. Initiate your connection to the primary characters by playing with them in your mind; get to know them through their experiences as told within the tale.

In a group setting, a whole new world of exploration can be at your fingertips. Individuals within a group can be designated a character to work with, to imagine. They may write their imaginings, paint them, draw them, sing to them, whatever it takes to be involved and immersed in the experience. When the group reforms, each individual can express their connection: what they saw through the eyes of the characters, how they felt, what the landscape looked like. It may only be imagination, but you will be tapping into a world as real as this one.

As you imagine, take the following points into consideration:

- What is the character wearing? How does the fabric feel against the skin?
- Is the character barefoot? If so, what does the ground feel like?
- What are the ambient conditions, i.e., what is the weather like? Is it cold, warm, raining?
- What sounds are present in the vicinity?

- As the character, do you feel tall or short?
- What tasks are pressing in the character's mind?
- What does the surrounding landscape look like?
- What is the character feeling emotionally?

These are simple questions and observations, yet they will provide you with an extraordinary insight into the tale and initiate your exploration of its mysteries.

With that in mind, we can now move on to an examination of the primary characters of the tale, how they interact with it, and what message they have to bestow upon you.

Unravelling the Mystery

◆ ◆ ◆

I have been a multitude of shapes before I assumed this form:
I was a drop of rain in the air; I was the brightest of stars;
I was a word among letters; I was a book in my prime.
I was a path, I was an eagle, I was a coracle on the sea.

Taliesin: The Battle of the Trees

◆ ◆ ◆

At the heart of Welsh Celtic magic and myth, this particular tale has the ability to transcend concepts and sear the spirit and body into a lucid, rapturous relationship of pure enchantment. It does this on several levels; each component is as vital as the other, each one a fundamental step in the dance of initiation. The tale unfolds its layers to reveal archetypical personas and metaphors essential to the initiatory journey. Each individual component has its own song, its own dance, in the drama of transformation; they are each responsible for bringing something unique and necessary to the process of initiation.

In Celtic mythology nothing appears by accident; the concept of "padding out a tale" does not exist; none of the concepts are arbitrary, and each has a vitality that is essential to the transformative process. To ignore or neglect a component is to dismiss part of the story's spirit. What appears on the surface of Celtic myth or legend is quickly transformed into something entirely different when one scratches at the surface. Nothing is ever black and white; the Celts, being lovers of riddles, have ensured that the multilayered nature of our tales remains a task to decipher—it requires work, commitment, and devotion, and rightly so. To embark on this journey is to tap into a font of wisdom and knowledge that was old when the world was new.

Every individual facet of this tale contains within it keys to access the mysteries of the universe in its entirety. Some of the archetypes may seem to play only a minor role in the unfolding tale, but this is no indication that the strength or message of that component is limited or inferior to another. Sometimes there is great magic in what is given little attention. True magic is never obvious; it calls us to ponder, consider, and above all to explore and learn. These tales invoke a deep, old magic that is reminiscent of the circles of stones from millennia past. The tales do not speak of simple elemental magic but of a deeper kind that utterly transforms the initiate by connecting him or her to the origin of their spirit.

Imperative to the understanding of the following interpretations and for the mysteries to become applicable is your ability to immerse yourself totally as an integral part of the tales' essential components. Stories are generally observational; we read an account that someone has written of an action or situation that occurs somewhere else. We may see images in our minds or feel an empathic connection to the characters—all of this makes for a good reading experience. The Celtic myths differ, as I have noted previously, for they are not intended to be read; they exist within their own right and must be lived. However, a common problem is that a new practitioner of the Celtic mysteries is unused to this type of immersive quality, which is essential to grasp the mysteries contained therein. We cannot access the magic of the tale if we begin the journey as observers. We must be active components of the tale. To achieve this requires a shift in the way we perceive the world of words and creative storytelling.

To perpetuate, utilise, and disseminate the myths of our Celtic ancestors is, by proxy, to honour them as vital forces in the process of spiritual development. The total immersion in the subtle powers of the myths and tales of the old Celtic world is a process that heightens our own subtle powers of awareness. It allows us to become better practitioners of the mysteries and effective magicians who take their learning from the continuous wisdom of the past made applicable to the twenty-first century. There is an immanent quality to the tales, and it is this quality that makes them applicable and authentic tools of profound spiritual value.

To fully access the mysteries and allow the process to be immersive, you must first realise that the tale is speaking about one person, and one person only: you! This is the immanent quality that is vital to a true exploration where we are affected on a soul level. The magic contained within the tales are timeless; the written formats may only be a few hundred years old, yet the sense one gets when immersed in them is that of pure timelessness.

This quality ensures that the tale is applicable to the journey or quest of any explorer who approaches them with good intention and integrity. They are not observational for the sake of pure entertainment; they act as manuals that guide you, the querent, to a place of initiation and transformation.

Each component of this process is explored in the following chapters; together we will look at their qualities, what they bring to the journey, and how they guide us. The apparent separate nature of the spirits and archetypes in the tale begins to blur upon their practical exploration—they may have individual qualities and attributions that define their purpose or role; they also exist within each other. Every component is a vital cog upon the wheel of mystery, and if one should fall off, it would render the mystery unfathomable and defunct. Keep this in mind as you journey through the tale: every facet exists as a vital aspect. They are not singular powers; they are part of the whole.

In conclusion to this introduction of the primary themes and components, I ask that you throw passive observation to the wind. If you are willing and wanting to embark on this remarkable journey, begin by perceiving this as YOUR tale. This concept will be reiterated throughout the following sections. You are the initiate, and the cauldron and the witch goddess are waiting for you. Your encounter with the magical components of the tale will go beyond the descriptions that follow, which are by definition limited by my ability to articulate them in words of dry ink. I ask that you abandon the normal interaction we have been programmed to accept when in the act of reading; cast aside all thoughts of separation. This is no longer a tale that happened to "someone else"—it is happening to you right now.

Divine Intoxication
THE THREE BLESSED DROPS

◆ ◆ ◆

Three drops, of all the multitude of herbs,
would spring forth. And upon whichever man they would fall,
she would see that he would be all-knowing in all
the arts, and full of the Prophetic Spirit.

Ystoria Taliesin

For all that follows to make sense, we must first look at the quality of the brew that Cerridwen strove to create. This was not a task she took lightly: a year and a day of toil and work, of utter commitment, ensured that the final product would do exactly as it said on the can! It would imbue the seeker with wisdom and the Prophetic Spirit. This is the heart of the Celtic mysteries; this is the vitality and the force that brings life to the entire universe and all who dwell within it. The essence of the brew and its fundamental properties has its counterpart in almost every culture around the globe. In the Celtic nations this essence or spirit is called Awen.[11] The name, although almost impossible to literally translate, can be described as the divine flow of spirit. The University of Wales's *Dictionary of the Welsh Language* describes Awen as "the poetic gift, genius, inspiration, the muse."[12] However, the word can be seen to be composed of two parts: *aw*—which forms the root of words such

---

11   A tip to effective pronunciation: *ah-when*—both syllables are pronounced rapidly, with no accent, to elongate the sound.
12   Bevan, *Geiriadur Prifysgol Cymru (A Dictionary of the Welsh Language)*, 240.

as *awel*, meaning "breeze, light wind" and can be synonymous with breath; it is translated to mean "fluid" or "gas." The suffix *-en* shares the same root as the prefix of the word *enaid*, meaning "soul" or "spirit." So, in light of this, it is reasonable to translate Awen as meaning "a fluid, gaseous flowing spirit." Awen is omnipresent; in fact, an effective way of describing it is that everything exists within Awen. It is not out there, ready to be invoked; we swim within it. To make sense of this, imagine, if you will, the following:

A Celtic goddess laughs loudly as she kicks a football towards her fellow deities; it bounces sharply off the forehead of her Nordic counterpart, whose stunned expression causes her to laugh ever louder. She watches in enjoyment and tilts her head upwards, becoming aware of another force. She looks at the fluffy white clouds that decorate the sky, the sun shining brightly and dazzling her blue eyes. The green, soft grass of the pitch upon which the gods play calls to the mountains beyond; their heads, swollen by days of rain, sing to the same song she hums in her spirit. The breeze brings brine to her lips from the sea that hides just out of view beyond the hillock behind her; she nods in reverence as her eyes meet the circle of stones that decorate its summit. She licks the salt from her lips and smiles as she feels the oceans of the world dance within her.

It is Awen she feels; she is within it—it surrounds her and everything else within this vast universe. She hums its music as she breathes, feeling it in the very molecules of oxygen and hydrogen that descend to the fabric of her lungs. It bursts through cells, caressing the carbon molecules that she is constructed of. From there she senses the distant galaxies and their stars, the black holes that suck all matter back into the field of Awen. Awen is all of these things. The tiny insects at her feet, which crawl through grass in search of food, move through the essence of Awen.

Her eyes close as its song rises within her; the other gods stop and turn towards her. She is singing its praise, and they respond. Their voices lift in unison; lost in the rapture of Awen, they sing to the people who revere them, to the cultures and civilisations that bring offerings to their altars. They too swim in the divine oneness of Awen. For a moment, the world stops and lifts its voice—from the deep, energetic soul of the universe, Awen sings too, as it will for all time.

Where Is Awen? Can We See It?

Yes, in various forms it is obviously manifested through the expressions of artists in the apparent world. Awen exists in our songs, artwork, writing, poetry, dance, and craft, all of which enable us to articulate the soul-deep connection we have to this universal force, where the universe experiences itself through myriad lives that live within its embrace. The act of bringing forth Awen can only realistically be expressed through our creativity, where we access the vast cauldron of potentiality and make manifest what was previously unmanifest.

The concept of Awen is a central tenet within the Druidic tradition but is not restricted to it alone. It is a concept that can be incorporated into any of the current Pagan traditions and utilised to enrich their practises and rituals. A deep, soul-filled understanding of Awen will act as a guide to effectively incorporating it into your daily practise, group practise, development circles, and seasonal celebrations. This spirit or essence underpins the Celtic mysteries; it lies at the heart of Celtic myth and magic. It is the force that unifies the mythology of a place and of a people with the universe as a whole. It is imperative for any exploration of Celtic magic and of Druidry to embrace and be fluent in the language of Awen. It is the Holy Spirit of Celtica.

Awen is imbued within the three sacred drops that explode from the cauldron to transform the innocent Gwion Bach. When Gwion's transformation leads him to another incarnation in the shape of the prophet Taliesin, he sings of the quality of this flowing spirit of inspiration and wisdom. It is in the poetry of the prophet in the deliciously profound Book of Taliesin that we first encounter the term Awen in written form. Within the poem "Angar Kyfundawt" (which translates as "the hostile confederacy"), we find the following verse:

Awen a ganaf, o dwfyn ys dygaf

Auon kyt beryt: gogwn y gwrhyt,

gogwn pan dyueinw, gogwn pan dyleinw,

gogwn pan dillyd, gogwn pan wescryd.

Gogwn pet pegor, Yssyd y dan vor.[13]

Awen I sing, from the deep I bring it.

It is a river that flows; I know its might,

I know how it ebbs, and I know how it flows,

I know when it overflows, I know when it shrinks,

I know how many creatures there are under the sea.[14]

The above and all subsequent references by Taliesin to Awen imply that the attainment of the divine spirit gave the prophet the knowledge of all the worlds and of all existences. "From the deep I bring it," says the prophet, reiterating that Awen is an integral part of all things and that we swim within its flow. In the above verse and subsequent verses of "Angar Kyfundawt," Taliesin explains how he knows its extent and flow. He knows of its ebb, how it courses, how it retreats, and how many creatures there are under the sea. The conscious acknowledgment of Awen provided Taliesin with the ability to perceive all things at all times, for all things exist within its flow.

The above piece of poetry creatively expresses Taliesin's embodiment of Awen in a manner that demonstrates its all-pervasive, omnipresent quality. It exists simultaneously in all things, in all places at all times; it is not bound by the laws of the physical universe, for it exists beneath the fabric of the known, visible universe. It is the building block, the soul of the universe, which acts as a house for the countless spirits that move in and out of the physical dimension. Living, breathing, dying, returning, the ebb and flow of life lives as an expression of Awen, which rises from the depths of the unseen world. The denseness of our human experience can cause us to feel separate from Awen—that we stand alone in this world. Awen heals this condition by confirming that we are a vital aspect of the universe learning about itself. But

---

13   Evans, *Facsimile and Text of the Book of Taliesin.*
14   Translated by the author.

this process cannot be confined to cerebral or intellectual understanding. For it to move the spirit into lucidity, the essence of Awen must be felt, sensed. One must be utterly immersed in it to experience the connection Gwion Bach initially encounters before morphing into the prophet Taliesin. Initiation is required to be conscious of Awen; as the tales and poem recount: *"Ac yna yr ordeiniodd hi drwy gelfyddydd llyfrau Pheryllt i ferwi pair o Awen.* (So she took to the crafts of the book of the Pheryllt to boil a cauldron of Awen.)" In the same manuscript, the poet further elaborates that *"Mi a gefais Awen o bair Karidwen* (I received my Awen from the cauldron of Cerridwen)."[15]

The implication in the historical manuscripts is that knowledge of Awen, or the ability to know it, must be initialised by a creative process that leads to that act of transformation. This, in turn, is assimilated into cohesion, giving rise to the rebirthing of the individual as the Prophetic Spirit. This does not imply the same form of initiation popularised by modern covens and groves but a personal initiation into the mysteries by proxy of the archetypes involved. One is not being initiated into a group but rather into the heart of Celtic mystery and magic. In the case of our tale, Awen is achieved by brewing a magical potion, the constituents of which swim in the essence of Awen. The ingredients are chosen for their ability to impart upon the initiate the spark needed to embark on a conscious journey into Awen. The latter verse connects Awen to the cauldron of the witch-goddess Cerridwen, and it is her wisdom and the knowledge of the elusive priest caste known as the Pheryllt that initialise the potency of the brew. The fact that Cerridwen embarks upon this journey and can shapeshift at will implies that she is a well-versed and practised initiate of the mysteries of Awen; more on this later.

Earthly components are utilised for the attainment of Awen, for it already exists within them—it is not some far-flung force that exists "out there" in an unfathomable void. The entire tale informs us that the ability to perceive it, conceptualise it, and know it is all around us. We may need the guiding hand of another to show us the way; we may need to consult the instruction of

---

15   Excerpt from Hanes Taliesin, Peniarth MS 111, and translated by the author.

our ancestors as we are in the exploration of the tale in written form. But, fundamentally, Awen is everywhere; we do not need to physically travel anywhere to find it. We need only discover the keys that heighten our awareness of it. You hold such a key in your hands.

For decades, scholars have argued over the origin of Awen: is it a Pagan or a Christian concept? This has mostly been fuelled by a line in Peniarth MS 111. In the Hanes Taliesin section, it states that the three drops of Awen are *bendigedig* and arise from *rat yr ysbryd glan*, which translates as "blessed and from the Holy Spirit." However, the Celtic scholar Patrick K. Ford states that these words appear "to have been added over an erasure; the ink is different, and the letters, though carefully imitative of John Jones's hand, are different."[16] The rewritten words serve to conceal words beneath the text that read *ysbryd proffwydoliaeth*, or "the Prophetic Spirit."

This blatant attempt to conceal a Pagan concept with an overtly Christian sentiment serves to demonstrate the trials these manuscripts have endured through the centuries. We may never know the actual reason why this occurred, but it is intriguing that whoever performed the task did not bank on the scrutiny of the twenty-first century. It may be that the Pagan concept was a threat, or that secret members of the bardic schools strove to hide this material in the prophetic knowledge that future generations would eventually find the truth hidden beneath it.

Further demonstrating the ability of Awen to survive differing ages, conquests, and religions can be seen in its acceptance within the Christian tradition. The National Eisteddfod of Wales movement is, on the surface, a typically Presbyterian affair that celebrates cultural poetic expression and the beauty of language. It is also Christian in nature by proxy of the Welsh Presbyterian Church's influence in preserving our language. However, the concept of Awen moved along from its Pagan origin and became firmly entrenched in the Christian tradition. To this day, Awen is spoken of and acknowledged as a force worthy of attention and expression. Awen is a gift, a trust that is acknowledged and subsequently expressed by the initiate. But

---

16   Ford, *Ystoria Taliesin*, 133.

the question remains whether Awen is derived from the Holy Spirit of the Christian tradition or from the bubbling depths of Cerridwen's steaming cauldron. Seemingly, in Wales at least, both concepts are equally valued. However, within the old chronicles of the Celts and particularly within the works of Taliesin, it is the magical origin of Awen that is celebrated. Within the ancient texts we gain a snapshot of a complex period in time where the Pagan and Christian traditions were, for a time, swimming in and out of each other—each one borrowing from the other, each with its own agenda and motive—yet through all this change and turmoil, Awen survived.

During the latter part of the eighteenth century, Awen was given a symbol to represent its attributions, which has since become recognised and associated with the flowing spirit. It can be seen as the emblem for groves, covens, and orders; worn as jewelry; and adorning the ritual items of the Welsh cultural celebratory body known as the Gorsedd of Bards of the Islands of Britain. The primary source for the symbol comes to us from circa 1792, and it is now widely used as what represents the essence of Awen. The insignia is drawn thusly:

Devised by the genius poet Iolo Morganwg, the father of the National Eisteddfod of Wales and to quite an extent the inspirer of modern Druidic practise, the symbol represents the sun at its various stations. Other references imply that the symbol may be significantly older than the inventions of Iolo Morganwg, with similar symbols appearing in Greece and in Egypt, especially within the Temple of Horus at Edfu. The Welsh monk Nennius also presented a symbol startlingly similar to the Awen of Iolo Morganwg as part of an alphabet in the ninth century. It contains a glyph that resembles the three columns, although they are joined at the top.[17] It is said to represent the Latin word *ego*, which is ascribed the phrase "I am that I am." Nennius in his Historia Brittonum also uses the term Awen in reference to an individual called Talhaearn Tad Awen ("Iron Brow Son of Awen"), which indicates that

---

17   The manuscript concerned is viewable online at http://image.ox.ac.uk/show?collec tion=bodleian&manuscript=msauctf432.

the term Awen and its significance was utilised in the early Welsh language, and no doubt for centuries before within the oral tradition.

Lovingly referred to as the three rays, the central ray represents the sun at its zenith during the summer and winter solstices, the left ray the sun at midday on the vernal equinox, and the right-hand ray at noon during the autumnal equinox. These delightful correspondences connect the symbol to the cycle of the sun and the season. The columns are explained by Iolo Morganwg:

> Thus they are made; the first of the signs is a small cutting or line inclining with the sun at eventide, thus / ; the second is another cutting, in the form of a perpendicular, upright post, thus | ; and the third is a cutting of the same amount of inclination as the first but in an opposite direction, that is against the sun, thus \ ; and the three placed together, thus / | \.[18]

Iolo Morganwg also elaborated on the columns by explaining that each one vibrates to a vowel sound that intones the name of the creator. Alas, Iolo was outwardly a nonconformist, yet seemingly, deep down, he was in love with Paganism. The intoning of the vowels of Awen in a Pagan sense can be seen as a manner by which we sing in praise of the universe, and they are sung thusly:

- The first column / resonates to the vowel O
  (pronounced as a long "oh" sound)
- The second column | resonates to the vowel I
  (pronounced as a long "ee" sound)
- The third column \ resonates to the vowel W
  (pronounced as a long "oo" sound)[19]

The bardic record shows that it is from the sound of Awen that all language is derived, and that this occurred in response to the utterance of the universe's voice. In the depth of the infinite chaos, the universe uttered its

---

18 *The Barddas of Iolo Morganwg*, 21.
19 To avoid confusion, note that the Welsh language has an additional vowel in the form of W, pronounced as the "oo" in *zoo*.

mighty name. From that utterance all the galaxies, all the worlds, and all life upon them sprang instantaneously into existence with a shout of joy. As the universe sang its name, three blinding shafts of light erupted from its core. Each shaft of light resonating to a sound, which in combination imitates the song of the universe singing in praise of itself. As the universe let free its voice, Iolo offers the following description:

> ...and with the utterance was the springing of light and vitality, and man, and every other living thing; that is to say, each and all sprang together. And Menw the Aged, son of Menwyd, beheld the springing of the light, and its form and appearance, not otherwise than thus / | \, and in three columns; and in the rays of light the vocalisation—for one were the hearing and the seeing, one unitedly the form and sound; and one unitedly with these three was power... and since each of these was one unitedly, he understood that every voice, and hearing, and living and being, and sight and seeing, were one...[20]

In the vocalisation of Awen there is great power and mystery. Try intoning the vowel sounds whilst visualising the columns, or rays, of Awen. Feel how they affect and resonate in different parts of your body; sense that you are connecting to a concept that is centuries old. According to the Celtic revivalists, Awen causes us to know truth, to maintain truth, and to love truth. Its primary tenet, which can still be seen on the banners of the National Eisteddfod of Wales, is "The truth against the world," meaning that within Awen swims the river of pure truth. Iolo Morganwg describes this as

> ...that is to say, they are called the three columns, and the three columns of truth, because there can be no knowledge of truth, but from the light thrown upon it; and the three columns of sciences, because there can be no sciences, but from the light and truth.[21]

The Celtic revivalists, in particular Iolo Morganwg, have been scorned over the centuries and even branded forgers, but it can truthfully be stated

---

20 *The Barddas of Iolo Morganwg*, 17.
21 Ibid., 67.

that without them, modern Paganism and Druidry would have a different face. The likes of Iolo Morganwg gained nothing from their endless collecting, musing, and writing; he was long dead by the time his works came into print. They have inspired not only the love the Welsh have for frightfully long sentences (I am now acutely aware of the length of my own!) but also for exploring the wisdom our ancestors left behind for us to decipher. The old manuscripts and the Celtic revivalists continue to perpetuate the value of the material at hand.

The non-Pagan National Eisteddfod of Wales utilises the three rays alone, whilst the Pagan traditions incorporate a dot above each ray to depict the three sacred drops from the cauldron of Cerridwen, which denotes the origination of Awen within our indigenous mythology. By the simple addition of the three sacred drops, the symbol creates a chain of imagery that directly bonds it to appropriate and relevant myth. This further exemplifies the essential nature and sacred relationship between the tribe and the land. The very act of adding to a symbol, giving it meaning, serves to demonstrate the living, breathing, adaptable nature of the current Pagan traditions. Awen facilitates and encourages maturation and the evolution of traditions that work with it; it is not a stagnant force but an eternally moving stream of energy. Adapting Awen to fit and express modern life has no rules as long as a degree of sagacity and a good smattering of integrity is utilised.

> We are like islands in the sea, separate on the surface but connected in the deep.[22]

Imagine yourself as one of these islands, a vast stretch of sea seemingly separating you from the person next to you; it is a state we find ourselves in daily—the belief that we are separate from one another and separate from the world and the Divine. Nothing could be further from the truth. Awen connects us to everything: it is the water within the ocean; it is the land that reaches out beneath it to connect all to the other. The mind-boggling and sometimes befuddling world of particle physics and quantum mechanics seems to be exploring concepts that mystics and sages throughout time have

---

22   William James, philosopher.

long accepted. The current theories of the vacuum state, also known as the zero-point field, describe how, even at minute levels, deep within the fabric of the cosmos, there is vitality, a force, that connects every visible and invisible part of this universe to each other.

Particle physics takes a journey to the dawn of creation and to the point of singularity, to the seconds before the big bang. It explores the magic of creation as the universe became aware of itself and exploded in galactic glory, creating worlds and stars, trees and rivers. Quantum mechanics looks deep into the miniature world, into the space between spaces, where it peers into a singular universe that is a seething mass of energy and potential. The scientific community is suddenly aware of a singular field of energy that connects every possible thing in the universe with one another. In a pseudo-scientific sense this is called the zero-point field, and it demonstrates that ultimately there is no such thing as separation; we all exist within a field of infinite potential.

This field of potentiality gives birth to everything in the universe; when we gaze up at the stars, to other worlds beyond our reach, we stare at the magic of Awen. It holds within itself the memory of the universe in its entirety; swimming within its flow is all the memories of all the worlds since the dawn of time. Everything that can exist, has existed, and will exist is within this field, and we have direct access to it. We are not and never have been separate from it; it is only illusion that keeps us apart. The great thinker and scientist Ervin László gives this field an intriguing title: he calls it the Akashic field or A-field, a term I rather like, and I have adopted the A-field to mean the "Awen field" within my own spiritual practise. According to László, this A-field is "the fundamental energy and information-carrying field that informs not just this universe, but all universes past and present."[23]

Deepak Chopra explains that we cannot step out of the ocean of potential, out of the zero-point field, for it contains us and everything else in the universe, known and unknown. We are unable to step outside of it and therefore find ourselves in the same position as a fish attempting to prove that the

---

23   László, *Science and the Akashic Field.*

ocean is wet.[24] We have spent so many years under the spell of separation that we find it almost unfathomable to comprehend the concept of oneness, but we can. The mysteries of Awen, the zero-point field, the A-field, or any other name we give it is hidden within our mythologies; we need only seek it out.

EXERCISE

Awen is the soul of the universe, it is the house of the spirit, and we are an essential component of it. Soul—derived from the Proto-Germanic word *saiwalo*, meaning "coming from the sea or belonging to the sea"[25]—gives rise to the exercise that follows. This meditative journey may be performed physically or contemplatively. Ideally it will involve a physical journey to the sea wherein the journey itself becomes part of the overall experience.

Take yourself to a beach; if possible, plan your arrival to coincide with dusk or dawn or midnight to utilise natural liminality as part of the exercise. Be safe; ensure there is someone close by to watch over you. Remove your clothing and walk slowly into the water until you are waist deep. Immerse yourself in the contact between flesh and water: sense the temperature, feel the texture of the seabed beneath your feet. Breathe in tune with the lapping of waves. Extend your arms away from your body, palms outward, and assume the pose of the three rays of Awen: / | \.

Take a deep breath and visualise the central column; a blinding ray of light descends from the sky above you to pierce your body. Hold the image for several seconds. Take another breath and visualise another beam of light at 45 degrees penetrating your body from your neck and down through your right arm. Hold the image for several seconds, and then repeat the visualisation for your left arm. Imagine yourself as the three rays, glowing brightly as the waves embrace your lower body.

Raise your voice and intone the three sacred vowels O, I, and W as directed on page 58. Allow the sound to cascade from your lips and fall into the sea

---

24   Chopra, *Life After Death*, 202.
25   *Chambers Dictionary of Etymology*.

that you stand in. Allow your mind to expand with the sea; acknowledge that you are standing in the same body of water that laps onto the shores of distant lands. It sits frozen at the polar caps and crashes onto the rocks of storm-wracked beaches. You and the sea are as one; it mirrors the quality of Awen. It is in all places at all times. You are not an island that floats isolated; like the seabed at your feet and the briny liquid that laps at your skin, you are a part of all these things. You are Awen singing in praise of itself.

Allow the vowels to resonate for as long as you are immersed in the experience. Then come back to the present, allowing the sound to dissipate and flow into the sea. Bring your awareness back to the present, yet take the immersive quality with you. Walk gently back to dry land, knowing that the sea can teach you the quality of oneness whenever you feel separated. Record your experience in your personal journal.

Cerridwen's Cauldron

THE WOMB OF ENCHANTMENT

◆ ◆ ◆

Come and taste of the cauldron's brew,
and magic she will give to you,
You will dance in the eye of the storm;
you're Cerridwen's children,
the cauldron born.

Damh the Bard, "The Cauldron Born"

Standing in central position is the great cauldron of Cerridwen. This vessel, although non-anthropomorphic in nature, is one of the primary archetypes of the tale. The symbol of the cauldron is commonplace in the modern Pagan movement, but why? Where does it come from? Is it enough to simply state that it is just a symbol of the Goddess? A deeper understanding of this symbol is required.

The cauldron at the centre of our tale is the vessel that contains the essence of the transformation experience. It epitomises several qualities that are of great importance to the process, which will be discussed a little later. Primarily it is the vessel that contains the essence of the three sacred drops; it holds Awen until it is ready to be taken by the initiate.

I begin by exploring the cauldron in reference to the divine feminine and its pertinence to our tale. For centuries the cauldron has been a symbol of the feminine, especially in relation to its semblance as a womb or a receptacle that holds within it the essence of spirit or life. On a purely physical level the cauldron symbolises the hearth, food, and sustenance; it epitomises the heart of the home. Every round and long house from the Bronze Age and through to the Iron Age would have had a cauldron at its centre, held by chains that supported it above the hearth's warming fires. It is only a small leap from that function to adopting the cauldron as the symbol of what nourishes us. Akin to the body of a mother who sustains us for nine months before we are birthed from her "cauldron"—our initiation into this life—she becomes the physical and spiritual representation of the cauldron. There are two words in the Welsh language for cauldron, *crochen* and *pair*; the word *crochen* shares the same prefix, *cro*, with the word *croth*, meaning "womb."

If we take the above into account, it can be perceived that Cerridwen and the cauldron may be seen as one and the same thing. The cauldron is simply an externalisation of the nourishing properties of the witch goddess's womb. Suffice it to say that the cauldron, in its central position, represents the potential of Awen as the vessel that holds it, implying that within the womb we swim knowingly in the magic of Awen. It is our birthing into this world—the breaking of the waters within the cauldron—that causes us to forget our connection to this unifying force of the universe. However, for a time within our infancy we continue to swim in the oneness. To a babe in arms, the mother is the universe in its entirety, and the baby is an integral part of that; it is one with its mother.

Alas, we grow independent of our source—of what symbolises the connective magic of the universe—and we fall into the illusion of "I" and "Other." We become separated from our origin, from the truth of connection that our birth and infancy expressed. For many what follows is the journey to discover oneself, when, in fact, we were never lost to begin with. Mythological allegories arose in response to this, and our ancestors in their wisdom developed methods and techniques that would reunite us with the source of our spirits. In the Celtic continuum this naturally developed as the symbol of the cauldron and found its way from the home to the schools of mystery, epitomised by the witch goddess and the initiate prophet.

"I received my Awen from the cauldron of Cerridwen," said Taliesin. He received Awen from the cauldron, from the extension of the Great Mother's womb. In relation to the cauldron as a representation of the divine feminine, it can be seen within the story that there are, in fact, *three* cauldrons.

Initially the symbol is blatantly apparent in the form of a gigantic iron cauldron, which hangs from a great chain and swings above a roaring fire. This stands in an initial position within the tale; it is the vessel that invokes the essence of Awen into itself; it is the physical introduction to the subtle qualities of magic. For the student of the sublime—for a potential initiate whose only experience in the world is of worldly things—the introduction to the occult world must begin on an earthly level or nothing that follows will make sense. Before we can ascend into spirit, the descent into matter must be complete, meaning that in order for us to understand the spiritual experientially, we must first understand and be fully immersed in the world in which we live. To attempt to fast-track the physical would be foolhardy and dishonour the connection we have to the here and now, to the planet that sustains us. It also implies that the keys to understanding the spiritual are held within the physical. When we consider this in relation to Awen, it makes perfect sense: everything in the world swims in Awen; it is only illusion that causes us to believe we are separate.

The cauldron, therefore, stands as the symbol to a multitude of connective relationships, but primarily it acts as the physical vessel that is indicative of our place in the world. We gather materials from this world, ingredients that we can hold, smell, taste; they are physical and yet they resonate with Awen. They are acknowledged for the relationship they have with their locality; their personalities teach us the diversity of the world whilst simultaneously celebrating the oneness of this organism that we are an inexorable aspect of: earth. They are subsequently cast into water, which symbolises sustenance and oneness. The vessel is teaching us about our world—about the magic that we see in the physical. To create the brew, the world must be observed, the dance of sun and moon informing us of when the bulbs of snowdrops stir within their earthly tombs. It shouts in proclamation of spring as the apple blossom gracefully unfolds from tiny buds. Campions raise their glorious heads towards the sun, singing of life, calling to the bees to suckle at nectar. This is magic! This is the awe-inspiring, gob-smacking wonder and sheer magic of the world we inhabit. All of it is singing—every single ingredient of the brew and the creatures they interact with raise their voices in sheer praise of the world. In our quest we reach down and breathe in tune with a primrose that has been singing its little head off in praise of the sun that sustains it; we feel and sense its part of the story, and within it an explosion of magic unfolds. As we acknowledge its presence, its role in our brew, we sense the beating heart of our nearest star, burning with heat beyond imagination, its nuclear fusion and radiations pelting our planet, reaching through the atmosphere to be reflected in the tiny flower we hold in our fingers. This is why the tale begins with such a physical emblem. It teaches us to look for the magic around us; otherwise, how can we possibly find the magic that lies between the worlds?

Being fully immersed in the world is to know the magic it holds—to see the wonder in a sunset, to gasp in awe at the power of the tides. To watch the ebb and flow of the perpetual cycles of life, death, and rebirth in a tree outside your window is to sense the magic that causes our ascent into spirit. And then, all at once, the waters break—the cauldron splits, and the chase begins. We are ascending into the realms of the subtler senses, and we run ahead of the witch goddess who instigates our transformation. Having tasted Awen, we begin to know it, and, with hearts thumping and threatening to shatter the sternum, we run, changing form as we do so, knowing that another fate waits in this cycle of initiation.

The initial cauldron lies broken, its contents deadly toxic; its magic is not designed for another. The tale is meticulously sequential; nothing is happening on a whim. The initial cauldron leads us to another, this one more directly linked with the mother. As the spilt liquid of the cauldron cools on the wet grass, the initiate concludes the chase and is pecked into the belly of the black crested hen, the shapeshifting witch goddess Cerridwen. As a seed battered by the chase, exhausted by our dance through the drama of the elements and the seasons, we descend into darkness. The hen breaks her form, her feathers becoming the black fabric of a flowing robe as Cerridwen stretches from a bird to a woman. As she stands, a cloak of feathers falling about her shoulders, she screams as she senses the seed implanted in her womb. The fires of creation are kindled yet again. In the womb-cauldron the initiate rests, fed by the flowing spirit of Awen that transfers its omnipotence from placenta to babe. Cerridwen's womb is the second cauldron of the journey. The process takes time; gestation is required to absorb what the initiate has been taught thus far. Previously we stirred the waters of Awen; we familiarised ourselves with its properties. Now we swim in it—it is the primary experience of knowing we are at one with it, but it is not the last.

As Cerridwen's cauldron breaks open and she screams the initiate into being, lifting the stunned babe from between her legs, she too is transformed by the power of the cauldron. Her heart filled with empathy and knowing, she fulfils her duty as initiatrix and conceals the initiate into yet another cauldron—the *bol croen*, the coracle, skin-belly, or womb. Cast onto water—a recurring theme—this cauldron carries the initiate into the song of Taliesin.

It is apparent by examining the above that there is a connection, both culturally and literary, that sympathetically and symbolically links the cauldron and the womb. This tale demonstrates the vitality and function of the divine feminine in initiatory mythology, beautifully tied and bound to that most enigmatic of Celtic symbols, the cauldron. For any exploration of the significance of the cauldron to be in any way comprehensive, it is imperative that we explore its occurrence within the Celtic mythological and cultural continuum.

The archaeological and literary records clearly demonstrate the importance of cauldrons both physically and spiritually in Iron Age Celtic culture. Enormous cauldrons have been discovered throughout the British Isles and northern Europe in lakes, pits, and peat bogs. The cauldron was a vessel of dual significance, expressing a physical and spiritual attribution; however, the cauldron was also a symbol of power and wealth. Celtic chieftains were renowned for their generous hospitality in providing their guests with a feast of gargantuan delights, affairs that expressed pride and duty to their fellow tribal leaders. The amount of food prepared and the quality of it demonstrated the wealth and the efforts of the chieftain to entertain and impress. No doubt an aspect of this hosting was the continuous act of outdoing the hospitality of one's competitors. Central to this tenet was the cauldron and all the ornaments and tools that decorated the hearth, the heart of the chieftain's kingdom. According to the archaeologist Frances Lynch, the hearth with its accoutrements, firedogs, and cauldrons became the focus of the amount of power the chieftain possessed and his ability to reward those loyal to him.[26]

The Gundestrup cauldron from Jutland is perhaps the most ornate and visually stunning cauldron to have survived the ages; this gilded silver vessel is covered in mythical depictions of deities and archetypes, including a cauldron! One of its panels depicts a ritual act of immersing an individual into a cauldron, a motif which appears throughout European Celtic mythology. Archaeologists have since concluded that the iconography upon the cauldron is of pre-Roman origin and that the images portray deities and archetypes pertinent to the Celts of that region.[27]

To understand the essential nature of Cerridwen's cauldron, it is useful to be introduced to other similar vessels that share a magical lineage. I have chosen the following two examples—namely, the Second and Third Branches of the Mabinogi legends, and the poem "The Spoils of Annwn" from the Book of Taliesin—for good reason: Taliesin appears in both. They are directly linked to the initiate of Cerridwen's cauldron.

> For I will give unto thee a cauldron, the property of which is, that if
> one of thy men be slain today, and be cast therein, tomorrow he will
> be as well as ever he was at the best, except that he will not regain
> his speech.[28]

The above is taken from one of Wales's most enigmatic of tales, known collectively as the Mabinogi, which can be translated to mean "tales of youth." These consist of several tales, four of which are collectively identified as the Four Branches, that are steeped in allegory and hidden meaning. Akin to the tale at hand, they also serve to guide the querent on a profound spiritual journey. They are filled with archetypes that assist the hero on his

---

26 Lynch, *Prehistoric Anglesey*.
27 Green, *Exploring the World of the Druids*.
28 Taken from the Second Branch of the Mabinogi of Branwen, translated by Lady Charlotte Guest in 1838.

or her quest into the realms of the spirit. Within the Second Branch of the Mabinogi we encounter a young woman named Branwen, daughter of Llyr; one of her brothers is called Bendigeidfran ("blessed crow/raven"). Llyr is a British chief god of the sea, and his family is collectively known as the Children of the House of Llyr—they represent the sea and are those who protect Ynys Y Kedeirn, the Island of the Mighty, a synonym for the British Isles.

The story narrates the tale of the king of Ireland, who sails to Britain to ask for Branwen's hand in marriage. Unfortunately, he fails to ask her brother Efnysien's permission (a figure who bears semblance to Morfran Afagddu, who will be discussed later), and in retaliation he mutilates the king's horses. To compensate for the crime of his brother, Bendigeidfran presents the king of Ireland with a cauldron that will bring the dead back to life; it is the cauldron of rebirth. When questioned as to the origin of this cauldron, Bendigeidfran explains that it came from Ireland, from a place called "the lake of the cauldron," and it was carried upon the back of giant. The cauldron was forcibly obtained and eventually given to the king of Ireland.

Alas, the tale takes a tragic turn with the mistreatment of Branwen; she turns to nature and trains a starling to fly across the Irish Sea to warn her brother Bendigeidfran. A battle ensues, but the Irish have an added advantage with the cauldron of rebirth; however many men are killed, they are resurrected by the cauldron. The properties of the cauldron render the resurrected warriors dumb, perhaps to prevent them from speaking of what they experienced within the depths of the magical vessel. Also of interest is the period of gestation within the cauldron: they are cast in on the day of death and resurrected the next. They seemingly must spend a period of darkness in the womb of the mother before they are reborn. This has parallels with the initiation rites of our tale; this act of immersion and gestation in cauldrons, or vessels of the feminine, is a recurring theme throughout Celtic mythology. The battle continues until the instigator of the initial conflict, Efnysien, the shadow, places himself into the cauldron and stretches his limbs within it, thus shattering the vessel and rendering it useless. In the process his heart is torn, and he perishes. The battle ends, and only seven survivors return to Britain. Among them is Taliesin.

Losing the power of speech is a common motif in Celtic mythology—it implies the secret, individualistic nature of initiation and integration of the mysteries. One cannot speak of what occurs within the cauldron; the quest makes sense only to the one who is being immersed within the experience. To speak of this would be foolhardy in that it would make no coherent sense to a noninitiate and would dishonour the mysteries themselves. The next branch of the Mabinogi, called the Mabinogi of Manawydan, continues this theme of enforced dumbness. Here we witness the tribulations and ultimately the magical binding and disappearance of two deific characters, the enigmatic Rhiannon and her son Pryderi. In turn they are led to a magical *caer* (meaning "fort"), wherein hangs a giant cauldronlike bowl that swings from four chains that reach beyond the sky. It is said of Pryderi:

> ...as soon as he touched the bowl, his hand stuck to it and his feet became fixed to the slab beneath him, and the power of speech was taken from him so that he was unable to say a single word. And there he stood, unable to move.[29]

Rhiannon, in search of her son, discovers him and foolishly touches the same bowl and suffers the same fate. This single paragraph in the Third Branch conceals a staggering amount of hidden meaning and intertextual references that allude to the mysteries, the wisdom and the magic of the Celtic chronicles. Its pertinence to our tale is beautifully narrated by the medievalist Will Parker:

> The bowl in the caer belongs to the same family of symbols...as the Peir Pen Annwfn (the cauldron of the Head of Annwn) which boils not the meat of a coward...These are essentially goddess motifs: symbolic of the nurturing/sexual qualities of the feminine...[30]

The importance and magical significance of the cauldron is continuously reinforced and perpetuated throughout the mythology of the British Isles and Ireland; therefore, it is no accident that it plays such a vital role in the tale of Cerridwen and Taliesin. Regardless of the age of the actual manuscripts,

---

29   The Mabinogi of Manawydan, Son of Llyr, translated by the author in 2011.
30   Parker, *The Four Branches of the Mabinogi*, 418.

the themes and iconography it contains is evocative of a school of mystery that has persisted for millennia.

There are obvious similarities in the above tale to that of Cerridwen and Taliesin, in that it concerns a mother and her child. In the case of Rhiannon and Pryderi, they represent the Mare of Sovereignty and her foal, who are indicative of the land and the relationship the tribe has with it. This enforces the sanctity and sacredness of horses as symbols of the divine feminine in the British Isles. The cauldron is indicative of the mystical, a vessel of knowledge wherein our route to total immersion in the flowing river of Awen lies. It is the symbol of the divine feminine as a vessel of transformation. Whereas the horse is the feminine symbol of the fertility within the land itself, this diversity of symbology is demonstrative of the plethora of attributes that connect us and the gods to almost every possible aspect of the human condition and potential. The cauldron of Cerridwen opens a gateway to the other cauldrons of Celtic myth that are worthy of exploration. Alas, I can only realistically give a brief account within the confines of this book, but it's enough, I hope, to whet your appetite.

In the previous quote by Will Parker, you will have noted reference to the Peir Pen Annwfn, or the cauldron of the Head of Annwn—this is from a poem in the Book of Taliesin and is designated the title "The Spoils of Annwn." It recounts the heroic journey of Arthur and his warriors, along with Taliesin, on an epic journey to the underworld in search of the cauldron of the Head of Annwfn,[31] the ultimate Celtic magical cauldron. There are as many interpretations of the poem as there are words within it—it is appropriate, however, in this section to give you a brief description of its meaning.

Within my own order, the poem, along with the tale of Cerridwen and Taliesin and the Four Branches of the Mabinogi, are the primary tools of teaching. Within each we find a cauldron. Each cauldron brings a different quality to the quest of the hero; it imparts its wisdom in a manner that

---

31 *Annwn* is from the Welsh *annwfyn*, meaning "very deep" or "not-world." It exists beneath the world and connected with Taliesin's inspiration. Haycock, *Legendary Poems from the Book of Taliesin*.

prepares the initiate for the next phase of the journey. Within "The Spoils of Annwn" we encounter seven magical forts to which a specific journey is made. The vessel that is used is a ship called Prydwen, a typical feminine deific title in the Welsh language that contains the suffix *-wen*, meaning "pure," and denotes a creature of deific attribution. This vessel carries the hero on a tumultuous and perilous journey into the underworld and to the seven different island forts in search of the cauldron. The poem tells us something of the nature of the cauldron:

> My first words were spoken concerning the cauldron; from the breath of nine maidens it is warmed. It is the cauldron of the Head of Annwn, what is its purpose with its dark rim and edged with pearls? It will not boil the food of a coward; it is not destined to do so.[32]

The inclusion of one verse that relates to nine maidens further emphasises the feminine nature of the cauldron, but it also implies that the journey will be difficult—a coward will never access the mysteries of the cauldron. To effectively descend into its depths, we are required to be strong and brave, qualities epitomised by the presence of Arthur, who is also indicative of the flawed nature of man. To accept and acknowledge our flaws is to lessen their power over us. Wisdom and insight are necessary for the quest, and it is Taliesin who brings this quality. He is the radiant light of knowing, who instinctively guides us through the subtle worlds in search of the cauldron. Prydwen, the vessel, is the Goddess herself who guides us across the sea of discovery, to "berth" us at each island.

The Anglesey Druid Order devised a system of teaching from this poem that interprets it as a journey into "self." It is the descent into matter and the exploration of the nature of who we are, why we are, and what we are. Almost all spiritual traditions incorporate methods of exploring the self—it is not exclusive to Celtic traditions; even the temple at Delphi has the inscription "know thyself" carved above its door. This poem provides an effective tool for the evisceration of the self, which by definition is not an easy journey or quest; it is not intended to be. The Celtic schools of mystery teach us

---

32 Preiddeu Annwfyn, "The Spoils of Annwn," translated by the author.

a programme for living consciously and lucidly and with authenticity. They provide us with keys that teach the nature of "self" and that human nature, our nature, is a part of the whole and worthy of celebration. When we embark on a spiritual quest, we embark on a journey into the self, for as the cauldron teaches us, the self is a part of the whole; to know it is to honour it.

The system that hides within "The Spoils of Annwn" is beautifully complex yet paradoxically simple. Each of the *caeri* (forts) represents a vital aspect of the human condition. They define us as individuals and are facets of our personalities and experience in this world. They also define how damaged or intact we are upon arrival in this life and how we navigate the waves of our lives. Journeys to the forts can teach us the nature of who we are; by allowing us to "see the wood through the trees," we step outside of our normal boundaries and venture inwards as a traveller who observes. We may note the strengths and defences of our individual forts and will also learn of their weaknesses and the manner by which events may have compromised them. There are times when wounds from the past can be of such force that they obliterate the walls of our forts; disconnection ensues. When this occurs, there is no mechanism or reserves available for us to rebuild our defences. When our forts have been compromised, we may develop self- perpetuating patterns of behaviour and inappropriate coping strategies, which indicate the damage done. The journey to knowing ourselves takes all of these into consideration, but we are guided and protected through the quest by powerful and ancient archetypes. We do not embark alone; there are forces that help us.

Within the poem there is an eighth fort, which no journey is made to. It is called *Caer Pedryfan*, or the "four-walled enclosure." It is simultaneously interpreted as the island of Britain and as the boundary of Annwn; it is that which contains the experience. In a physical sense, it would be your auric field. It is the serpent's egg that surrounds your boundary; it is the first point of defence. This powerful fort represents protection, control, and vitality. It is the outward expression of our functionality and the manner by which we respond to the apparent world. The apparent characteristics of this fort can be seen emulated in the body's immune system, which is determined by our thymus gland, which in turn dictates before our birth our immune capabilities. A chink in the armour of our immune system can indicate the compromised state of one or more of our forts.

It is by this association that each of the subsequent seven forts has corresponding endocrine organs. This provides a system of energy centres akin to the Eastern chakra tradition but grounded in applicable occidental mythology rather than the dependency on oriental teachings. This brings a subjective concept into the body and makes it apparent; we are able to feel the effects physically. In slight contrast to the cauldron of Cerridwen, which initiates us into the mysteries of our origination and oneness with the universe, the cauldron of Annwn takes us on a journey into our human selves. It provides us with the ingredients for the experience of life. Both journeys are vital for spiritual development; each complements the other. To assist the conceptualisation of the journey to Annwn, it is necessary to engage your imagination:

Close your eyes and imagine an enormous cauldron, large enough to almost swim in! You climb a ladder that rests against its belly and peer over the edge. Within the cauldron you see an ocean, upon which float a series of islands. Cast yourself over the edge and feel yourself falling towards the sea. You seem to float momentarily, and see a ship beneath you: Prydwen. Your feet land gently upon her deck. Seagulls fly overhead. The sky contains a glowing sun and a silver moon; both smile down upon you. At the prow of the ship, standing side by side, are the stationary figures of Taliesin and Arthur; courage shines from the eyes of the king and wisdom gleams from the forehead of the prophet. With a bump, the ship arrives at the first island.

Caer Siddi: The Fort of Necessity

This fort is represented by the pituitary gland, the master gland. Its fort is a single tower, steadfast and strong; it revolves of its own volition and is surrounded by fire in which instruments are playing of their own accord. Above it is a fountain of youthful illusion, and around it is the wellspring of the sea. It is a place of illusion and repetition. It is the assumed earthly state. We are imprisoned here and held by heavy grey chains until we see and acknowledge its illusory nature. It is immovable and steadfast; it is the place of influence. Its illusions can convince all other forts of its truths and untruths. Yet it is the place of the fire in the head—we can see through its illusion as simply a fort that strives to maintain the status quo.

Does the cauldron reside here? If so, what is its nature? What does the mystery of this place and the search for the cauldron convey to your spirit? Contemplate the nature of the cauldron that may be located in this and the subsequent forts.

Prydwen calls you to journey to the next island.

Caer Feddwit: The Fort of Mead Intoxication

This fort is represented by the thyroid gland. It sits on a floral island, its towers rising from a sea of green; bees buzz busily about its turrets. Guard bees protect its entrance, and the queen hums from within. This is the place of communication and expression; it is the manner by which we converse with the world. It presents us with what nourishes but also what poisons; its intoxicating nature can convince us to believe our own illusions. Yet all that we find pleasurable lies here, and in it our ability to laugh and be joyous, to carouse and be entertained and to entertain. It can be addictive. This is the point where we express our emotions; it is the gateway from the forts to the world beyond.

Does the cauldron reside here? If so, what is its nature?

A beacon of light from the brow of Taliesin alerts you to board the ship. Prydwen sighs as she docks at the next island.

Caer Rigor: The Fort of Hardness and Rigidity

This fort is represented by the adrenal glands. This tall, mountainous island rises sharply from the sea; its flanks are decorated with wildflower meadows, woodlands, and green plains. A single fort sits precariously on a cliff top whilst ruined buildings adorn the lowlands. This is the place of stumbling, of harshness and falling; it is the place of the ego. It is the most dangerous of all the forts. Here we may fall into the "I'm not good enough" or "I'm right and you're wrong" mentality. Our principles lie here, and our ability to stand and fight or take flight. We may be immovable and stubborn on this island, overly protective of the cauldron. Our impulses are controlled here, whether they are rational or irrational. Rigor can cause us to be stuck in our ways, to become petrified. Herein lie our personal strengths and our determination; the ability to make things happen is here. We may construct from this point and also destroy. If we stumble, do we fall? If we fall, do we succumb to defeatism or do we rise to our feet, dust ourselves off, and start again?

Does the cauldron reside here? If so, what is its nature?

The bellows of Arthur's lungs call your name from the edge of the island, and you return to Prydwen. The sea laps gently at her bough as she berths at the next island.

Caer Wydr: The Fort of Glass

This fort is represented by the thymus gland. This island blinds you—it is made entirely of glass, some of it rounded and smoothed by the sea, others pillars sharp as a sickle and gnarling from the island's bedrock. Its towers are made entirely of clear glass, its staircases, floors, and rooms visible through its walls. Upon its walls thousands of faceless people stand watching you; you call to them but they do not answer. This is the point of being "you"— it is the centre of the self, your point of perspective. It is the place where you believe what you see, not knowing that you are looking through glass, which, although transparent, alters your view. This is the place of liminality; it sets all inherited patterns, how and when we die, and what we are susceptible to. This is fate, which is unknown; all uncertainty exists here, but so does our potential to access its mystery. Caer Wydr affects the manner by which we perceive all the other forts.

Does the cauldron reside here? If so, what is its nature?

Prydwen's sails flap in the breeze as you board once more and cross the expanse of sea towards…

Caer Goludd: The Fort of Guts and Impediment

This fort is represented by the endocrine function of the pancreas. The towering heights of Goludd rise from flames as bright as the sun, which burns to the west of it; in the east is the fullness of the moon. These are the fires of your passion and anger; it is what we feel in the pits of our stomachs. It is ruled by fire. This place represents our riches, both physical and spiritual, and also our material wealth and gain. However, it is also a place of frustration and may imply gloom, for it is a place that floats between light and dark. Here we reward ourselves after trials we have won. It is what defines how we learn, what we learn, and what we allow to influence us. Our vanity comes from here, as does our smugness and snobbery. It is here that we encounter all our fiery emotions—sexual impulses are invoked here; our lustfulness and the primal drive of carnality rise from this place. Our passion—which in turn can lead to anger, grief, despair, and the influx of energy that compels us forward—stems from here. The song of Goludd can be sensed in the gnawing claw that we feel in our solar plexus when confronted with extreme emotions.

The fires of Goludd can only be tempered by our ability to control them. They may instill fear that implies we do not always like what we feel deep within ourselves at times.

Does the cauldron reside here? If so, what is its nature?

Prydwen's wooden body creaks against the next island as you disembark onto...

Caer Vandwy: The Fort of Mystery

This fort is represented by the reproductive glands, the ovaries and the testes. The island rises brightly and magnificently from the sea, its base a single piece of pure gold; an impossibly high tower made entirely of crystal reaches into the sky. Steps hewn out of the gold lead you to the tower. The floor of the tower is adorned by a Celtic cross carved into the gold; beautifully elaborate, its knots twist and turn with glorious precision. In the centre, where the arms of the cross meet, is a brilliant beam of blue light, like that from a neutron star. It arises from a pit of utter darkness. There is music here and power beyond comprehension. This is the fort that combines all other forts into cohesion; it is the place that sings of our origination. All the wisdom and knowledge of all the worlds are within its walls; the light is the music of magic and creation. This is the place of knowing, where we make sense of the mysteries. Its danger is inexperience, foolhardiness, and arrogance; its message is that one cannot conceptualise what one has no concept of. Yet it teaches us that we are the sum totality of all that has been before us. Does the light stream from the cauldron?

Does the cauldron reside here? If so, what is its nature?

You embark the ship for the final crossing to…

Caer Ochren: The Fort of Edges

This fort is represented by the pineal gland. The sky is dark here; the castle sits gloomily and silently amidst the rocks of grey and black. Its towers are many and dimly lit by an unknown source. Within the fort is a perplexing array of mirrors—seemingly every wall, each ledge, floor, and ceiling are constructed of mirrors. In the centre of the vast hall sits an alien animal; its silver head holds a lantern between its horns. Once lit, the fort shines brightly as light reflects sharply from the mirrored surfaces. Like the third eye, the pineal gland, this place is activated by light. The secrets of the moon hide within this place. It is the home of mirrored observation; the ebb and flow of personality live here. This is the place where we think we see ourselves. In actuality, we see only a reflection, which is an image in reverse. From here we reflect what we want to present to the world; we may fall into another's footsteps here and become sheep. Remember, the moon does not shine by its own light, but by another's. By whose light do you shine? Is it your own? We may judge ourselves harshly in Ochren, but remember that what we see in the mirror is not a true representation. Perception and effectuality live here, as do the limitations of our intelligence.

You sense Taliesin and Arthur beside you. They ask you a question: "Is the cauldron within this place? What is its nature?"

They lead you back to Prydwen. From her decks you raise from your feet, above the sea of Annwn, and back into your mortal coil.

◆ ◆ ◆

The above system serves to demonstrate the complexity of cauldrons within the Celtic continuum. Although the journey appears to navigate through a sea of islands, it is, in fact, a journey into the cauldron; the entire experience is contained within it. And Prydwen, like Cerridwen in our tale, is the divine feminine power needed to ensure a successful and fruitful journey that deeply transforms. Utilised as a template for exploration of the self, this technique aligns one to the wisdom of the past made applicable to the modern age.

The cauldron teaches us the nature of isolation as a valued and necessary tool for development. We may share experiences collectively as a group, a grove, or a coven. But the journey into the womb of the witch goddess or into aspects of the self must be conducted alone. Support is essential, but a guiding hand is limited to being on the periphery. The isolation we sense within the cauldron is tantamount to death before the necessary rebirth as an initiate of the mysteries; this is further elaborated upon in the section devoted to Gwion Bach. The cauldron embodies the darkness before birth; it heightens our insecurities, our fears and demons that are projected onto the dark walls of our psyche. The period of gestation, as in any form of training, is lengthy; it does not occur overnight. Instead we must endure the solitude, the isolation, and the darkness in order to understand our fears, flaws, and compromised personalities, and acknowledge them as essential components of the whole. A journey into self and into the mysteries is not intended to destroy or negate our multifaceted personas, but instead it facilitates the acceptance of what and who we are in relation to our tribes, our families, our friends, nature, and the universe in its entirety.

EXERCISE

Take a moment to imagine the great cauldron of Cerridwen sitting on flames that relentlessly lick at its belly. The surface of its contents simmer, casting great pillars of steam into the air; the fragrance of a thousand herbs and berries tickles your nostrils. The cauldron is enormous, large enough to accommodate eight men. From its edge you cast yourself into its belly, the boiling liquid searing your skin, and you descend into the darkness. The cauldron has no bottom—it is endless, it reaches into the subtle realms of Awen; each molecule of your body responds, and in a flash of light, your body disassembles into its component atoms. Your body vanishes yet your consciousness remains, though not quite in the same manner as in the apparent world—it knows more, it is more than the sum total of the body. It is all that was, all that ever will be—all the sciences, magic, and wisdom of all the worlds are known to you at that point, as they were prior to your spirit condensing into the density of your human body. You possess no eyes to see by means of light, but you sense the apparent world above the simmering surface of the cauldron's contents; moving towards it, the molecules of your body reassemble, and you emerge, body unscathed, from the bubbling vessel. Floating as if carried on a plane of glass, you rise into the air and descend gracefully onto the soft green grass near the lakeshore. A smile caresses your features as you utter, "I am from the cauldron born."

Record your meditation in your journal.

Morfran Afagddu
THE DANCE OF DARKNESS

♦ ♦ ♦

Morfran, the son of Tegid—no man laid his weapon in him
at Camlan, for he was so ugly, everyone thought him to be
an attendant demon; he had hair on him like a stag.

Culhwch ac Olwen[33]

The brightest of lights cast the darkest of shadows. The journey to the spirit is one we embark on alone; we may share the company and warmth of others, but ultimately it is a solitary quest. These roller-coaster adventures will eventually cause us to encounter the shadow, or the "Other"—the darker side of the spirit, which casts long, sigh-filled shadows. This is the place of melancholy and anger, of shame and loathing—the place of pain and torment, passion and secrets. The shadow emulates the merciless aspects of the natural world, where nature acts simply in accordance to its nature. This is the teaching of Morfran Afagddu.

We are told very little about this elusive character within the manuscripts. The inclusion of a few words in the script alludes to a complex character who tells us more about ourselves than we may care to admit. It seems on first glance that we are informed of his existence only in relation to his mother's concern for him—his ugliness is the catalyst for the brewing of Awen. He is the reason behind Cerridwen's devotion to the spell she conjures. We are told nothing of his nature but only of his appearance; he is the darkness

---

33   My translation.

that is in direct opposition to the light and radiance of his sister, Creirfyw. To begin to understand the nature of Morfran Afagddu, we must initially look to the meaning of his name. Within the text we are introduced to this character thusly:

> …they named him Morfran, but because of his ugliness they called him Afagddu (meaning "utter darkness").[34]

We are not offered any other explanation as to why the child, within one single sentence, has his entire persona brought into question. Consequently he is stripped of his birth name. We are informed that he is named Morfran—this title consists of two Welsh words, the first being *mor*, meaning "sea," and the second *fran*, which is a mutation of *bran*, meaning "crow" or "raven" or another bird of the Corvid family. The modern *Dictionary of the Welsh Language* also describes the word as being synonymous with cormorant. Typically within the Welsh language, names are not bestowed on an individual flippantly and without reason (unlike name-giving in the twenty-first century!); they are normally descriptive of a person's disposition, standing, profession, or rank. They tell us something about the person before we even meet them. In this case, we are told that this individual, this child, was initially given a name synonymous with the sea and with the Corvid family of birds. The word bran, according to the University of Wales's *Dictionary of the Welsh Language* is in direct relation to black carrion birds, which alludes to the title of darkness that is eventually bestowed upon the child.

We are also informed that the name as a whole can be related to cormorant, which upon closer examination tells us a little more about the nature of Morfran. The cormorant is a black, glossed bird, tinged with bronze and deep blues. Their uncanny ability to dive to significant depths in search of food has been exploited by man for centuries; in fact, King James the First had a Master of Cormorants on the Thames. Alas, their feathers can become waterlogged, which accounts for the heraldic posture they assume on land in order to dry their plumes. Metaphorically, the cormorant dives into the sea—the "mor" compound of our character's name. We have already noted

---

34   NLW MS 5276D. Translated by the author.

how the sea in Celtic myth is synonymous with the spirit, and, within "The Spoils of Annwn" it holds the islands of the "self." Celtic lore also stipulates that the spirit, upon the death of the body, dives into the Western sea to the lands of youthfulness that lie beneath the waves. The cormorant interacts with the realm of sea, the place of mystery, and the implication is that this child is a creature synonymous with the sea.

The suffix *bran* gives us another useful reference. We previously touched on the divine family of Branwen and Bendigeidfran and the fact that they are the children of Llyr. Not only do their names suggest the Corvid family, they are also linked to the sea by means of their father Llyr, the sea god, a quality shared in the name given to Morfran. This implies that the quality of Morfran is indicating his importance within the watery, salty realm of the sea and of his penetration into it. He interacts with this world, but in a manner that is not immediately obvious or straightforward.

Afagddu—from the Welsh *y fagddu*—is given the description "a night of unordinary darkness" in the *Dictionary of the Welsh Language.*[35] It is also described as meaning utter darkness, extreme blackness, and gloom, and has been used figuratively to mean hell. Surely just being a little ugly or having a face that only a mother could love does not justify changing a child's name to meaning "he of utter darkness"—it seems somewhat dramatic, to say the least! But Cerridwen and Tegid do this for good reason; they are aspects of the mystery, and they understand the nature of their child and what he represents. At some level even Cerridwen knows that he will not receive Awen; it is not fated.

In the epic tale of Culhwch ac Olwen, one of the earliest Arthurian sagas, we find a reference to Morfran Afagddu that can be found as the subtitle of this section. In it he exudes a supernatural quality that is otherworldly; his appearance strikes fear in the hearts of men, who do not even attempt to destroy him. His ugliness is apparent here, as is his seemingly demonic nature. The men in battle do not attempt to slay him for good reason: he is representative of their shadow, and on some level they understand this. Yes,

---

35   Bevan, *Geiriadur Prifysgol Cymru*, 1266.

he is vilified, but within this vilification they perceive themselves. To destroy him would be to destroy an essential aspect of themselves. Immediately after the sentence relating to Morfran Afagddu we see a counterbalance, akin to his sister in the original tale. It reports a figure named Sandde Pryd Angel and how "no one laid his spear in him at Camlan because he was so beautiful, everyone thought him to be an angel."[36]

This reinforces the fact that without light there can be no darkness; without darkness there can be no light. They are essential; we may perceive them as antagonistic qualities when, in fact, they are not—they complement the other, they need each other in order to exist. This polarity is further exemplified in another reference to Morfran Afagddu that is found in the *Trioedd Ynys Prydein: The Triads of the Island of Britain*, a vast collection of wisdom, teaching, and history presented in a tripartite format. Triad number 41 states:

> Three beloved horses of the Island of Britain: …and silver-white,
> proud and fair, the horse of Morfran the son of Tegid.[37]

This further reiterates Morfran Afagddu's inherent connection to his opposite quality. He rides atop a silver-white horse, black and white in perfect balance. We are informed of fairness—a quality of the light half—and pride, an attribute of the shadow; seemingly, they dance in perfect harmony. And atop these qualities is their epitome, Morfran Afagddu—the shadow.

What does this tell us? How is this essential to the brewing of Awen?

The primary message of the shadow is: "Deny it at your peril." For the brew to be effective, we must consume it knowing who we are down to the minute detail—even what instills shame and embarrassment must be acknowledged for the elixir to work. This is the role of Morfran Afagddu; he is there to teach us the essentialness of our darkness. He is not alone in this teaching; other archetypes in Celtic myth serve to fulfil this role, and pertinent to our exploration is the character of Efnysien. When we explored the cauldron, we briefly encountered this creature, whose name means "hostile

---

36 Bromwich, *Culhwch ac Olwen.*
37 Bromwich, *Trioedd Ynys Prydein: The Triads of the Island of Britain*, 109.

enemy" or "un-peaceful," when he mutilated the horses of the Irish king. He too is a powerful representation of the shadow.

The practise of Paganism is not all sweetness and light. Buttercups and roses have their place, but we take the good with the bad. The beauty of the Pagan traditions is that it allows us to explore the darker side of our nature without fearing it. Beauty and awe is one thing, but we also need to be dropped from a height into a festering pit of excrement from time to time. To truly understand the wonder of nature and mystery, we must also face its less likeable side, including our own. Thankfully we have archetypes and deities who provide effective guides for exploring the darkness; we do not need to venture alone. They are there for good reason: to help us.

The personification of the shadow appears in every culture and is present in dreams and mythology as something that is feared and despised. The shadow comes with power, a power that we fear greatly; it may arrive with little warning, and vanquishing it is never easy, if it's possible at all. We may brand the shadow as evil—something that is counterproductive to our well-being. Its tendency to act on instinct scares us; to examine it makes us uncomfortable, causing us to squirm. The majority of us do not like our shadows, and we certainly do not want to engage with it, lest it break free from the chains of civility, rationality, and politeness that we bind it with. We fear the shadow aspect, for it epitomises our weaknesses, our instincts, and our shortcomings. All our unexpressed emotions—our tempers, loathing, and hatred—seethe within it. It represents that gut feeling we try to suppress when we listen to that woman in the office who annoys us. We smile insipidly when we actually just want to rip her arms off and smack her with the wet ends! To function in society, we suppress these extreme emotions (thankfully!), yet they are still an undeniable force within us. Left unchecked, our anger can lead to frustration, which in turn can lead to rage, which is a state of helplessness that nobody really wants to venture into too often in life.

We may not like our shadows, but we must recognise them for Awen to flow unhindered, lest it meet the barriers of ignorance set up to protect ourselves from ourselves. To deny the shadow—the Morfran Afagddu within—

we risk repressing it without due consultation and tempt it to raise its head, almost against our volition. When this occurs, the shadow may find the cracks that appear in our "pleasant" veneer and suddenly start to express its ways in disturbing manners. Its power over us can, at times, be overwhelming as we find ourselves behaving irrationally or out of character; generally, this is indicative of the fact that we have attempted to suffocate our shadow. It retaliates, it wants to be acknowledged, and if we don't allow it to be, it will turn and bite us on the backside. Its sheer force and rage has the potential to break free of the restrictions we place upon it. But the shadow is not evil, per se; its role is to challenge us, to provoke and explore the darker aspect of our psyche. If we work with it—if we honour and value it for the qualities it gives us—we diminish the power of its most terrible attributes. The purpose of our shadow is to push our buttons, to challenge us from the darkest recesses of its domain; it affects our relationships with others both socially and sexually. We may sometimes come across people that we just don't connect with; something about them repels us or grinds at our nerves, causing us to be irritated by their company. These are the times when we are confronted by Morfran Afagddu; we can be assured that when we are annoyed by another, they are simply holding a mirror that reflects the darker parts of our own shadows. Yet our shadows can enhance and enrich our creativity, which Jung suggested in the early part of the twentieth century when he said, "In spite of its functions as a reservoir for human darkness—or perhaps because of this—the shadow is the seat of creativity."[38]

The outward expression of our shadow in the form of creativity honours its power and alleviates its hold over us in a negative sense. Many artists create out of pain, passion, anger, or frustration, so rather than subdue the shadow, they give it a voice, thus placating it and lessening its influence to affect us in spite of ourselves. By ignoring the shadow, we fail to acknowledge and assimilate its positive qualities. Our instincts lie in the shadow and our sense of discernment, our ability to act on a hunch that, in hindsight, may have been the correct reaction to a given situation. There is a great deal

---

38   Jung, *Memories, Dreams, Reflections*, 262.

of authenticity within our shadow; and it can sometimes relate to life in a manner that is far more genuine than the tamer personas we have been programmed to present to the world. But with the shadow comes responsibility and the ability to respond to our darker sides without having to apologise for them. The great mythologist Joseph Campbell once said, "Don't give up your vices—make your vices work for you—if you are a proud person, don't get rid of your pride, apply it to your spiritual quest."[39]

We may judge ourselves harshly when faced with our shadows; we may punish ourselves unnecessarily when, in fact, there is no need. We may get angry at times, but this reflects our passion; to dismiss it would atrophy what drives us. To shout it into dark recesses will cause it to bark like a dog cornered. So you like to procrastinate? I certainly do. Why punish yourself; use it. That pious, thin bloke who sits opposite you in the office really, really gets on your nerves, and nothing would please you more than to tie him to a radiator and force-feed him donuts! Just ask yourself why—what is it in him that you dislike in yourself? What is the nature of the mirror he holds in which your reflection is cast? We are generally good people and strive to be polite, civil, and well mannered in life; our shadow does not threaten this, it just wants to be heard. A child that is not given a voice will rebel; lock something away, and it will find a way out. So the best course of action is to just leave the door slightly ajar and address it like a friend. Shadows are generally much larger than the objects that cast them, and maybe this tells us an awful lot about the nature of our shadow—how much do you know of your own?

What relationship do you have with your shadow? The majority of us may willingly examine this dark half, but I would imagine that this practise will cause a great deal of discomfort. But its message is clear—do not attempt to vanquish the aspects of yourself that you do not like or the things that make you cry out in frustration or anger. Don't supplicate the shadow by patronising its power over you or by attempting to ignore it with the typical "I am not that kind of person" attitude. Our shadow can work for us. Instead of turning a blind eye to it, acknowledge that some aspects of your

---

39   Osbon, *A Joseph Campbell Companion*, 135.

personality—albeit not very nice perhaps—are, in fact, an essential part of you. To ignore it is to tempt it to rebel. To dismiss the shadow is to fail to bring all our qualities to the cauldron.

Morfran Afagddu epitomises the qualities of the dark, or waning, part of the year—in stark contrast to his sister, Creirfyw, who symbolises the light, or waxing, half of the year. For Awen to be an effectively acknowledged and expressed force, it must contain aspects of the shadow. But the task can be difficult, elusive; the exploration of the shadow may be riddled with pitfalls and obstacles, a fact that the ancient Celtic chronicles record in the poem "Angar Kyfundawt" from the Book of Taliesin when it says "until death Afagddu's declamation shall be obscure."[40]

This line implies the difficult nature of the shadow and that for many its voice will go unheard. The dark speech is essentially powerful and a vital aspect of the querent's journey. Whilst the chronicles provide us with a warning—the danger of suppressing the shadow—they also provide us with hope that the shadow is indeed essential. In the poem "Marwnat Vthyr Pen" we find the following lines: "I am a poet; my art deserves praise, and may it be with ravens and eagles and raptors—Afagddu, to him there came a great experience, since good men suspend themselves between two poles."[41]

Whatever great experience Morfran Afagddu encountered remains unknown, as much a mystery as his essential nature. But what is important is the fact that Morfran Afagddu and his shadow aspect are perpetuated throughout the Celtic chronicles, and within each quote, each line and verse, he is perceived as being a creature of supernatural erudition. The above verse has been dissected by Celtic scholars for centuries, yet nobody, it seems, can shed light on the latter section: "Men suspend themselves between two poles." In my visions I am reminded of the Long Man of Wilmington, who resides on a hillside in the English county of Sussex. This chalk figure has for countless centuries stood proudly, his hands resting upon two poles, or holding a doorway open so that one can step through into the hollow hills of the ancestors, to the halls of wisdom that lie within. Perhaps this is the

---

40 "Angar Kyfundawt" (The Hostile Confederacy) in the Book of Taliesin.
41 Haycock, *Legendary Poems from the Book of Taliesin*, 321.

great experience of Morfran Afagddu: he acts as catalyst that opens doorways to our darker self, to the dark speech that rises from the abyss and sings in praise of the mysteries.

EXERCISE

What is the nature of your shadow? What are the things that drive your passions and your anger? Are you familiar with your own shadow—how it developed, what voice it has, how it seeks to teach you or compromise you?

This simple exercise serves to demonstrate the nature of your shadow, to give it a voice that it otherwise would not be given. It allows you to spend time exploring it and listening to its voice, where you gain a deeper understanding of its essentialness.

Take yourself to a room that can be darkened; close all curtains and illuminate the space by candlelight only. Spend some time preparing the room for the exercise, creating shadows and corners of darkness. Arrange yourself at the foot of a length of wall-lining paper cut to your height. Ensure that the majority of candles are behind you in order that your shadow may be cast onto the paper before you. Stand at the foot of the paper and adjust the candlelight so that your shadow is visible on its surface. In a group setting, the outline of the shadow could be drawn onto the paper itself.

Reflect on your shadow and the fact that bright lights cast dark shadows—the stronger and brighter the light, the longer and darker the shadow. The shadow cannot exist without light to cast it; what does this tell of the nature of light and shadow? Ponder and meditate on your dark half, the traits and aspects of your personality that are generally avoided. Can you name them? Do they pain you or bring elements of shame and embarrassment to mind? How has the past—your childhood, your relationships and connections—altered or given voice to your shadow? Do you suppress it or do you allow it to sing?

Look to the shadows within the room you occupy. Contemplate the dark and its powers: how it can cause us to feel insecure or afraid. Watch and note that the demons you perceive on the walls of darkness are from within.

Observe your shadow on the paper before you—it is separate from you, yet an inexorable part of you. It cannot be denied.

Take to the floor, on knees or cross-legged, and with a large marker pen or several markers of different colours, express the nature of your shadow directly onto the paper. Give voice to your passions and lust, to your anger and loathing, to your bitterness and envy. Draw symbols and patterns that represent the things that drive you and give your life determination and stubbornness. Allow what pains you to dance from the pen to paper, filling in the shadow, giving it voice. Ponder on these things; give them the time they deserve as vital cogs on the wheel of your story. Do not denigrate them or belittle them; attempt not to judge them; simply give them voice. When you have exhausted yourself, the paper, or the pen, sit back and look at the whole picture. What does it reveal about your shadow?

Do not destroy the paper, but instead fold it and keep it in a box, wrap the box in paper that reflects the nature of your shadow, and tie a ribbon about its form. These are your shadows; they are as unique as you are. Keep them in a secret place, and every three years or so, unwrap the package and look to see what has changed or what may be added to its patterns.

Record your experience in your journal.

Creirfyw

THE HEART OF BEAUTY

◆ ◆ ◆

And they had a daughter named Creirfyw,
and the fairest maiden in all the world was she.

Hanes Taliesin

Creirfyw does not appear in the Elis Gruffudd's text; when we do meet her, it is in the hand of John Jones's manuscript, where he writes *"a merch a elwit y Greirfyw a thegkaf merch or byt oedd honno* (and a daughter named Creirfyw and the fairest maiden in all the world was she)."[42]

It tells us very little of her nature, unlike her brother, Morfran Afagddu, yet she appears in several manuscripts that contain fragments of the tale. However, the writers have recorded two versions of her name—Greirfyw and Creirwy.[43] So first we must examine the nature of this elusive creature's name.

The prefix *greir-* is a mutation of the word *creir*, which in turn is derived from *crair*—according to the *Dictionary of the Welsh Language,* this is taken to mean "a relic, a holy thing, talisman, treasure, a richly decorated article; object of admiration or love, darling."[44] The addition of the suffix *-fyw* is a mutation of the word *byw*, meaning "alive, living, having life, animate, quick, existing, actual." With this in mind, the name of Cerridwen's daughter can be taken to mean "living treasure." Accompanied with the description that

---

42   Peniarth MS 111.
43   *Creirfyw* will be used throughout this book.
44   *Bevan, Geiriadur Prifysgol Cymru,* 578–79.

she is the fairest maiden in all the world, we begin to get a sense of Creir-fyw. However, other manuscripts have her name ending with the suffix -*wy*, meaning "egg," so in that sense her name can be taken to mean "a holy egg" or "treasured egg." But what does this tell us of her nature?

When we first meet Creirfyw in the text, her associations are bright, full of life and vitality; her name sings of treasure and relics and things that are valued. The terms *love*, *darling*, and *admiration* hide within her name—there is a lot of light here; she is a creature who radiates beauty and wonder. When we look a little deeper into the chronicles of the Celts, by the magic of inter-textual references we find Creirfyw in her Creirwy guise within the *Trioedd Ynys Prydein*: "*Teir Gwenriein Ynys Prydein—Kreirwy merch Keritwen, ac Aryan-rot verch Don, a Gwen verch Kywryt mab Krydon*. (The three fair (royal) ladies of the Island of Britain—Creirwy, daughter of Cerridwen; and Arianrhod, the daughter of Don; and Gwen, daughter of Cywryd, son of Crydon)."[45]

The inclusion of Creirfyw's name in this triad is immensely important to our understanding of her. She exists beyond the tale, and the implications of this reveal something of her nature. The triad specifies that the ladies men-tioned are royal, and according to the scholar Rachel Bromwich the term *gwenriein* has an extended meaning of "royal lady or princess."[46] Yet we are not informed of this royal lineage within the original tale. The only infor-mation we are provided with is Cerridwen's standing as a wise woman or enchantress and that her husband was a nobleman. There is no indication of royalty, yet Creirwy is listed in the same triad as two significant royal women.

Arianrhod, the daughter of Don, is another creature of supernatural eru-dition; she is the child of a goddess, one of the chief mother goddesses of the Britons. She herself has powers beyond that of a simple mortal and can be found within the Fourth Branch of the mystical Mabinogi legends. In this tale she steps over the wand of a god/king and gives birth immaculately to two babes, one of whom instantly escapes to the sea, diving beneath the waves. The other grows into a man who undergoes a series of supernatural and transformative processes and is ultimately initiated into the mysteries by

---

45   Bromwich, *Trioedd Ynys Prydein: Triads of the Island of Britain*, triad 78, page 208.
46   Ibid.

proxy of a sow who devours his rotting flesh. According to the triads, Arian-rhod's father is none other than Beli Mawr, the ancestor deity of the Island of Britain, from whom the leading deific dynasties are descended. Within the native tales of Wales, Arianrhod appears as a magical being of royal-godly parentage, yet she lives amidst mortals; she is a demigod who, by the pro-cess of apotheosis, has become a fully fledged goddess of the modern Pagan movement.

We are also introduced to another royal lady, Gwen, the daughter of Cywryd, son of Crydon. This seemingly obscure family is directly descended from a list of ancient British kings who are the ancestors of Beli Mawr.[47] We have almost come full circle; it seems that these royal princesses are some-how linked, one to the other. Each share a commonality in that their parents are either supernatural or are in possession of magical abilities. If Arianrhod is descended from a god and a goddess, and Gwen is also a descendent of the same father god, then it would be reasonable to suggest that Creirfyw's parents are also of supernatural or godly origin. This is demonstrative of the paradoxical and sometimes contradictory nature of the Celtic material.

Creirfyw shares her title as the fairest maiden in the world with another lady of significant lineage who appears in the Welsh romance of Culhwch and Olwen. Within this epic tale we are introduced to:

> Creiddylad, daughter of Lludd Llaw Eraint, the most beautiful maiden there ever was in the three islands of Britain and her three adjacent islands. And for her affection Gwythyr, son of Greidol, and Gwyn, son of Nudd, fight each May Day forever, until the day of Judgment.[48]

Here we are introduced to two men of supernatural quality who repre-sent the light and dark half of the year respectfully and may be the source of the popular Pagan myth of the Holly and the Oak Kings. Under orders by King Arthur, they agree to abstain from taking Creiddylad's hand and instead they meet at a time of liminality, between spring and summer, to fight for

---

47   Ibid., 327.
48   *Culhwch ac Olwen*, translated by the author.

her hand in marriage. Whosoever wins the battle on the day of Judgment will win the maiden's heart. Here we have the perpetual battle between light and dark playing itself out at the time of heightened sexual power and carnal lust. This symbol of beauty, Creiddylad, causes these two men to fight to the death for the sake of love. It can be seen as a metaphor for the overwhelming power that beauty has over the human heart. Beauty is something that is wanted, needed; humans lust for it, desire it, and, at its extreme, they will kill for it. When this battle for beauty is internalised, it can cause eating disorders, insecurities, and a constant war with oneself. On the other hand, it can imbue confidence and sureness; it can bring light and joy into the lives of others. This can be seen in the gifts that Creirfyw brings to the cauldron, and they are as essential as the shadow—they are imperative for the brewing of Awen, yet they are riddled with contradictions and obstacles.

Beauty is as fickle, fleeting, and subjective as the nature of Creirfyw herself, and with so little recorded of her, we are left scratching our heads in frustration. Or are we? The physical remnants of the tales are simply one side of the coin; there is another side, one which we access by means of the subtle senses. It is all very well to ponder over dusty tomes and manuscripts that hide in the shadows of libraries and archives, but these tales abound in magic and are perpetuated by magicians and adepts of the wise crafts. It would stand to reason, therefore, that one utilises the senses to discern what hides betwixt and between the lines of old ink on parchment. As this book has demonstrated thus far, this tale and myriad others perpetuate a body of wisdom and lore that predates the coming of the Catholic church and its missionaries and pertains to a time when the old gods walked hand in hand with mortals. They provide evidence of a residual Druidic/Pagan wisdom and source of knowledge that initiates of the mysteries can continue to access to this day. But this cannot be achieved by one method alone.

People are drawn to the beauty of words, to the fine lines of calligraphy on velum and parchment; they are sucked in and become immersed in a world of writing. As we have seen, this function served to preserve the material, but one must be cautious that the beauty of words does not distract the subtle senses or be to its detriment. The wonder and beauty of language, of its evolution and development, is a magnificent thing—a part of our history. But within the beauty of words lies the threat of literalism. This is a common syndrome in a world besotted by the written word, by the attitude that if it is written, it therefore must be true. These tales, which swam in the ever- moving rivers of the oral narrative tradition, did not belong to the world of the academic; instead, they were a tool of the magician, of the bard, and of the seer. We are all drawn to beauty in different ways, but we must be careful of its embrace, for it can overwhelm us and coerce us into strong opinions based only on one facet of the truth. Within the traditions of the ancient Celts, it was permissible to "fill in the gaps" by means of Awen and the divine connection the initiate had to the source. If we take Creirfyw, for instance, we quickly realise that we have very little information, so the best course of action for the querent is to journey with her—to summon this archetype, within context, from beyond the mists of time and directly communicate with her. Historically this visionary element was not frowned upon or condemned as inappropriate or lacking in authority; in fact, it was quite the opposite. A student and initiate of the schools of mystery was expected to use the subtle senses in this manner, to tap into the cauldron of knowledge and bring forth its wisdom, filling in the gaps that the centuries had forged.[49]

To journey with Creirfyw is to be immersed in the beauty of life, to see its wondrous, awe-inspiring light that radiates throughout the universe. If we look to nature or to the night sky, if we look into the depths of the ocean or as far as our telescopes can reach, we see beauty. This breathtaking face of the universe surrounds us continuously; we swim within its radiance, and yet sometimes the whole of existence can seem a dreary and dark place, threatening and unfriendly. Just like Creirfyw, beauty has another face: it commands respect and honour. The pure blossoms of the blackthorn are alluring, so much so that hands may reach out to caress them, only to find a vicious thorn that penetrates the flesh. The aquamarine seas of our planet are a sight of utter beauty, yet they can rise and destroy. The woman on the

---

49   Parker, *The Four Branches of the Mabinogi*, 100–101.

cover of a fashion magazine may be the object of desire and lust, but her airbrushed features only hide the pain of abstinence and hunger that embitter her. The pop star with his expensive clothes and rock-hard abs may find himself crying in isolation, his beauty of little value to him in an empty bed. Beauty can steer us into tight corridors of denial, of pretending to be something we are not; it can cause us to conform rather than sing our own individual songs. We may look in the mirror and despise what we see; we may dress differently, or hide behind an act so that the world accepts us. Feeling fat and unattractive, we may stop eating well in an attempt to emulate the perfect beauty on the cover of a magazine. Our vanity may isolate us from our responsibilities—it may force us into debt for the next fashion item or the new advanced surgical technique. Tighten this, smooth that, tuck this, and stretch that! Finding the balance in beauty is perhaps more difficult than accessing the shadow.

Creirfyw's song has another side; she tells us to look to the smallest pimpernel, to the bobbing head of a weed that graces the hedgerow, to a single campion that grows on an old pile of grit. If we look closely at the smallest things in life, we can see a humble form of beauty that may otherwise elude us. The lesson of beauty is balance—this is the song of Creirfyw. She teaches us to take stock of what we have—regardless of what we look like, where we come from, or how much money lines our wallets. We are inherently beautiful, we are a vital cog in the wheel of the universe, and it is amazing, yet simultaneously it is deadly. When we sing in tune with our being, we make music that is unique, individual; it expresses our place in the world as spirits that swim in corporeal vessels. You are beauty and ugliness, shadow and light combined; you are simultaneously amazing and deadly. This is a vital part of your song, and this is what Creirfyw asks that you bring to the cauldron.

Do you harmonise to the rhythm of your own music? Are the lyrics of your life song your own or in line with another? We may be inspired and influenced by those around us, but too often we allow this to sink to another depth, where we attempt to conform. We may change our behaviour, standards, and opinions to please someone else. We may dress to satisfy another's needs or suffocate our own expression in fear of judgement and ridicule.

We are all victims of these states to an extent, but we needn't be. They are not our songs. Your own is supremely more beautiful, for a simple reason: it is yours! Creirfyw asks that we look to the humble buttercup—its beauty lies in its ability to express itself with honesty, being true to itself. The buttercup does not wish to sing the song of dandelion or orchid; it has its own song of beauty and purpose. It is not reliant upon another. An oak tree does not wish to emulate the rowan, it wishes only to sing in praise of itself. The face of beauty in nature teaches us the lessons of beauty in human nature.

The light must be in balance with the dark—shadow and reflection, brilliance and dullness. When the songs of Creirfyw and Morfran Afagddu combine, we ascend into the realm of humility and integrity. By allowing the two voices of light and dark to harmonise, we start to sense and appreciate our own inherent beauty. Imagine how dull the world would be if we all looked the same, talked the same, dressed the same. Creirfyw and her dark brother do not oppose; they are not powers that antagonise each other. They serve only to give voice to our light and shadow—they are essential to our well-being. You may not have the wardrobe of a rock star or the muscles of an athlete or the hair of an actress, but these are only facets of beauty—perhaps falsely so, for they are perpetuated with an agenda. True beauty lies in the ability to balance the light and dark, to give voice to the brother and sister of opposites. Combined, they bring immense magic to the cauldron; apart, they can destroy it.

You are a part of the universe learning about itself, singing in praise of itself. You are more beautiful and wondrous than you give yourself credit for. Sometimes it can be difficult to appreciate the beauty of a star-filled sky when you feel like your own stars have been extinguished. But look to magic, look to wonder and enchantment, reach out to the siblings of light and dark, and they will help you rekindle the stars of beauty that have always resided within you. This life is your story; it is not prewritten, you are its author and its narrator, its producer and director. Creirfyw teaches us the value and nature of beauty; her brother brings us the message of the shadow.

Together they teach us to listen.

EXERCISE: LESSONS IN BEAUTY

Spend three days thinking intensely on the three things that you value most in your life. Create or find an item to represent each value; this will eventually be cast into water, so ensure that the item is of an expendable nature. Imbue it with the sense of what you treasure the most. Only you will know what each item represents; they could be your children, your family, your career or art, but they must represent what gives your life the most meaning and value. Make sure that you can identify each item without confusing one with another.

Then choose a place that you consider the most beautiful—a favourite valley or wood, a glade or a plain, but it should contain a body of water, be it a lake, a river, or a pond. At a time that suits you, take yourself and the three items you have selected to this place. Get as close to the water as you possibly can. Settle yourself and invoke the following image into your mind:

See the body of water in your mind's eye and imagine that upon its surface there is a mist. From that mist a human figure appears; it is half naked and incredibly ugly. Its hair is matted and unkempt, and blisters and scars cover its body. It approaches you and says, "Give me what you cherish the least!"

At this, the figure sinks into the body of water. Open your eyes and reach for the item that represents what you cherish the least. Cast it into the water.

Settle yourself once more and recall the same mist that hovers above the water's surface. This time you imagine a figure of great beauty, male or female or a combination of both. It is the epitome of physical attractiveness; everything about it is perfect and alluring to you. Imagine that it walks towards you, its hands outstretched as it says, "Give me what you cherish the least!"

The figure vanishes beneath the water, and you must again reach for the item that represents what you value least. This is no easy task; much of your love and connection to something vitally important to you is symbolically attached to this item, and you are being asked to throw it away. Feel its separation from you as you cast it into the water.

Close your eyes once more and recall the mists. This time from within its depths comes a figure of two halves—one side radiates light and beauty whilst the other is dark and obscured by shadow; a river of pulsating grey light beats at their joining. The figure approaches you, its hands outstretched, and as it slowly sinks beneath the water, it says, "Give me what you cherish the most!"

Relinquish your final and most treasured possession into the waters.

What are you without the things you value the most? How do they define you? Having spent some time pondering over them, evaluating them, and then giving them up to the spirits of light and shadow, how do you now perceive yourself? When all that we value is stripped away from us, we are left with the bare bones of our personalities and qualities. We are all defined and define ourselves by what we treasure. The purpose of this ritual is to challenge that definition, to allow you time to reflect on who you are as an individual stripped bare of the constraints and values that have been placed on your life. At this point you are a child of the cauldron, naked, vulnerable.

This allegorical offering of your values and treasures causes a shift in consciousness that may not be immediately apparent. Allow messages of light and shadow to enter your subconscious through meditation and dreams. Note the feelings and senses that you encountered during this exercise in your journal. Give thanks to the archetypes of light and shadow and to the spirits of this place of beauty.

Record the experience in your journal.

Tegid Foel
NOBILITY AND STRENGTH

◆ ◆ ◆

In the days of Arthur, there was a nobleman
who lived in the land called Penllyn.
His name was Tegid Foel, and his home
was the body of water now called Llyn Tegid.

Ystoria Taliesin

You will note that the following interpretation of the Tegid Foel character is subject to a similar treatment as that of his offspring. Very little is recorded of this masculine figure, yet he is essential to the telling of the tale. In a similar style to the exploration of Creirfyw, Awen must be utilised, in conjunction with research and written sources, to tease meaning from this mysterious character. Although his presence within the tale is limited to the first paragraph alone, this is no indication that his role is unimportant. In fact, one can find attributes of immense value that contribute to the overall meaning of the tale. With the exception of Tegid, every other archetype and component within the tale has a definite supernatural quality. Their contributions are those of magic, of deep human qualities and attributes; they bring the gifts of acceptance and learning, liminality and innocence to the cauldron. These qualities are subjective and fluid; they have no defined parameters or borders and can blend with one another. Tegid's properties are very much the opposite: they are steadfast and based entirely in the physical world. Tegid Foel is the personification of the material plane.

His name appears in the old texts as Tegit Uoel[50] and Tegid Voel[51]; both variations appear in modern Welsh as Tegid Foel, meaning "Tegid the bald." He appears briefly in other Welsh genealogies, where we are informed of other children whom he fathered. We are not, however, provided any further information about them or their lives.[52] One may immediately note the peculiarity of the term "bald"—why such a reference to his baldness? As with all names in Celtica, nothing is used by accident or without meaning; his baldness is indicative of something. Surely his title is not a nickname directly related to male pattern baldness! But baldness does denote something specific to our exploration of Tegid—it implies high levels of the male sex hormone dihydrotestosterone. This hormone is produced in the male prostate gland and affects the hair follicles; it denotes increased virility and sex drive. These males' body types are generally hirsute, but the side effect of such a powerful hormone is the ultimate loss of head hair. If we take this into consideration, we are presented with the image of a tough, sexually powerful, and fiercely masculine figure. He is the epitome of manliness. We are told that he is noble, and a further folk legend presents him as vicious and cruel. These masculine traits all point to a "god" type figure, the polar opposite of the feeling, emotional, instinctive aspects of Cerridwen in her aspect as Goddess.

In Pagan lore, Tegid Foel represents the energy of the Lord, with all his authority, stability and the setting of boundaries. Without this aspect of the God, the inspiration of Cerridwen's cauldron lacks the ability to be manifested on the physical plane. Tegid provides the structure and discipline necessary to hold the energy of inspiration being produced or channelled by Cerridwen. The energy symbolised by Tegid is present throughout the tale, but he is not always obvious, as he is not always represented as an anthropomorphic being. The physical boundaries he represents can be seen as the structure and material of the cauldron that holds Cerridwen's potion. This provides the boundary and holding function necessary to contain

---

50   Peniarth MS 111.
51   NLW MS 5276D.
52   Wade-Evans, *Vitae Sanctorum Britanniae et Genealogiae*, 320.

Cerridwen's catalytic and magical work, symbolic of the constraining and disciplinary function of Tegid. Tegid can be seen as the "holding" aspect of the land during the chase sequence. He represents Awen made manifest through the structure of the physical world.

The coracle, or skin-bag, contains the transformational forces being experienced through access to Awen; without the principle of structure, authority, and boundaries, there is nothing to contain and focus the transformative energy being experienced. Without the principles represented by Tegid, the forces of inspiration that lead to the act of transformation would dissolve and return to the void. Tegid is an essential component that "holds" the tale in place and provides it with a physical stage upon which to play out. Pure inspiration remains ethereal and unmanifest without the structuring nature of the physical world. Without the boundaries and limitations imposed by the physical, our inspiration remains just that: unmanifest. We need Tegid Foel to manifest them onto this plane. Without his influence, the tale would be devoid of security and stability—it would descend into anarchy and become disarranged. Awen would be too fluid and would run through the fingers to be absorbed by the void; Tegid provides the cup that contains our Awen.

Tegid is the tutelary archetype of the lake, and yet the waters themselves are representative of the Goddess aspect—unconscious, formless, emotional, and otherworldly. But for the qualities of the Goddess to be made manifest in this realm and for us to connect to the elements that embody her, she needs the containing boundary of the surrounding banks, which provide the structure, discipline, and boundaries—i.e., the material world. Both these elements combine to provide a link between the manifest plane, represented by the masculine force, and the unmanifest: the feminine force. Neither is greater than the other, but both are essential for making manifest the mysteries and bringing them to applicable cohesion. Ultimately the mysteries are useless unless we are able to set them on a stage that makes them manifest, tangible; anything less than this would simply be a mental exercise. All the other archetypes bring subjective, supernatural qualities vital for the assimilation of mystery, but without the principle of Tegid—the steadfastness and sureness of the physical world—they would lose their cohesion and dissolve into abstraction.

Tegid Foel is our connection to the physical plane and our localities; he represents the qualities of support and security, of stability and strength. He is an allegory for community and tribe, family and friends; he connects us by means of bone and blood to the soil and sap. We are all supported in one manner or another, whether in our personal, professional, or spiritual lives; support is vital for us to be nurtured and permitted to develop. In this light, Cerridwen and her children are supported within a family unit; if Cerridwen is out foraging every day for over a year, someone is maintaining the larder. This role is fulfilled by her husband; he supports the witch's skills by providing for his family. He maintains the physical, visible world to enable Cerridwen's pursuit of the occult arts. The roles here are not those of dependency, but rather of honourable reciprocation. For relationships to grow and fruit they must be symbiotic, each to his or her role, each one contributing to the family or spiritual unit in a manner that is conducive, not predatory or parasitic.

Tegid Foel represents what holds us and gives our lives structure and support. There is a degree of practicality here, for without support we may be unable to fulfil our goals or responsibilities. When we look at our own lives and examine the details that make up our everyday patterns, we will note the structures of support and stability, security and encouragement that bring meaning and reciprocation to our relationships. These are essential for us to be permitted to pursue our dreams, studies, career paths, and life choices in the knowledge that we are supported. This is not a selfish notion, for the concept of reciprocation must be utilised for these relationships to be symbiotic. We may need the support of a spouse or partner to look after the children whilst we pursue our studies with our covens and groves. I reiterate that this is not dependency, it is practicality. We live in a world where nothing is given to us on a plate; our lives are restricted by finances, working patterns and shifts, and family obligations. We may all dream of being full-time priests to the gods, but that is not the world we inhabit; our devotion to the old ways must be balanced with the sheer practicalities of twenty-first-century life. And to enable this we must have support systems in place that mould the physical environment around the spiritual in a beneficial manner.

Generally our support systems go unacknowledged—they morph gradually into the humdrum of existence, and we take them entirely for granted. The message of Tegid Foel is the conscious acknowledgment of the physical, material systems that give our lives the structure and support they require. The anarchic spirit may find this concept utterly anathema and condemn it at first sight, but to do so would be to dishonour the nature of relationship. As children we are supported by our parents and their interaction with the world—they nurture, house, and feed us. We reciprocate by caring for our parents in later life and raising our own children; the cycle repeats. In our educational years we are supported by our peers, encouraged by the unit of friends that arise from intense periods of schooling. These folk become the shoulders upon which we cry in our darkest moments and the invokers of laughter and the joy of love-filled companionships. Our careers are supported by the systems that enable the smooth running of any operation or task; nothing truly happens independently. Within our spiritual development, we are equally supported by means of our spiritual family groups— the covens, groves, groups, and orders to which we belong. Without these structures in place, we would be hard-pressed to maintain Awen's form, and it may become too fluid to form shape and substance. To be in receipt of support is to also provide it—a one-sided relationship based on what one can gain is doomed to fail from the offset. To be in sacred, meaningful relationship is to swim in symbiosis.

The physical location and materials that make up our nonhuman support systems are also vitally important for our well-being. They provide us with a sense of place, of being, by connecting us physically with the world around us. We tend to choose our physical habitats carefully. A house is more than just a series of bricks and mortar to a practitioner of the mysteries; it is a home, an extension of the persona that inhabits it. An untidy house is an untidy mind, says the wisdom of the grandmothers, and there is a certain degree of truth in this old wives' adage. Our states of mind affect the physical, and good mental health is reflected in good physical health.

Our emotions are able to affect our environments in manners that are very real. The saying that "you could cut the atmosphere with a knife" is not a whimsical notion but one based on the activation of the subtle senses, which perceives something beyond the ordinary. The subtle world directly affects the physical world and vice versa; the proper and effective maintenance of both realms is an essential task for any student of the mysteries.

For this to take place, we need systems that guide and support us. We need teachers who can guide us, partners and friends who provide us with the time and energy to commit, and the physical materials needed to practically enable us to develop. For the modern Pagan, however idiotic the notion may seem, a car is equally as essential to those in isolated communities as the ability to imagine. We are communal pack animals; we thrive in community and need this aspect to be human. We are products of our time, and we cannot deny the world as it currently exists, warts and all. It is our world, and it supports us; our communities and families sing of exquisite connection to the material world whilst simultaneously reaching into the subtle realms. To acknowledge our relationships is to deeply honour them, so next time you feel like screaming at your mother for annoying you or verbally attacking your partner for leaving laundry about the bedroom floor, stop and think of what forged that connection in the first place. Examine your relationships and what effect they have on your physical/material world.

In some Eastern spiritual traditions there exists the function of denying the physical, of rising above and beyond the limitations of this dimension. This is not a function of the Celtic systems, which celebrate the essentialness of this experience as something that brings richness and individual expression to the overall knowing of the universe. Tegid Foel is our connection to the here and now; his message tells us to be of the world, for we *are* of the world—our spirits may exist between dimensions, in the space between place, but our corporeal forms exist in the here and now. This planet, this physical earth, is a vital cog on the wheel of experience, and by observing the cycles of nature, we glean an understanding of human nature and the wisdom that that entails. The physical and the spiritual cannot be separated whilst we are within human form; they are not destined to do so.

EXERCISE

What is the nature of your support systems? What are the systems you have in place that enable you to participate in the world? What are your relationships based upon?

When you study your life and the complex web of relationships within it, how do they appear? Chances are that you have probably never sat down and examined the nature of your support systems. This exercise gives insights into the functionality of our relationships and what role we play within them.

Contemplate your relationships by initially focusing on the most poignant ones. Take your journal and note the structure of the most immediate relationship in your life. Ask yourself these questions:

- What is the basis of the relationship?
- How did it form?
- What basic need does the relationship fulfil in you?
- What needs are fulfilled in the other by you?
- Who is the more assertive partner?
- What are the defining qualities of you and the other?
- Is the relationship based on an emotional connection or by means of obligation?
- What support does the relationship provide?

Contemplating the above will cause you to deeply question the nature of your relationships. The danger within any relationship is stagnation; the prevention of this is dependent on our ability to acknowledge the value—and sometimes the destructive elements—of them. Love and hate share the sides of the same coin; they are not opposites, for there is still a connection there—the opposite of these is indifference. Indifference in relationships causes the breakdown of the supporting systems that they contain. The Tegid element is removed. Consider:

- What are your Tegid traits—how do you connect to the masculine forces?

- In what way do you honour them?
- How does your virility and sexuality express your inner nature?

Record your experience in your journal.

Morda
THE KEY TO LIMINALITY

◆ ◆ ◆

And she took a blind man to stoke
the fire beneath her cauldron,
and he was named Morda the blind.

Ystoria Taliesin

When we encounter Morda in the tale, only a single sentence alludes to his being. We are informed that Cerridwen "employed a young boy called Gwion Bach from Llanfair yn Caer Einion in Powys to tend the cauldron, and a blind man named Morda to tend the fire beneath it, and she entrusted them to not allow the boiling to cease until a year and a day had passed."[53]

In Elis Gruffudd's account, we are given the following snippet of information:

> The story says that she took an old blind man to stir the cauldron
> and to tend it, but it says nothing of his name any more than it tells
> us who the author of the tale is.[54]

Another account, in the hand of Llywelyn Sion from the National Library of Wales, gives us another variant on the name: "and Dallmor Dallme to tend the fires beneath the cauldron."[55]

---

53 Peniarth MS 111.
54 NLW 5276D.
55 Manuscript NLW 13075B.

The examples above, taken from three different manuscripts, provide us with a range of information about a character who is only privileged one sentence within the tale. So why the variation?

You will note that Elis Gruffudd's account tells us nothing of his name. However, Elis also has the task itself presented differently. The majority of the manuscripts that contain the tale state that the blind man tended the fires whilst Gwion Bach stirred the cauldron. Elis claims it to be the reverse. It is possible that this is a scribal error and that he simply recalled the tasks in the incorrect order. We must also consider that Elis Gruffudd did not entirely agree with the obvious Pagan nature of the tale, as he clearly states in his version that it is "against reason and contrary to faith and piety." With this in mind, it can be deduced that some of the information in his manuscript may be suspect and biased. Sion, on the other hand, gives us an entirely different name, yet it's indicative of the character's disability—*dall* is Welsh for "blind." Therefore, before further analysis of the character's attributes is explored, it is necessary to briefly examine the name of this seemingly elusive individual.

The name Morda does not appear in the *Dictionary of the Welsh Language*, but closer examination of its construction reveals subtle clues to the nature of this being. His name is composed of two elements: *mor*, meaning "sea," and *da*, meaning "good"; combined, they can be interpreted as "good or fair sea." You will already be familiar with the concept of the sea being a catalyst for Awen, for spirit and connectivity. Morfran Afagddu also shares a link to the sea, and Morda serves to reiterate this intrinsic connection to the realm of the spirit. However, the key to understanding the message he conveys is secreted within his proclaimed disability: he is blind. He appears in some manuscripts as Dallmor Dallme or Dallmor Dallmaen, meaning "blind sea, blind stone," although it must be stated that nobody has yet satisfactorily interpreted the "Dallme" component except that it contains the prefix *dall*, meaning "blind." However, in some texts where it appears as Dallmaen, the suffix *maen* can be taken to mean "stone" or "standing stone." Morda the Blind exists between the worlds—he is a part of this world yet is somehow detached; he brings to the cauldron the magic of liminality. Liminality—

from the Latin word *limen*, meaning "threshold"—is, I believe, the most important component of any spiritual quest, journey, or personal development. For it is within liminal space that we experience and connect; it is here that our concepts and misconceptions break down, where the spirit is challenged and the mind set free to explore what exists beyond normal human comprehension and experience. Morda had no external visual data to inform him of his surroundings; he was reliant upon his liminal senses to guide him.

◆ ◆ ◆

The waters of Lake Tegid dance for four miles, a hidden world beneath its surface. The normally fast-flowing yet nonthreatening river that flows through this sacred landscape had, on a cold day in October, been transformed into a beast of uncompromising nature. The lake, prone to dangerous flooding, had forced the river to expand beyond its banks. Moody and lost in the rapture of her own being, in her own incapacity to remain on course, she stormed towards the sea. I closed my eyes, recalling the task that Morda had been given. I breathed with his mystery, listening to the tumult about me. A small footbridge stretched across the expanse of the river, a sturdy old thing but tired and in need of some repair. I have stood upon this bridge a few times over the years, but never had I experienced such power as this day. From over two hundred yards away the rumbling river pulsated the air, a distant heartbeat reaching out into the world, making herself heard, warning those who would approach of her mood. Soggy ground gave way to pools of yellow water as I approached the river herself, the air thick with mist, the thundering sound of the river now beating against flesh and bark. Normally the river cannot be seen until one stands upon the very bank and peers over the edge, but this day what seemed like thick, yellow clouds reached out of her body, some twelve feet above her normal level. The speed was terrifying, as was the deafening thunder of her course pumping through the land and all who stood near her. It seemed as if the trees leaned away from her in terror.

The bridge was sodden; water dripped endlessly from her iron railings, causing smaller rivulets to appear and flow across the wooden walkway. In places the wooden boards had been compromised, eroded by decades of wind and water; through these gaps I could see the raging river beneath, beating her way eastward. I had company this day; three of us stood upon the bridge watching the sheer power of the river as she turned the corner just ahead of our vantage point. What would normally be a ten-foot water-fall now defied description. A seething tumult of peat-stained water bulged from the landscape, fat, angry, and intent on one purpose: to force its way to the sea.

The power of her voice prevented any form of human verbal communication; however loudly one shouted, nothing could be heard. The bridge pounded beneath us, groaning against the constant punishment, begging for mercy. The beating voice of the river had a physical effect on our dense human forms—it began to hurt. We became lost in the story of water, of river and mountain, of rain and cloud. Standing on a bridge that crossed a threshold between the worlds, we found ourselves betwixt and between, neither in one reality nor another. The song of Morda rose from the maelstrom. The crashing river lay beneath us, yet she reached above us, around us, through us. Watching the water beneath me, my companions seemed to dissolve into the mist and spray, lost in their own rapture. Beneath me I watched the passing of time as water caressed and beat at rock and tree root. Stories of times long past and the terror of the present reached out to batter the senses from the banks of the river and from within its depths.

I stood above the raging torrent, watching it all flow beneath me, an observer. Yet lost in the rapture of the waters, trapped in liminality, I became immersed in the story unfolding beneath me and around me. My own perception of reality was about to be changed, to be defied, as all defined boundaries lost their cohesive ability to articulate their perimeters, to sing from the stability of their place within this sacred landscape. Perceptions and concepts began to dissolve within the maelstrom. My own mind lost its ability to remain within the confines of my skull—it lost its hold on the body it felt secure within and slipped, almost unwillingly, through the back of my head. As mist and vapour engulfed me, the blindness of Morda and his watery attributes overwhelmed me.

The water within my own veins, within my vital organs, reached out to caress the spray and peat-stained tumult beneath me. My consciousness became one with the elemental power of this place; I felt both secure and insecure all at once, content and terrified simultaneously. Unable to articulate the experience or to rationalise it, I could only surrender to its power, to its ability to shatter my own perception of reality. This place of liminality had inadvertently caused my spirit to sing with what I was immersed within; rapture and bliss became the aftertaste of this remarkable, unplanned experience.

◆ ◆ ◆

The Pagan arts are steeped in traditions filled with magic and mystery, and we as its priests are the walkers between the worlds. We are those who guard the wisdom and knowledge of our ancestors, who reach out into the world of men to inspire, and we do this by proxy of our connection to worlds and realities beyond ordinary human comprehension. But in order for this connection to exist in the first place, one must adequately be able to perceive the spiritual realms of existence, the dimensions beyond the vastness of the universe, and those beyond the minuteness of the atom. This task is not as difficult as people would initially imagine. There are many within the Pagan traditions who feel a certain degree of inadequacy when it comes to spiritual practise and experience. Many feel that if they do not experience cinematic, 3D vision quests, they are doing it wrong or cannot do it at all. Others feel that because they have never heard a god or a spirit speaking to them through their human ears, they are simply no good at it. People fail to understand that experience of the spiritual is subtle; the spiritual dimensions are accessed through the senses of the body in a manner that we are unused to in everyday reality. Liminality is the key that unlocks the doors onto experience and relationship with the subtle forces of the universe and our place within it.

Society teaches us to observe silently, to passively accept information from differing medias, which asserts a reality that is acceptable to modern society. We watch, we react in a passive manner; there is no assertiveness to the stream of teachings that we accept from the modern world. We are taught that concepts such as imagination are great if you fancy being a novelist, but that is as far as it goes—it isn't really "real." Society disempowers the tribe in this way, creating apathy and a sense of inadequacy; to some extent even elders of spiritual traditions can have the same effect with accounts of fantastical, cinematic spiritual encounters, leaving potential explorers feeling inferior. The spiritual dimensions are not difficult to access; one must begin gently, easing the consciousness into a practise that it has hitherto been unfamiliar with. Active imagination and physically or metaphorically being present within a liminal space increases the mind's ability to shift awareness, resulting in connection to subtle spiritual dimensions.

Liminal states are surprisingly common in our everyday lives, yet we pay very little attention to their significance or symbology until we actually require them for attaining an altered state of consciousness. Achieving a state of conscious liminality is essential for the construction of ritual and for vision questing and journeying to the subtle realms of the spirit. When we consciously and with intent create a sacred space or venture out into nature to connect, the majority of us inadvertently choose either liminal times or liminal places in order to shift the awareness from the everyday humdrum of human existence. These choices may not be clear to the beginner; it is almost as if something within us is instinctively drawn to liminality, knowing that it will assist the process of alteration.

Liminal Times

Our ancestors have always acknowledged the liminality of time, some more than others. Noon or midday is considered liminal, for it is neither morning nor afternoon but a unique period of time that is transitory in nature. Midnight can be assumed to hold the same liminal quality. As the witching hour, it is the exact moment between days; it is neither Monday nor Tuesday, today nor tomorrow: it is betwixt. It is that mysterious border where time seems to cease, where the very fabric of space is transfixed within an unknown place, a place of mystery and magic. Nothing is definitive during these periods; they exist as a threshold, a place of potentiality. The festival of Calan Gaeaf (Samhain) is perceived as a liminal time, the very rules of ordinariness are suspended during this period; anything, it seems, is possible. It is neither autumn nor winter but rather a place where existence itself seems to hold its breath and wait for the coming darkness to devour the world in its blanket of reflection and potentiality. Akin to twilight, where it is neither day nor night, Samhain intrigues us; it sparks the imagination and allows it to sail to heights never before imagined. The veil between realities is said to be thin upon the night of Samhain; as it is during twilight, spirits and ghouls roam, freely able to pass from one reality to another, to infringe upon the land of the living. To this day we continue to dress as spirits and monsters, itself a liminal state, where the identity of the dresser is somehow suspended for that period between dusk and dawn. It is a common tradition in Britain that during Samhain, and indeed during certain rituals at other times of the year, men cross-dress as women. They adorn a liminal state where aesthetically they are asexual; they stand between gender identities and relish in the pageantry and drama of it.

Twilight is particularly liminal; the peculiar half-light can cause our imagination to soar from the confines of normality and challenge us to question what we sense or perceive. It is neither day nor night but somewhere in between; the eyes strain against the coming darkness. Hormones that induce sleep are released into the bloodstream, causing us to yawn and feel lethargic and sleepy. The primary human hormone that is directly affected by the liminality of twilight is melatonin. This hormone is released by the pineal gland into the bloodstream; it is an endocrine hormone that is inhibited by light but permitted by the arrival of darkness. A process known as DLMO (dim light melatonin onset) informs the body that the brain requires rest; this is dictated entirely by the approaching darkness of twilight. This liminal hormone affects every living creature on the planet and does so during liminal times. Melatonin is commonly referred to as the hormone of darkness.

The natural world and this period of liminality have a profound effect on the mind and the body, causing us to react involuntarily to our surroundings. This strange time balanced between night and day is perfect for ritual and ceremony, for works of deep magic and transformation. The brain itself responds to this half-light, and as a consequence the mind is more willing to accept that all is not as it seems, allowing us the liberty to break free of our conformity to normality and descend into the sublime world.

When an individual dies, there is a liminal period between death and disposal, a time when the family grieves for their loss, trapped in a period of time that is unfamiliar, strange. Time itself seems suspended during this period, and we are separated from the mortal remains of the deceased for what may be several days leading up to the funeral. In times past, the entire community would have involved themselves in the honourable preparation of the deceased, helping the transition of the spirit from one state to another and also the grieving process of the bereaved. Understanding and immersing oneself in this liminal period assisted the bereaved and empowered them. In modern society the potentiality of this liminality has become anathema or somewhat taboo—we are denied involvement and are coerced into accepting the help of strangers to alleviate the burden. This lack of connection to liminality and the belief that we must relinquish control to strangers whose primary concerns are monetary has further distanced us from the importance of the liminal state; apathy and dishonour soon ensue.

The Pagan traditions motivate individuals to empower themselves and their tribes by making use of liminal periods and utilising the energies and potential that lies within them. They are an essential component of connection. In the tale at hand, Morda occupies a liminal time frame—he steps out of ordinary existence and resides in liminality for a year and a day. The extraordinary activity of kindling the fires of a magical cauldron removes him from the life he knew previously, placing him in a time and place between the worlds. Although he occupies this place full-time without recourse or respite, this does not imply that we must do the same. Partial liminality is all that is required to taste the mysteries; to become permanently liminal would be detrimental to our human experience.

Perhaps the most demonstrable periods of liminality of which we are all familiar with on a deeply personal level are the hypnagogic and hypnopompic states. These are the technical titles given to states of being that we find ourselves in up to four or maybe six times in any twenty-four-hour period, depending on lifestyle. The hypnagogic state is what is balanced between wakefulness and sleep, hypnopompic being its opposite, the state between sleep and wakefulness. They are liminal states, for they cannot be defined or classified as the common, widely understood states of wakefulness or sleep. They are the mysterious states that lie outside our common points of reference. A varied range of anomalous experiences may be encountered during these states, from vivid imagery, disembodied voices, and the sensation of floating or flying to the sudden, involuntary body jerks that can shock us back into the normal wakeful state. Experiences during these states will feel immensely real and have a nondreamlike quality to them. It is not uncommon for people to report apparitions, sensing the spirits of the dead, or to suffer sleep paralysis and the sensation that someone is either sitting on them or on their beds. Imagination is immensely effective during these states where imaginary scenes or landscapes take on a profoundly vivid quality; they may appear as solid and as real as the wakeful world one has left behind. Our perception of time and place is greatly altered, and although we may appear to have a degree of awareness and may be convinced that we are not actually asleep, a significant and surprising amount of time may well pass by.

No doubt many of you reading these words will have experienced dozing off on the sofa, where the seemingly annoying mental baggage of everyday life stops for a while, and you drift into a pleasant state of imagination and imagery, of memories and comfort—until an involuntary jerk or a text message on your mobile phone shatters the blissful state and you awake, heart pounding, to find an hour and a half has passed.

During these peculiar states of mind, the subconscious is more readily accessible and easily influenced; words or suggestions given to someone in this fragile state will sink deep into the mind and remain there. We can learn in this state; it is a common practise for those learning a new language to listen to recordings via headphones as they fall slowly into sleep. Whilst in the hypnagogic state, the mind is more capable of absorbing information without the irrational aspect of the mind interfering and perhaps denting our confidence or ability to learn new material. As Pagans we are not unfamiliar with these states and, in fact, may consciously induce them. Think of the last time you were in ritual—not the celebratory ritual of tribal gatherings but your own deep rituals of connection and journeying. Or recall an episode where you were led, perhaps as part of a group, into the imagination of guided meditation. You will recall that a similar state is achieved to those described above; in fact, any trancelike state begins by shifting brain frequency from the normal, rapid irregular waves of high frequency to a slower frequency, the hypnagogic state. As we descend into trance, the brain's frequency decreases to around 8–12 Hz; this state may also be referred to as the alpha state. The body slows, muscle tone relaxes, yet we are acutely aware of our surroundings, even if our temporal awareness is compromised. It is here where we begin to see the images narrated to us during a guided meditation; it is here where we reach the landscape we have preprogrammed our subconscious to encounter on a journey to the otherworld. They are as real as the book you are holding in your hands. As we descend further into our vision, into our encounter with the subtle realms of the inner senses, they become more defined—they take on a life of their own and are not necessarily influenced by our own imagination—and we begin to interact with spontaneous anomalous stimuli. This state is known as theta activity, where the frequency of the brain has decreased even further than in the alpha state—it has now reached the depths of 4–7 Hz, yet we are not asleep. What we have done is consciously induced liminality in our own body, and by doing so— and immersing ourselves in the experience—we retain a certain control over posture and other things, not allowing ourselves to fall fully asleep.

It is here where we meet our gods and the archetypes of our tribes and ancestors; it is here where we access the otherworld and the inner realms of spirit. We do it each and every day, but we do it without consciously utilising its power, without even realising that we can and are able to manipulate this liminal time to our own spiritual advancements. I have heard so many people claim that they have never seen the otherworld, never encountered the spirits of place or the archetypes of our ancestors. I do not doubt them, but I firmly believe that their inability to understand common human states as being passageways or conduits to the spiritual realms is simply because they have not been taught how to do it. From my own experience of these states and their ability to act as keys to doors that may otherwise remain locked, I firmly believe that anyone can and is able to achieve these states and benefit from them. When we consciously fall into these states of liminality, it is surprising the amount of common themes that result from each individual's experience—it is almost as if the world within these states contains the whole of human experience from the beginning of time combined with the common experience of the universe as it learns about itself.

The priests and teachers of the Pagan traditions occupy a liminal space; those who have encountered and experienced the subtle realms of the spirit are obliged to share that wisdom with their communities, inspiring them to also reach these states and further develop their spirituality. But even here there is danger, for although liminality is essential for accessing the inner senses, we can also become trapped within it and become permanently liminal, a state where we can no longer function normally within this world. We become too otherworldly, too liminal for the majority of people to know what to do with us or how to interact with us. Those trapped in permanent liminality lose their humanity and their ability to empathise with the world around them and with those within their tribes. They eventually become outcasts, and in ancient times they would have been banished to the outskirts of the village. Modern secular society may identify hippies, gypsies, and Travellers as those who are living on the edge of society, outcasts; in other words, they have been made permanently liminal. Within the priesthood, permanent liminality is a dangerous state that should be avoided at all costs. An effective priest must find a point of balance; she must be able to adequately understand and utilise liminality without becoming trapped within it. Being trapped between and betwixt isolates us from our kin; we begin to lose the fabric of our humanity and will ultimately become lost in the darkness of between-ness. Forever trapped in liminality, Morda teaches us the importance of this sacred state and also acts as a warning beacon. The spiritual landscape can be unfamiliar and treacherous to those who step forth unprepared. Morda and his companions serve to guide us; they are akin to consulting a map prior to a hike: they teach, prepare, and guide.

Liminal Places

We are all familiar with places that have an air of mystery to them or a magical quality that is difficult to define or articulate. Our culture is full of references to places that are liminal, imbued with an ancestral knowing that they are somewhat different. In traditional Celtic lore and mythology, liminal places are features in the landscape that provide access to the subtle realms of being, to the hidden worlds that lie interwoven with our own. Tales abound of dark, dappled groves where the adventurer steps into the unfamiliar territory of otherworldly beings—of fairy mounds and cairns that act as gateways or doors to other dimensions. These places of liminality are embedded in our racial consciousness; they are a part of who we are, and remarkably we continue not only to be drawn to such places but to have an appreciation of their value.

Places that act as thresholds between elements—such as bridges, neither in water nor on land, neither in air but somehow transfixed between the worlds—carry us to places betwixt and between. These places of liminality are more than able to transport us deep into the subtle dimensions of the infinite mind. They have a peculiar "feel" to them; some may feel downright dangerous or threatening, such as cliff tops where the sylphs of air tempt us to leap into nothingness, where we sense the abode of the spiritual realms more clearly than in mundane localities built by man.

Perhaps one of the most significant of liminal places that has waned in power over recent decades is the between-ness of the crossroads. The place where two roads meet and intersect has always held great power to our ancestors; it was believed that the ancient druids would gather at crossroads during the eve of Samhain to listen to the voices of the dead. Altars were erected to various deities, especially during Roman times and their feast of Ludi Compitalia, which was held between the fifth and fifteenth of January.

Hecate, the great goddess of the witches, was believed to be the goddess of crossroads, and altars would be erected at them in her honour. Perhaps it is not surprising that the gibbet, or gallows, would be erected at a crossroads for the public execution of criminals, whose bodies would then be interred at the same location. They were reputedly places of power where witches and gypsies would gather to cast spells and conjure. Some of the more unfortunate among them might also be strung up at the same spot!

Dark caves stand at the junction between land and sea, their deep, gloomy interiors booming with the echo of the tide. Light very rarely enters these domains of the Goddess where her bones are laid bare, sore and tender. Within my own landscape I sense the ford a few fields away from my home—it is road and river, a place of offerings and appeasement, a place traditionally associated with the fair folk of the island. Similarly a great lake swims within a clearing in the forest to the south of my home; it is the lake of fairy, an entryway to the otherworld. The estuary only a hundred yards away, a mysterious boundary between land and sea—it feels dangerous; it challenges anyone who dares venture onto it. These places of liminality evoke a deep darkness wherein swims the memory of all who have ever lived. Akin to the peculiarity of a crossroad or a patch of shoreline at low tide that would otherwise be inundated by the sea, liminality sits at the junction of time and place, a location that is not defined, not clear. There is nothing to conform to here, no set rules or regulations; even the law itself seems to have been suspended at these places or taken to their extreme perimeters of acceptability. Yet these places and times ensnare us in their enchanting quality, they have been vital components of our cultural heritage and expression. They have influenced and inspired our mythologies and traditions; they are a part of us. They allow us the opportunity to step out of ordinariness and leap into the uncharted territory of the spirit; they are both simultaneously familiar and unfamiliar.

Liminality is a crucial aspect of Pagan practise; it animates our tradition and brings colour to what may otherwise be a struggle to sense the otherworldly quality of this colourful and vibrant tradition.

EXERCISE

How do you experience liminality? What songs of liminality exist in your immediate surroundings? This is an exercise in familiarity, in finding the liminal places that surround you. These may be surprising things, places, and times that you have encountered a thousand times in your life, yet perhaps not afforded them notice.

Begin with your home; find the liminal places within it. What defines its portals and thresholds? Are you aware of them? Perhaps they are places where you have guardians in position: totem deities pertinent to you, your family and tradition. Explore the liminal thresholds of your home and pay attention to them. In Wales there is a tradition that if the liminal thresholds are dirty, the *pwca*—notoriously mischievous nature spirits—will run amuck and cause havoc within the home. To prevent this, the doorsteps, window frames, and sills must be cleaned frequently or risk calamity by the hands of the pwca. Consequently, doorsteps are cleansed and the open portals are smudged with sweet-smelling incense rich in pine resin and mugwort, vervain and rowan berry.

Do you have a garden gate, a wall, a fence or other enclosure? The borders of your home are liminal places—they are the locations where guardians can be placed to protect and defend the home; they are powerful places steeped in mythology and lore. It is commonly believed that negative or destructive influences cannot easily cross a protected liminal threshold, hence the belief that vampires must be invited.

Spend time at the liminal thresholds of your home during liminal time, at dusk, dawn, midnight, and midday. Sense the subtle energies that reside there. In the nature of Morda, do this blindly—wrap a scarf or blindfold about your eyes and rely on your subtle senses to perceive the energies that abound at the thresholds of your home.

Extend this practise further afield by visiting the liminal places you can identify in your surrounding neighbourhood or countryside. Bridges and stiles, structures steeped in liminal mythology, seethe with subtle energies of between-ness. Waiting rooms and departure lounges at ports and stations and airports are all liminal places where people await transition. Lakeshores, seashores, towers, and hills—all these places sing the songs of being betwixt and between. Visit them, feel them, and when you next cast your circles, relish in the liminality that you are creating, a place that is between the worlds.

As an individual or within a group, embark on journeys to explore liminality. Lead a workshop in which all participants lie on their backs in a darkened room with a heavy stone placed upon their bellies. Breathe in to the count of four and out to the count of four. Allow the mind to drift close to the hypnagogic state, to that place of liminality where we are closer to the source of all being. Immersion in this state will bring subtle visions and messages that filter from the abyss of potential to the conscious mind.

Become aware of the liminal times, states, and places that affect your Paganism and practise and how they enrich your rituals and devotionals. Note them in your journal.

Cerridwen
IN SEARCH OF THE WITCH GODDESS

◆ ◆ ◆

When the chairs come to be judged,
My own will be the best of them.
These are my songs, and this is my cauldron,
These are my rules.
In the court of Don I am a knowledgeable one.

The Chair of Cerridwen

Our story brings us to the throne of the witch goddess, the initiatrix, the great devourer of the profane. To explore the meaning and substance of this enigmatic character involves a journey deep into the heart of Celtic magic. When we approach the cauldron, we find ourselves pivoted between it and Awen, and facing us are the deep, wisdom-filled eyes of the witch goddess Cerridwen. She stands as sentinel to the mysteries; she is the initiator, the conjurer of the flowing spirit; knees may bend before her in reverence, yet she is inherently knowledgable of the human condition and its limitations. She is by no means intimidating or frightful, but she takes no prisoners; to approach her is to be challenged.

By definition of the content of the tale and the teachings that lie within it, one cannot avoid a connection with the witch goddess; a relationship with this component of the mystery is imperative to immersion and transformation. However, it would be foolhardy for the querent to approach her without due study and a spirit that is receptive to her teachings. To approach the witch goddess is to open a doorway into the heart of mystery. Cerridwen bridges the gap between the profane and the sublime; she is the vehicle that transports the querent through the tumultuous maelstrom of the human condition. She opens the heart to deep magic that immerses the querent in the intoxicating elixir that bubbles within the cauldron. She challenges, she provokes, she imbues wisdom and experience—she guides and subsequently devours the profane aspect of the querent prior to engaging her powers as the great mother who births a child of magic.

Much has been written in relation to the witch goddess Cerridwen, and I am conscious of the risks of falling into patterns of repetition. The following exploration and interpretation will be equally based on an academic dissection of the witch goddess and how she is portrayed in the chronicles of the Celts. The other vehicle of exploration is by means of the subtle, subjective mechanism of the visionary mind, the power of magical connection. One can become befuddled by pure academic exploration, and too much of the subjective would serve to imbalance the material; therefore, both aspects must be combined in a manner which, I hope, is complementary rather than antagonistic. Before I embark on the examination of her name within the ancient language of Wales, I feel it necessary to share my own personal thoughts on Cerridwen's significance.

To stand on the shores of her vast lake, surrounded by the Berwyn Mountains, whose feet dip gently into her waters, is to stand in the presence of Cerridwen. In my visionary mind I see her walking towards me across Lake Tegid's waters; the robes embracing her body seem to be fabricated from the crystal-clear water itself. Her skin is as white as snow, and her dark hair runs in rivulets about her face and shoulders, falling from beneath a crown of sweetest honeysuckle. As she steps from water to land, the greens and browns of the trees and grass reflecting in her fluid robes, she smiles gracefully. Her eyes are as black and deep as the lake from whence she came. She has no sclera, no whites in her eyes; they are the pools of old magic, of the old ways of these lands. Her eyes are the windows to the soul of the universe.

Visions of Cerridwen compel one to feel a deep sense of sovereignty; the head bows and the knees bend, only to find that the witch goddess reaches out, indicating that such action is not required nor necessary. She radiates a beauty that words are unable to articulate, and yet within her deep eyes there is a sense of the Dark Goddess. This aspect has been placed upon her in recent decades, as have other titles such as Grain Goddess and Pig Goddess. They are not cast aside or dismissed; instead, they are gathered up in her robes and embraced. She pulses with power—its fronds can be felt by the heart and pull at the senses; her eyes see beyond your physical form and touch the edges of your spirit. It stings as the wonder and energy of the witch goddess combines with one's own; shivers run, and the goose raises its head in a sea of pimples that tickle the skin. To be in the presence of Cerridwen is to stand in the halls of ancient magic and mystery.

I recall a time when I was lost in the rapture of Cerridwen, surrounded and in the company of priestesses who have devoted themselves to her. The witch goddess watched on, observing and reveling in the dance of devotion. I stood back, my consciousness half in this world and half in the other, and observed her nature. What was apparent was her totemic aspect, her role as the queen of witches and of Witchcraft. Prior to her ascension as a goddess, a theme that will be explored a little later, she was primarily a witch. She stands as the epitome of the magical crafts, of the wisdom of Witchcraft, spellcasting, conjuration, and sorcery. She sits at the heart of Celtic magic; she is teacher, mentor, and guide; she is the Mother Witch of Britain and of its Witchcraft. To take her hand in learning is to walk through the landscape with the wisdom of ages, to learn what no book can teach. She takes the initiate to the ancient halls of learning and teaches us that we are the sum totality of that font of knowledge and that its wisdom can be accessed if the heart sincerely seeks it. One can become entangled in the belief that Cerridwen's role is restricted to the process of transformation alone. This is untrue. She has numerous aspects: she is initiator and witch, she transforms but also teaches and serves the Craft of the Wise. She is a valuable asset to any witch or practitioner of the Celtic mysteries.

When we consider the source material, we find that Cerridwen is not limited to a single tale; she appears in several manuscripts, which affirms and confirms the importance of the witch goddess. Before we embark on examining her significance, though, we must explore the etymology of her name. A warning here: the following material can appear to be somewhat complex (no great surprise, considering it involves one of the most enigmatic figures of the Celtic mysteries); many of the words and constructs may be alien to you, and your tongue may struggle in the attempt at pronunciation. Fear not! I have attempted to provide a comprehensive a guide without being too verbose or overcomplicated. However, it may take a few readings before you are better acquainted with the lyrical dance of the Welsh language. The pronunciation guide in this book will serve to assist your efforts.

The Black Book of Carmarthen, compiled in its current form during the thirteenth century, records two significant instances of Cerridwen's name: *"Hervit urten autyl kyrridven ogyrven amhad*...(according to the sacred ode of Cyrridwen, the Ogyrwen of various seeds...)"[56]

The above line is repeated in another poem of the Black Book of Carmarthen, which tells us that she was considered a component of inspiration. In both instances the poem, in full, recounts the importance of poetry and the magic of the bard or minstrel. It speaks of their exalted speech and the nature of poetic harmony. The poets described within the collection seem to take their authority and their inspiration from the witch goddess herself— she appears as a patron to those in possession of the bardic or Prophetic Spirit. However, something unique arose from the single line that appears above, and we first encounter it in the epic collection translated by W. F. Skene and entitled *The Four Ancient Books of Wales*: the term "Ogyrwen." This title or name appears in works attributed or concerning the prophet Taliesin. In the Book of Taliesin we are informed that "Ogyrwen" is connected to Cerridwen and her cauldron, and the poem describes oblations and offerings to this mysterious creature. Within the Book of Taliesin we find the following verse:

---

56   Evans, *The Black Book of Carmarthen.*

Neut amuc yg kadeir o peir Kerritwen; handit ryd vyn tafawt yn adawt gwawt Ogyrwen, Gwawt Ogyrwen uferen rwy digones, arnunt, a llefrith a gwlith a mes.[57]

The eminent W. F. Skene translated the above as:

May my tongue be free in the sanctuary and praise of Gogyrwen; the praise of Gogyrwen is an oblation which may be satisfied by them with milk and dew and acorns.[58]

In stark contrast to the above, which contains the term Ogyrwen, he adds the letter G to the name, implying that Ogyrwen is a mutation of Gogyrwen. However, Skene is obviously influenced by the poetic genius of Iolo Morganwg, who coined the term Gogyrwen to mean a creature of elemental or spiritual value or personification.[59] When this is considered in relation to the suffix *wen* commonly found in the majority of Celtic female archetypes, it seems likely that Mr. Skene assumed therefore that "(g)Ogyrwen" was a goddess. Consequently, his translation within *The Four Ancient Books of Wales* of the Black Book of Carmarthen's poems informs us that "according to the sacred ode of Cerridwen, the goddess of various seeds."[60]

But, as one can see in the original text, we do not find the Welsh word for goddess—*Duwies*—instead we have Ogyrven. *The Dictionary of the Welsh Language* interprets Ogyrven[61] as "Awen, inspiration, poetry." However, Iolo Morganwg defines this entity as something of greater mystery; he defines it as a personification, a being of immense power and inspiration. Ultimately, very little can be deduced in relation to Ogyrwen by academic measures alone, and we must look to the subtle. The groundbreaking scholar D. W. Nash remarked that it is not entirely clear what is meant by the term Ogyrwen, but he notes that many previous academics and linguistics have deduced that it is likely to mean a "spiritual form or a personified idea" in a

57   Evans, *Facsimile and Text of the Book of Taliesin*.
58   Skene, *The Four Ancient Books of Wales*.
59   Bevan, *Geiriadur Prifysgol Cymru*.
60   Skene, *The Four Ancient Books of Wales*, 498.
61   Note that in modern Welsh the letter V is replaced by the letter F.

similar manner to Iolo Morganwg's interpretation.[62] Nash directs the attention to a line in the Book of Taliesin poem "Angar Kyfundawt (The Hostile Confederacy)," which states *"Seith ugein Ogyrven yssyd yn Awen* (there are seven score Ogyrven in Awen)."[63]

We must be subjective here and resort to utilising the subtle senses alone; this may well imply, as Nash suggests, that there may be seven sources for Awen, the knowledge of which has been lost to the mists of time. It could imply that there are seven dutiful deities, archetypes, or goddesses that serve the function of Awen, bringing it from the fluid ethereal realm of Ogyrwen and making it manifest on the earthly plane. Providing the querent with identifiable mechanisms with which to access the mysteries, the adept—in this case, Cerridwen—acts as a guiding hand, the bridge between the conceptual and the incomprehensible. It is possible that the source of Awen is too vast, too big for our puny human minds to digest; the seven- score elements of Ogyrwen may well be the instruments that prevent the total losing of our minds by grounding us in culture, land, and community.

One can safely assume that the translation by Skene may have played a significant role in the later development of Cerridwen as a goddess, and there may be elements of truth here. By all accounts the poems link the magical power of Cerridwen via her cauldron with Ogyrwen. In my opinion and visions, Ogyrwen is a deity whose legacy has been lost to us, yet clues remain to tantalise and inspire our meditations upon her. She may represent the Mother Goddess of Awen, the one whom Cerridwen receives her abilities from; they certainly share something by proxy of their names, as we have seen in the suffix *wen*. It is therefore my opinion that Cerridwen is directly connected to this ancient Mother Goddess, who may not have had an earthly component other than her representatives on this plane. I have often imagined that Cerridwen and her initiates are in magical succession to this primary Goddess of Awen. The identification of Cerridwen as a goddess in the above translation has led to her subsequent deification and serves to demonstrate the complex and colourful nature of this archetype. However,

---

62   Nash, *Taliesin or Bards and Druids of Britain*, 195.
63   Evans, *Facsimile and Text of the Book of Taliesin*.

some scholars of the past were nothing short of insolent when it came to her academic examination. The Celtic scholar Ifor Williams, who wrote extensively about the figures of Celtica, discussed Cerridwen in his work on the tale of Taliesin. In it he takes the form of her name as it appears in the poetry of the Black Book of Carmarthen and denigrates her title to mean "bent, crooked one"and further elaborates in a rather impudent manner that:

> Cerridwen was not the witch's real name, it is too sweet and loving a name to be put on the likes of her! In the old manuscripts, the Black Book of Carmarthen, she is called Cyrridfen. This consists of "fen" to mean wife and "Cyrrid" is derived from "cwrr," meaning something crooked. You know what kind of nose a witch has, well I suggest that Cerridwen, with her body all bent and crooked, her hooked nose and twisted hands, were as wrongful as her craft![64]

Mr. Williams certainly did not hold back his prejudices and was keen to brand Cerridwen as a twisted old hag, more typical of a Hollywood production than an initiate of the mysteries. But one must also consider the overtly Presbyterian nature and faith of the majority of Celtic scholars. He was, perhaps, biased, for he simply had no other point of reference that could place Cerridwen in a position of wisdom and knowledge. That, in a similar thread to Elis Gruffudd's opinion, would be against all faith and piety. I may be a little harsh on old Mr. Williams here, but it is likely that he was influenced by the restraints of the Presbyterian environment of the early twentieth century. He may have found Mr. Skene's rendition of Cerridwen as a goddess a little difficult to swallow.

Thankfully, this explanation for the meaning of Cerridwen's name has been rejected by modern Celtic scholars, who are generally sympathetic to the Pagan nature and pre-Christian themes hidden within the material. However, prejudices are still voiced concerning the mysteries of Cerridwen, particularly in relation to her standing as a goddess. It seems that the only evidence put forward by academia to discredit her rank as a deity is the fact that there exists no proof of a previous cult of Cerridwen. Prejudices run

---

64   Translated by the author from *Chwedl Taliesin* by Ifor Williams, 1–2.

deep and arise from various agendas. One of these fountains of doubt was the attitude of the mostly male poets of the Middle Ages. They were seemingly reluctant to accept that the source of Awen was ancestrally denoted as arising from Cerridwen's cauldron. With the church strengthening its hold on society and suppressing native material, the bards moved away from the magical connotations and the female-driven source of Awen, preferring (or, rather, conforming) the font of Awen as the Christian God. Satirical poetry that denigrated the old ways as consorting with the devil and the old witches who lived in the good old days of Cerridwen arose to further belittle the mysteries. The Welsh themselves (my own family included) turned their backs on the old ways, and the likes of Cerridwen and her mysteries went deeper underground.

◆ ◆ ◆

If we take the various forms of her name, they can be listed thusly:

- Kerrituen
- Ceridfen
- Cereidven
- Cyridven
- Cerridwen
- Caridwen
- Cridwen
- Cridfen

The manner by which her name is spelt has been changing for centuries, dependant on the narrative or preceding manuscript the current scribe used as source material. This must be seen in perspective, and one must bear in mind that the majority of scribes were not overly familiar with the native tongue and dialects, allowing greater room for error. Yet it can be surmised that the majority of variations are slight and that her name remains similar in sound and meaning. Eventually her name was modernised in the eighteenth century to the consistent form we know today as Cerridwen.[65] According to the Celtic scholar Rachel Bromwich, her name consists of two syllables, the prefix *cerid*, taken to mean "love" or "loved," and the suffix *wen*, meaning "fair" or "pure." In combination, she translates the witch goddess's name as "fair and loved," in stark contrast to the ghastly translation by Ifor Williams.[66]

As we have seen, Cerridwen's name is as multifaceted as she, and this gives further depth to the witch goddess. But what of that title "witch goddess"—surely she must be one or the other? Can one be a witch and a goddess simultaneously? You will have noted that I use the term witch goddess throughout this book, and it is here that I present to you my justification for doing so.

Cerridwen as Witch

It is important to stress that within every manuscript—with the exception of the *Ystoria* or Hanes Taliesin scripts, which form the heart of this study—Cerridwen is not described as a witch or a magician. Within the books of poetry she is presented as the owner of the cauldron of Awen and that all poetic and prophetic abilities and powers emanate from this vessel. She is presented as its guardian; it is only in the later tale that she is directly associated as the creator of the brew that imbues the knowing of Awen into the querent. But, as we have previously seen, the themes exhibited within the tale of the prophet and the witch are remarkably older than the surviving manuscripts; therefore lines become blurry and the edges of knowing frayed. It is at this junction that Awen must be utilised. Within the early poetry attributed to Taliesin, we are provided with tantalising snippets of information that belie Cerridwen's position as a sacred archetype. She is often described as a component of Awen, in succession or as an aspect of Ogyrwen. She demonstrates that she is in possession of supernatural abilities, and yet her tale portrays her as a mortal woman.

---

65   Haycock, *Legendary Poems from the Book of Taliesin*, 312–19.
66   Bromwich, *Trioedd Ynys Prydein: The Triads of the Island of Britain*, 312–13.

The element that makes her human—and, indeed, identifiable—is the fact that she is flawed; she got it wrong. The brew was never intended for Morfran Afagddu, but in Cerridwen's mind it was meant for him. When the situation takes a surprising turn, we are subjected to her rage and retribution. The very presence of these traits informs us that she is as flawed as we are; she may be in possession of subtle powers, but she is still human, not an ethereal force that is beyond our reach. The original transmitters of the mysteries had obviously noted that in order for a human being to transform, one must have something tangible and recognisable that the mind can adhere to. With that, the children of the gods were born, together with individuals adept in the magical arts, to guide mortal hands into the dappled groves of mystery with a simple message: "You can; we will help you."

The old manuscripts refer to Cerridwen and inspiration, to the cauldron and Awen; they are forever forged in unity. Yet when we investigate the scripts that contain the tale of Cerridwen and the birth of Taliesin, we are given a greater insight into her nature. In the manuscript recorded by Elis Gruffudd we are provided the following wonderful description of her abilities: *"a oedd geluydd a dysgedic ynn y tair Kyluyddyd, yr hrain yssyd y'w henwi: hud, witshkrafft, a sossri* (and she was learned in the three arts of magic, witchcraft, and sorcery)."[67]

Here we have a direct reference to her standing as a learned magician. Cerridwen is not presented as an amateur; she is an adept of the subtle arts, which the text specifies as magic, Witchcraft, and sorcery. She is identified here as a practitioner of the Craft; she is a witch. She is the totemic witch queen of Celtic/British Witchcraft, the mother of every witch and druid who lives and practises the arts of Celtic magic. A remarkable legacy that current practitioners possess and are able to tap into is this vast cauldron of ancestral knowledge, and at its head is a Witch of profound wisdom. All current practitioners of Witchcraft throughout the Western world can trace their Craft back to the islands of Britain and claim Cerridwen as their patron. The same can be said for all modern-day students and initiates of Druidry,

---

67   NLW 5276D (my translation).

for she is the mother of the cauldron, the one that gives substance to the quest for inspiration.

Pause for a minute, and consider the stereotypical image of the witch—she stands aloft, a wand raised high above her head; words of power fall from quivering lips to be carried by steam. This steam floats from the surface of a bubbling cauldron, its contents singing the songs of the natural world. With her free hand she stirs the cauldron, her chanting increasing in tempo.

This image is evocative of Cerridwen; she is the original witch, whose actual place in time is as mysterious as her relationship with the Ogyrwen. But one can rest assured that each time you reach for your cauldron and gather about it, as a grove or a coven you are imitating the sacred dance of the witch Cerridwen. It is evident from the tale that her cauldron is the original and true witch's cauldron, the contents of which are boiled according to magical direction and skill known only to her and the initiates of the mysteries. She is not a selfish witch; her knowledge is not restricted but can be accessed and studied by those who approach her cauldron with good intent and integrity. Her role is to teach and to guide; she may also chastise and rebuke, as all mothers must do.

We have previously explored the nature and significance of cauldrons in Celtic culture and the discovery of countless vessels in bogs and lakes throughout northern Europe. But here we are introduced to the iconic witch's cauldron, a tool that continues to be used today by practising Pagans. What is remarkable is that the vessel, as a symbol and as a tool, has survived for countless centuries and continues to exist as a magical implement that offers direct access to the witch goddess. The next time you use your cauldron, ponder on its connection, hold it between your hands, and rest assured that the witch goddess hears you and can be summoned with ease.

◆ ◆ ◆

In part 1, I explained how the Narrative Spirit has ensured the survival of the Celtic material, but it is not the only spirit at work. This may be a difficult statement for the academic to swallow, but I suggest that the spirit of the witch goddess, an entity who has been nurtured for centuries, lives on within the blood of the tribe and the land. She sings from the depths of lake and river; she is revered in groves from Anglesey to California; she chants with the covens of Middle England and the Midwest. She exists as a thought-form and is nourished by the devotion of her followers. We can become lost in the trappings of dates and the semantics of language; the witch goddess is older than these—she sings of a magic that predates the ink of scribes. She is the queen of Witchcraft; her sovereignty resides there. Welsh folklore abounds with references to Cerridwen as the queen or patron of witches, a quality that I believe would enrich the devotional aspect of any modern witch's practise. Welsh folklore perpetuates the belief that witches had the ability to transform themselves into animals, and that by certain incantations and magic they could change the form of other individuals. There is an account of a Welsh witch called Betti'r Bont who was rebuked by a servant man who disbelieved her supposed powers. He lived to regret his insolence and awoke one night to find himself in the form of a hare. To his horror, he was subsequently set upon by a greyhound, which he managed to escape the jaws of but was thereafter subjected to the same chase until spells were cast to release him from his torment.[68] This tale and a hundred others beside it continue to be retold in the villages of Wales, each one mirroring the magical aspects of Cerridwen's tale.

The trial and confession of Isobel Gowdie, a Scottish witch tried in 1662, echoes some of the transformation sequences in Cerridwen's tale. Her vivid account offers a detailed and unique glimpse into the practise of Witchcraft during the seventeenth century.

> *O I shall go into a hare, with sorrow and sighing and mickle care, and*
> *I shall go in the Devil's name, aye, till I be fetched home again. Hare,*
> *take heed of a bitch greyhound, will harry thee all these fells around,*
> *for here come I in our Lady's name, all but for to fetch thee home again.*
> *Cunning and art he did not lack, but aye her whistle would fetch him*
> *back. Yet I shall go into a trout, with sorrow and sighing and mickle*

---

68   Owen, *Welsh Folklore.*

doubt, and show thee many a merry game, ere that I be fetched home
again. Trout take heed of an otter lank, will harry thee close from bank
to bank, for here come I in our Lady's name, all but for to fetch thee
home again.[69]

The witch's powers are clearly demonstrated in the section of the tale
commonly referred to as "the chase." I shall briefly touch on this aspect in
relation to Cerridwen and will further elaborate on its interpretation in the
section devoted to Gwion Bach. Cerridwen evidently displays her superior
talents as a witch by wilfully changing her shape; the sequence begins after
Gwion Bach has ingested the blessed drops. In her rage and immediately pri-
or to the chase, we are informed in one manuscript that she strikes the blind
man, Morda, on his head with such force that one of his eyes falls from its
socket. This striking of a creature of liminality may imply that she is initiat-
ing the chase sequence—she is informing the querent that a liminal process
is about to begin.

Throughout the chase, Cerridwen retains her gender as she becomes a
greyhound, an otter, a hawk (the female of which is reputed to be the more
effective hunter), and finally a black-crested (or tufted) hen. In each case she
initiates the transformative process. Immediately before her claws seize upon
the escaping initiate, she forces him to transform, to leave the significance of
one element and enter another. The chase is a complex and symbolic process
that is controlled by the witch in her various guises. She is forcing the initiate
forward, and we can assume that in this liminal state the true meaning of the
entire sequence is made clear to her. Previously she was driven by the needs
of a mother, but within the chase she is partially liberated from her human
component; we are informed that her form is changed but not her nature.
Therefore, in the shapes of animals and birds, she maintains aspects of her
humanity whilst simultaneously accessing the source. Ultimately her task is
to initiate.

---

69 The trial and confession of Isobel Gowdie, taken from Robert Graves's *The White*
    Goddess, 401–402.

Her wisdom and the contents of the Celtic tales and poetry are suggestive of a reliquary of Druidical wisdom and knowledge that continues to be perpetuated in Europe and countries colonised by Europeans. The myriad motifs that we find within the Taliesin and Cerridwen material are indicative of early Celtic narratives and are culturally specific. They include shapeshifting, cauldrons of magic, and the ingestion of liquid that transmits the prophetic and/or poetic spirit; according to professor Patrick Ford, these motifs are particularly specific to the Celtic traditions.[70] This implies that the themes within the Celtic material arose within the islands of Britain, and although they may appear to be emulated on the continent, they are deeply specific to the Celtic cultural continuum. The material examined is riddled with magical significance and has adepts of the arts demonstrating their abilities and powers. This vast melting pot of historical documents and the narrative tradition can cause one to question what is what—are these the practises of Witchcraft or those of Druidry?

I would suggest that we are seeing both. It was generally accepted that the druids of the British Isles and Gaul were practitioners of the magical arts. Hippolytus, writing in the third century, said, "The Celts hold the druids as prophets and foretellers of future events because they can predict certain events by Pythagorean science and mathematics...The druids also use magic."[71]

The description given above in Hippolytus's *Philosophumena* suggests that the druid priests practised science and magic. It can be argued that the majority of ancient civilisations perceived magic and science to be one and the same thing, the theory being that magic is simply the science that we have yet to figure out. However, Hippolytus was not alone in his observations; other classical authors remarked on the magical qualities of the druids:

---

70   Ford, *Ystoria Taliesin*, 48.
71   Hippolytus's *Philosophumena* (AD 170–235) as translated by Philip Freeman and J. T. Koch in Koch's *The Celtic Heroic Age*, 35.

The Persians have men known as Magi...the Egyptians have their holy men. For their part the Celts have men called druids, who deal with prophecy and every division of wisdom.[72]

Furthermore, we have an account of the disciplines within the Druidic arts of which one is particularly pertinent to the discussion at hand:

Throughout these regions, as people gradually became more civilised, study of praiseworthy doctrines grew, introduced by the Bards, Vates, and Druids. The Bards sang praiseworthy deeds of famous men to the melodious strains of the lyre. The Vates endeavoured to explain the sublime mysteries of nature. Between them were the Druids, an intimate fellowship of greater ability who followed the doctrine of Pythagoras. They rose above the rest, seeking the unseen, making little of human mortality, for they believed in the immortality of the soul.[73]

You will note that in central position, balancing the arts of bardism and Druidism, is the sublime ranking of the Vates, modernised as Ovates. These were the magicians of the druid priest caste, those who walked between the worlds, seeking answers and clarity from the forces of nature and its gods. They were learned in the arts of magic, sorcery, and enchantment. Sound familiar? Cerridwen is also said to possess these qualities and to take the wisdom of nature and its mysteries in hand as an adept of the magical arts. It can therefore be argued that the Ovatic priests were the magicians of the druid orders. After the invasion by Rome and the subsequent suppression of Druidry in the British Isles, the philosophies of Druidry were amalgamated into the Roman culture to eventually blend with Celtic Christianity. The Ovatic arts, however, seem to have gone underground and survived in the folk magic of the British Islands, later to become known as Witchcraft.

This Witchcraft is not to be confused with the religion of Wicca. This was the Craft of the wise woman and cunning man; it was not religious observation per se. This wisdom passed the centuries by means of folk tradition,

---

72 Dion Chrysostom, Orations 49 (AD 40–112) in Koch's *The Celtic Heroic Age*, 30.
73 Ammianus Marcellinus (AD 330–395) in Koch's *The Celtic Heroic Age*, 31.

which survived because it existed outside the boundaries of religion. This magic, as old as the hills and valleys, continues to be perpetuated and reinvented by modern practitioners who, by means of subtle skills, tap into the vast cauldron of wisdom that is separated from us only by time. The revival of Witchcraft in the 1950s and the rise of Wicca served to preserve the folk magic of the islands of Britain within a religious framework, another example of the incredible ability this magic has to survive and evolve. It can be surmised that Witchcraft and Wicca embrace various magical traditions, whereas Druidry is defined by its course specifically within the Celtic continuum. I believe that the origin of Cerridwen stems from the Celtic Druidic era, and that the magic that she and the tales are, as Will Parker states:

> the final and perhaps most unambiguous evidence for a residual druidic element blended in with the biblical and classical traditions... quite unheard of anywhere else in Europe at the time.[74]

When we look between the lines—when we close our eyes and journey with the spirit—we meet the archetypes of the tales. It is by this method that we can understand and perpetuate the mysteries contained therein. Nothing is truly lost, and we are connected to the past by more than just culture and heritage. This globe is a closed circuit; all the wisdom of all the times are here, waiting for us to access them. We are fortunate that our ancestors provided us with keys to fit the locks of mystery; and one of those keys is the witch aspect of Cerridwen.

Cerridwen as Goddess

We have briefly examined this aspect of Cerridwen, but I feel that it merits further exploration. When Skene translated the name Ogyrven and interpreted it as "goddess" in the Black Book of Carmarthen, I doubt he had any insight into the future dilemma he was to initiate. Subsequent authors followed in his footsteps and sustained the belief that she was indeed a goddess.

---

74   Parker, *The Four Branches of the Mabinogi*, 100.

But where does this leave us? How do we define her role as a goddess, and does it have any merit?

Several influential romantic writers of the nineteenth and early twentieth centuries initiated the belief that Cerridwen was not only a witch but also a goddess. The translations by Skene were no doubt influenced by the works he consulted when compiling his *Four Ancient Books of Wales*. In *A Dictionary of Eminent Welshmen* compiled in 1852, Cerridwen is described as a British goddess and well-known personage in the Druidical pantheon. It elaborates further that "Cerridwen is a celebrated character in Druidical mythology whose attributes were similar in many respects to those of Ceres."[75] It is more than likely that the above sentiment was heavily influenced by an earlier work by the much-rebuked Edward Davies entitled *The Mythology and Rites of the British Druids*. Within this work, of which a generous section is devoted entirely to Cerridwen, Davies describes her as an ancient goddess of Britain and the first of womankind. He further elaborates, by means of several tangential diversions, that she is a representative of the moon, the ruler of bardism and poetry, the source of divinely acquired inspiration, the modeller of youth, a goddess of corn and grain, a botanist, and a sailing vessel. He expresses the notion that the history and character of Cerridwen

> is a mythological allegory upon the subject of initiation into the mysterious rites of Cerridwen. And although the reader of cultivated taste may be offended at its seeming extravagance, I cannot but esteem it is one of the most precious morsels of British antiquity, which is now extant.[76]

This statement, along with many others, invokes a wondrous image of Cerridwen as a goddess and seems to reflect modern attributes given to her. On first glance one may be inclined to be in agreement with Mr. Davies; alas, he mixes fact with a good dash of conjecture where he arrives at several incorrect conclusions. Davies argues that a cult to Cerridwen as a goddess did exist and that she was worshipped conjointly with the moon as late

---

75 Williams, *A Dictionary of Eminent Welshmen*, 73–74.
76 Davies, *The Mythology and Rites of the British Druids*, 186.

as the twelfth century. He remarks that her temple resided in the district of Caergyvylchi, modern-day Dwygyfylchi in the county of Gwynedd in North Wales. He claims that the Book of Pheryllt she consulted was, in fact, priests of the Pharaon, whom he describes as "the Higher Powers." According to Davies, the Pheryllt had a city among the mountains of Snowdonia that some may identify as the ancient fort of Dinas Emrys, anglicised as the Ambrosial City. He claims that the Pheryllt were the first teachers of the mystical arts and were immensely skilled in the arts of magic. However, Davies has been ridiculed by later academics for his outlandish remarks concerning temples, places of worship, and ancient priests of magic, of which there is no written or archaeological evidence to substantiate. D. W. Nash, in his *Taliesin or Bards and Druids of Britain,* seemingly embarks on a mission to utterly destroy and denounce the suggestions of Davies:

> This statement that the goddess Cerridwen had a temple at Caergyvylchi in Caernarvonshire is made with all the historical seriousness with which we might affirm that there was a temple of Diana at Ephesus, or of Jupiter at Rome. It is nevertheless destitute of the slightest foundation, and affords another example of the modern manufacture of the Druidical Mythology.[77]

Although I agree with Mr. Nash's criticism of Davies' imaginings, I cannot help but feel that something is missing from his argument—his condemnation of Davies' work and his lack of evidence is based entirely on the fact that no physical material exists to prove the theories set forth in *Mythology and Rites of the British Druids.* However, Mr. Nash and subsequent critics of the Celtic material have not considered local lore as worthy components to a body of evidence. The material examined in this book arose from locality- specific narration; the subsequent scribing of these tales is only one part of the story, for the Narrative Spirit continues to perpetuate these myths locally. Davies may have been liberal with theories, but I cannot help but feel that some descriptions tally with the locality specific legends and lore. How do we as modern Pagans judge what is appropriate and what is mere

---

77   Nash, *Taliesin or Bards and Druids of Britain,* 187.

conjecture? After all, we have access to sources that pure academia does not. Can we justifiably use lore and folk tales as evidence? If not, do we then simply conform to the standard that if it is not written, it is not so?

The area remarked upon above, and purported to be the site of the temple to Cerridwen in the Welsh county of Gwynedd, is abundant with folkloric history and legend, the majority of which concern witches, cauldrons, fairies, and ancient priests who inhabited a temple at the summit of the mountain that overlooks the current village of Dwygyfylchi, the descendant parish of Caergyvylchi, as mentioned by Edward Davies. Local legend records that this was the site of a temple to the goddess Cerridwen and that her priests resided in the city that stood atop the mountain. It says that 20,000 men at arms protected the priestly caste that resided within the fortification and were known only as "the watchers." With the coming of the Roman invasion, the watchers are reputed to have departed to the west, and with that they fall out of history. Now, among the aged of the area, it is still held that the watchers were none other than the Pheryllt, whose book Cerridwen consulted. This rich folklore is briefly mentioned by the writer Lewis Spence, who identifies the city of the Pheryllt as Braich Y Ddinas, which sat atop the mountain adjacent to Dwygyfylchi.[78]

These tales, rich in local lore and legends, can be at loggerheads with academia, for they may seem to contradict the written material. As we have seen, while the material of the Narrative Spirit may not have the strength of evidence that scholars prefer, it does, however, have merit. It is at this junction that the role of the witch, the magician, or the seer comes into play. The nature of the tale we are examining is an intricate allegory of transformation, but for that transformative process to take place all elements must be balanced—light and dark, liminality and physicality, content and form. It teaches that we must be balanced to see both sides of an argument, not preferring one over the other. This principle is vital for the exploration of the material; it is by means of all methods that we come to an authentic conclusion that is valid to our spiritual development and connection. The

---

78   Spence, *The History and Origins of Druidism*, 57–58.

components and archetypes that make up these tales are real, very real, but it is our connection to them that defines that realism. Mr. Nash and Mr. Davies, to name but two, had their own agendas and connection to the source material, and whilst we can admire and be inspired by their efforts and studies, we must be cautious that we do not fall into the unmoving territory of literalism.

It is by means of examining local lore, legends, and the written material that we can study Cerridwen's development into a goddess, and many influential individuals have been paramount to her deification. Their justification for doing so may be a little scarce on evidence, but nonetheless these opinions have moulded the modern-day practise of Celtic Paganism. The writer J. A. MacCulloch, when discussing Cerridwen, informs us that:

> the cauldron was first of all associated with a fertility cult, and Cerridwen must therefore once have been a goddess of fertility…She may also have been a corn goddess, since she is called a goddess of grain, and tradition associates the pig—a common embodiment of the corn spirit—with her.[79]

MacCulloch and his successors were influenced by various scholars before them—W. F. Skene, who as we saw previously attributed Cerridwen as the goddess of various seeds, being one of them. But of greater influence to the deification of Cerridwen and what has had the most impact on modern Paganism is the body of work called *The White Goddess* by Robert Graves. This work has been heavily criticised in recent decades, and although it may often draw inaccurate conclusions, it has become central to the myths of modern Paganism. *The White Goddess* is essential reading for any practising Pagan, for within it one can identify the source for the majority of modern Pagan myths and the deification of mythological archetypes. This does not devalue current practise but simply demonstrates the ability of modern practise to evolve and create new material pertinent to the spiritual quest.

Within the pages of *The White Goddess*, Graves introduced the concept that Cerridwen shares an antiquated origin with various other female

---

79   MacCulloch, *The Religion of the Ancient Celts*, 117.

deities. He forms bridges that elaborate on the notion MacCulloch had of her being a grain goddess and links her with Demeter and Cardea. He claims that the etymology of her name shares a similar root as the Spanish word *cerdo,* meaning "pig." With this, he presents Cerridwen as the white sow goddess, the barley goddess, and the white lady of death and inspiration. He also claims that other significant female deities of the Celtic chronicles are aspects of Cerridwen in her guise as the white goddess of life in death and death in life.[80] We can see by these associations how Cerridwen has developed into the commonly accepted belief that she is an aspect of the Dark Goddess.

Her associations as a white sow goddess do have allegorical merit, and this aspect of her can be utilised within the practise of modern Paganism with astounding connection and results. When we look to the legends and source material, we find numerous instances where pigs played mystical roles or sparked wars and battles between various tribes. It was commonly believed by the Celts that the pig was a creature of Annwn, the underworld. In the fourth branch of the collection of legends known collectively as the Mabinogi, we encounter a white sow that performs the task of devouring the profane aspect of the initiate. Central to the tale is the birth, life, death, and rebirth of the offspring of Arianrhod called Lleu Llaw Gyffes, meaning "light, of skilful hand." The fourth branch is perhaps the most mysterious and magical of the Mabinogi and is literally riddled with pre-Christian thematics and iconography; in fact, Will Parker suggests that "Lleu is literally a Druidic God in medieval clothing and we have definitive evidence of a pre-Christian cult."[81]

The story centralises around the divine children of the Mother Goddess Don. A war is initiated by the stealing of pigs, which calls the great magician Math away from his palace, where he resides with his feet in the lap of a virgin, unless he is at war. His lap maiden is brutally raped and consequently we are introduced to Arianrhod, who is interviewed to replace the virgin. When asked to prove her virginity by stepping over the magic wand

---

80 Graves, *The White Goddess,* 68–98.
81 Parker, *The Four Branches of the Mabinogi,* 447.

of Math, she gives birth to two babes: one slithers like a fish to the ocean and the other, Lleu, is secreted in a chest by his uncle, the great enchanter of the Britons, Gwydion, the son of Don. A series of trials ensue between the child, his uncle, and Arianrhod, who curses the child for the shame he brought upon her. Condemned to never marry a mortal woman, his uncle and Math create for him a bride from the flowers of the woodland. She, in turn, ultimately betrays him and falls in love with another man, and together they conspire to kill Lleu. However, he is not easily killed and demonstrates to her the complex situations that must be created to ensure his death. Alas, it is a trap, and a spear is driven through him, but instead of dying he transforms into an eagle and flies away. At this point in the tale we are told:

> ...and Gwydion discovered that upon each day a sow would break free from the swineherd and nobody knew where she went. Gwydion took to pursue her, and she went upstream, travelling beside the river in the valley now called Nant Lleu (in modern Welsh, Nantlle), and within this place she stopped to graze. Gwydion came under the tree where she fed and looked to see upon what she grazed. He saw that the sow was feeding on rotting flesh and maggots. He looked to the top of the tree and saw an eagle within its topmost branches. When the eagle shook its feathers, flesh and maggots fell from him to be devoured by the sow. It occurred to Gwydion that the eagle was Lleu, and he took to his spells to call him.[82]

This is not the only instance of a sow leading a querent on a journey. Another white pig leads the hero Pryderi and his mother Rhiannon to become trapped in the otherworld in the Third Branch of the Mabinogi saga. Pigs have long been associated with the indigenous underworld of the Celts, the realm of Annwn, and were believed to have free reign to travel between both worlds. In the account above, the role of the sow and its associations with Cerridwen mirror the actions of the witch goddess in the act of devouring the profane as she consumes the initiate Gwion Bach before his transformation is complete. In the Fourth Branch of the Mabinogi the hero

---

82 *Math Fab Mathonwy*, The Fourth Branch of the Mabinogi, translated by the author from *The White Book of Mabinogion* edited by J. G. Evans.

Lleu is also undergoing a sublime initiation, and it seems evident that the sow is a facet of this process, the component that devours the profane, dense aspect of the initiate. In light of this we can associate Cerridwen as a goddess who presides over the act of initiatory transformation. The sow is also seen in folk tradition and concerns a chase, which coincidentally emulates the initiation process. A *Calan Gaeaf* (Halloween/Samhain) custom popular in Wales concerned a black sow that would chase the villagers and threaten to seize the hindmost and devour them. This tradition, most common in North Wales, is believed by folklorists to contain residual elements of an ancient initiation ritual.[83] It may also account for the rise of modern trick-or-treat practise.

Within the sacred landscape of Cerridwen's realm we find another goddess of significant antiquity, and one whom Cerridwen and Gwion Bach directly interact with. This is not so apparent upon initial examination of the tale, for it hides within the magic of words and names. Within the chase sequence we are informed that the goddess pursues Gwion Bach, upon leaving his guise as a hare, *"ai ymchwelud tu ag afon Ayrwen* (and chased him towards the river Aerwen)."

This statement is important, and I must reiterate that every word within the narrative is chosen for its significance within the greater context of the tale. Here we are informed that the river in which part of the chase sequence is enacted is called the Ayrwen (*Aerfen* in modern Welsh). On first glance, a would-be initiate may see nothing of value or meaning—surely it is just the name of a river, right? Indeed, nothing could be further from the truth. The names of rivers and lakes, mountains and valleys have enormous significance within the language of Wales, and this river is no exception. If we examine the name, we discover that Aerwen is the title of a war or battle goddess to whom the river is sacred. No longer called by this title, she is now referred to as Afon Dyfrdwy (the river Dee); *Dyfrdwy* is composed of two words that combined mean "the river of the goddess." It is notable that the river begins its life in the mountains of Snowdonia and courses its way through this wild

---

83   Isaac, *Coelion Cymru*, and Frazer, *The Golden Bough*, 635–36.

terrain to eventually meet with the lake at Bala, the home of Cerridwen and her family. After a few miles she once more takes her form as a flowing river that continues through the famous Celtic Land of the Dead. This landscape of hundreds, if not thousands, of burial mounds and cairns in the Ruabon Mountains hosts the river Dyfrdwy as she seeks a path to the sea. The river has been considered sacred for centuries and was even recorded in 1188 by Giraldus Cambrensis in his journey through the landscape of Wales. It was said that a temple dedicated to Aerwen was situated in the current village of Glyndyfrdwy and that to ensure success in battle she required three human sacrifices each year.[84]

It has long been assumed that Gwion's shape in the river is in the guise of a salmon, although we are only informed that his shape is that of a fish. However, the river Dyfrdwy is famed for being the greatest salmon river in the British Isles; therefore, it is safe to assume that it was indeed the form of a salmon that Gwion took. It is also significant that we have the combination of two deities here, the goddess Aerwen and the deific aspect of Cerridwen. Cerridwen's later association of being the goddess of life and death may have been confused with those of Aerwen, who inhabited the same realm; in fact, it would be impossible to state which deity would be totemic of Lake Bala. It has been recorded that a previous name for the lake was indeed Llyn Aerwen (the lake of Aerwen). It has been suggested that Cerridwen and Aerwen may be aspects of the same goddess.[85] We may never know the true connection between these two archetypes, but the interaction between them is important to the understanding of the tale and the characters therein. Cerridwen and Aerwen share similar traits, and both are symbolic of a place and the relationship that human beings have with the land. In a visionary sense, Cerridwen is representative of the powers of magical transformation and the instincts of a mother. Aerwen is presented to us as a goddess of a natural force, the river, whose course cannot be altered or controlled. She is symbolic of nature and the relationship humanity has with it as it courses through the land touching and affecting. Cerridwen and Aerwen interact,

---

84 Blake and Lloyd, *The Keys to Avalon*, 144–45.
85 Ibid., 145.

and this relationship is important, for it grounds the characters within a place; they are imminent. Pertinent to this discussion is the fact that the identity of Aerwen as a goddess is an accepted fact, whereas it is by process of apotheosis that Cerridwen comes to us in the guise of deity.

It is by the means of apotheosis, the act of exalting a subject to a divine level, whereby Cerridwen indisputably has been deified and is currently revered and worshipped by devotees around the globe. We have explored the various mechanisms that may have given rise to her deification, and we have also witnessed the rebuke of her rank as goddess by various academics. But the fact remains that she is now perceived as a goddess and one who is applicable and appropriate to the new Paganism of the twenty-first century. It also serves to demonstrate the uncanny ability these archetypes have for survival, because no matter how often or how vigorously they are suppressed, denigrated, or devalued, they continue to exist.

The gods and goddesses of the current Pagan tradition will continue to be devalued and belittled, pulled apart and eviscerated to within an inch of decency, for they are still perceived as a threat. Paganism may be generally accepted, but it is still a fringe tradition seen as a threat to other institutions who would love nothing more than the demise of our deities. Thankfully these archetypes have significantly more power than the prejudices of little human minds, and try as some might, they will not succeed in suppressing these divine voices.

Many may argue that the gods bear no resemblance to those of the ancient world—that any bridge which linked us directly to the wisdom of the past has long since burnt. Many cry that the gods are not real but are merely romantic notions of fantasy and an unhinged mind. We may well hear the protestations that "They are not gods!" I would beg to differ. My gods are as real as I am, for I give my gods voice, as do you and the covens and groves that devote their spiritual practises to them. Nothing is inherently original; everything must evolve or suffer stagnation and annihilation; nobody would have the audacity to question the face or attributions of the Christian or Islamic deities, yet they too have evolved. Everything has to start somewhere, right? The gods of the revealed religions bear little semblance to the archetypes that gave birth to them. Our gods are new gods inspired by old gods; we are the new Pagans who give voice to this Paganism that we have created to emulate the past whilst consciously not trying to live in it. Cerridwen and her kin cause us to look to the future, to be inspired but not long for the past. We are encouraged to change and develop their allegories and tales and make them authentically applicable to the Pagan spiritualities of today and tomorrow.

Cerridwen as Mother

When we first encounter Cerridwen, her role is central to the transformative process. She is the initiator of the brew and its creator. She does this in direct response to the pain she feels for her child—she turns to the powers of magic to imbue within him the essence of Awen. This action expresses her instinct as a mother to sacrifice herself, her time, and her energy to a process that would ultimately benefit her child. This is what drives the tale—this is its purpose and reason for being: it begins with a mother. Only another mother would truly understand and empathise with this overwhelming call to do something so absolutely extraordinary for her child. Her motives are driven by the pain she senses within her son and the fact that he will never be truly accepted by society. Imagine what that must feel like. Consider for a moment the inexorable love that a mother has for her child and the subsequent torment she must endure in the knowledge that that child may never be accepted by the world. Her actions are indicative of a mother's drive to ensure the happiness of her child whatever the cost.

Regardless of which version of the story we encounter, it is safe to assume that significant to the virtue of the tale is the presence of a son and a daughter. We are not told if one is older than the other, but when one considers the nature of Creirfyw and Morfran Afagddu, it may be assumed that, in all probability, they are twins. Imagine, then, a mother's pain to gaze upon the wondrous beauty of one child and then to be forever faced with the hideousness of the other. Within the text we are provided the following insight into Cerridwen's state of mind:

Because of their son's wretchedness, his mother became very sad in her heart, for there was no obvious means by which her son would win acceptance amongst the learned men of the day unless he beheld qualities markedly different from his looks. And so to deal with this matter, she turned her thoughts towards her Craft to see how best she could make him in possession of the Prophetic Spirit and a great storyteller of the world to come.[86]

Morfran Afagddu is the drive; he is the catalyst for Cerridwen's creation of the brew, yet he is reliant on his mother's ability to transform him. This implies that the inherent powers within Cerridwen are learned, not inherited, otherwise it would make sense that her offspring be in hereditary possession of her powers. Seemingly they are not, but of course the tale has a dual aspect: we are faced with its merits as a tale of a mother's love for her son and also the sublime aspect where each character is already playing a vital magical role. The tale bridges the river between the profane and the sublime, enticing the querent with identifiable human motifs. It is by means of her identity as a mother that we are initially introduced to her, and this is a vitally important aspect of the tale, for if we fail to identify with her, we fail to effectively transform.

Cerridwen is a wife, a devoted mother, and a talented witch who has subsequently been elevated to the dizzying heights of a goddess. But her overriding human identity remains that of a mother who just so happens to be a learned witch. What follows is a sequence of magical events ultimately concluding in her familiar human role of a mother. So we begin with a mother and we conclude likewise. At the commencement of the chase we are subjected to the unadulterated anger of a mother scorned—everything she has struggled and worked for is destroyed. She is intent on killing the individual who spoiled her plans and condemns her son to a life of ugliness with no reprieve. When she eventually destroys him in her belly, during her entire magical pregnancy she continues to resent the unborn child, who represents what her son can never be. But when Taliesin is born, we are once

---

86   NLW 5276D, my translation.

again faced with the uncompromising, unconditional love a mother has for her offspring. His beauty is such that her heart cannot bring itself to destroy him, and so she gives him over to the powers of nature to nurture, care, and transform him further.

Here we have the combination of the mother, witch, and goddess singing in harmony. It is as though regardless of one's standing or experience, even the most adept and knowledgeable of initiates continues to learn. Cerridwen had her motives, but with the transformation of the initiate, something changed within her as she coursed through the slipstream of Gwion's initiation. The teacher is always affected by the process of teaching; the student learns from the teacher and the teacher, by proxy, learns something of him- or herself in the process. Cerridwen may be perceived as a superior goddess, yet her tale serves to tell us that she is also the expression of humanity; she is learning what it is to be human by being a mother. Cerridwen's own personal transformation is summed up beautifully by the Celtic scholar Angela Grant, who says:

> …Cerridwen who, having thereby been impregnated by the combined spirit of poetry, wisdom and prophecy, then becomes the "mother of wisdom" and is changed, in a manner at least, from the dark, angry and vengeful Witch to the wise and beautiful mother who knows her child needs the fosterage of the sea for forty years before he can be truly reborn as the archetypal poet and diviner.[87]

We are each born into the world having spent nine months in the wombs of our mothers—we grow, live, and some of us reach for the spiritual. Within that spectrum we find another womb where we gestate and are reborn into the world as lucid practitioners of the magical arts. Cerridwen serves as the nurturer, the initiator, and the gateway by which we access the spiritual continuum of the universe and incorporate it into our human lives. She is the mother as teacher and the mother as student; our relationship with Cerridwen must be reciprocal.

---

87 Grant, *Magical Transformations in the Pedeir Keinc y Mabinogi and Hanes Taliesin*, 56.

Imperative to a true and experiential understanding of Cerridwen or any other deity is our relationship with them. Without connection there can be no relationship, and without a deep and sacred relationship with our gods, we are condemned to a life of cerebral or armchair philosophy, with no real interaction. A study of the Celtic material quickly demonstrates the personable nature of the deities and their desire to connect with their adherents. They are not ethereal imaginings flapping about in some otherworldly plane that is beyond touch and concept, they are here and present. They are the divine, imminent aspects of us and the powers of nature, which are forever connected to the source of all being, to the constant river of Awen. They exist within us and without us; they are both internal and external, depending on how we interact with them. Cerridwen provides us with the keys to transformation by presenting herself to us as a human being, a mother, and every individual on the planet can identify with that. She teaches us the fundamental qualities of magic, of study, of nourishing our skills and talents; she guides us into the process of change and encourages us to nourish and nurture others who come to us for inspiration. She is not an entity who demands unquestionable worship; she works with us—if we commit to knowing her.

Within the practise of Paganism, the interaction with deity is necessary to the connection we have with the natural world and its qualities. But we may also be at risk of only developing a conceptual, shallow relationship with our gods, and this is not enough. Think upon a relationship within your life that is of great value to you; it may be with a parent, a lover, or a sibling. Now compare the intensity of that relationship with that of a deity; do they emulate each other? Do they differ? If so, how? The manner by which we connect to deity is incredibly personal, and it is something that develops with time. I consider the flippant calling or invocation of a deity just for the sake of it to be imprudent and foolhardy. We would not assume a reciprocal relationship with a stranger, and we cannot assume the same for deity. We must connect, and as we have seen this is achieved by first identifying with the mythology and the iconography and then the attributes of deity. We then begin to "get to know one another" in a manner that constructs reciprocation. Too often a relationship with deity may be overtly passive or simply observational, with no real substance. This is not enough for magic to occur. When we arise to meet the gods, we must do so with integrity, with honour, and with an appreciation of the sacredness of relationship. We do this by getting to know them. But this is not a simple task, for we are denied the physicality of the gods. We have no flesh to touch or warmth to feel; instead, we must sense their pulsing spirit within the fabric of our flesh and the land.

People cannot conceptualise what they have no concept of, therefore when we move to meet Cerridwen we must have a concept of who she is, what she is, and why we approach her cauldron. Our relationships with these archetypes begin in the same manner as our connection to other human beings—we are attracted to them. It is by analysing that attraction and moving into the energy of that archetype that we begin to know them, and essentially they begin to know us. A selfish, one-sided relationship is doomed from the offset; reciprocation is vital. We all have motives and reasons for being drawn to the presence of deity, but Cerridwen and her kin are not there to entertain. When we approach the cauldron, we must do so with confidence. When we look into the dark pools of her eyes, we must do so with conviction and integrity, where we begin a relationship that is forged with honesty and trust.

In conclusion, Cerridwen may be segregated as a witch; you may approach her entirely as the archetype of Mother or as the Great Goddess. More than likely she is all these things simultaneously. It is your relationship with her that defines and delineates the borders between each role.

Are you ready to embark on a journey into the embrace of the witch goddess?

EXERCISE

Developing a relationship with an archetype begins just the same as any other relationship: by means of introduction. We would not accost a total stranger in a supermarket, wedge them between ourselves and a wall, and demand that they suddenly be our friend. We would be considered a little unhinged at best, a raving lunatic at worst. Therefore the manner by which you move yourself into Cerridwen's energy must be gentle and, above all, polite.

We are not afforded the luxury of Cerridwen in the flesh; we must connect to her energy. At first glance this may seem an impossible task, but in actuality it is no different from recalling the memory of a loved one who has died. The dead and the gods exist beyond the veil that separates the realms of existence, and to meet them we must become adept at parting those veils. Think of someone whom you were close to who has since died. Recall their features and their voices; invoke memories of them and interact with the image. Call them to you from beyond the veils. This task is made easier by the fact that we have a point of reference—a memory, a photo, or a video capturing the deceased in life. We do not have those associations with Cerridwen, so we must forge new ones. But the images that we may subsequently invoke will be similar in nature to those we summon for our dead.

Begin by settling yourself in a quiet place where you will not be disturbed, and have your journal ready. Think of the witch goddess and her attributes and her role in the tale. Jot down some notes, a poem, perhaps maybe even an illustration of her features as you imagine them.

Now close your eyes and imagine before you a curtain, perhaps similar to the style in a theatre. These represent the veils between worlds. By the powers of your imagination, cause them to open. As they sweep gently aside, they reveal a woman who stands alone on a stage that your mind creates. Allow her to appear naturally without attempting to steer what appearance she assumes. This is Cerridwen.

Introduce yourself to her, talk to her, tell her who you are, where you live. Interact with her—chat with her as if you have just been introduced to a new person, which, in fact, you have. Don't try to be all mystical and spooky, just talk to her like you would any ordinary living person. Tell her where you went to school, what you do for a living, and who the members of your family are. Tell her stuff about you. There is absolutely no need to reel off antiquated words of worship or honour, no point falling to your knees with cries of "O great Mother, I bow before thee!" She may be a goddess, but don't idolize her; treat her with the respect that you would show any being, human or other. Stand in her presence and revel in the fact that you are starting something new. When you are ready to go home, simply bid her farewell and cause the curtains to close again. Every time you go to meet her, begin by invoking the image of the curtains; this will inform your subconscious mind that the subtle senses are being utilised and that something extraordinary is about to occur.

Try to avoid direct images of the otherworld, which may serve to confuse and frustrate you. Always use liminality to reach it; this is the purpose of liminality. The curtains act as a symbol of being betwixt and between; they form the bridge between your conscious mind and the subtle realms. However, do not be restricted to this suggestion alone; by all means use your own imagination to conceptualise and envision other symbols that are of a liminal nature.

It is useful to have an item that is representative of Cerridwen, perhaps a figurine, a talisman, or a statue—something that may be kept on your altar or sacred table or shelf that is evocative of her. It would be best to utilise Awen to create this item, so that as much of your own connection is imbued within it.

- Meditate on her qualities and how best you will represent them.
- Sculpt a figurine from clay or wood.
- Create a talisman with symbols that connect you to her image.
- Make a pendant that is indicative of her, and
  wear it during your rituals and devotions.
- Make a wall plaque that can be placed in a
  prominent position in your home.

- Plan a grove or coven day to create items that reflect her attributes.
- Paint her image and display it.
- Create heady, highly perfumed granular incense to burn in her honour.
- Write songs or poetry that invoke her, and share them with your working group.

Record all your experiences in your journal.

Gwion Bach

THE HEART OF TRANSFORMATION

◆ ◆ ◆

She employed a young boy called Gwion Bach from
LlanFair yn Caer Einion in Powys to tend the cauldron.

Ystoria Taliesin

When we first meet Gwion Bach, it is in his guise as an employee of Cerridwen, who recruits him from a life as a yeoman's son from a village to the south of Bala, in the neighbouring county of Powys, to tend her cauldron. The manuscripts specifically note that he is employed, which implies that Cerridwen is rewarding him for the task of cauldron tending. We are not informed if this is by means of payment or board and lodging, but it is significant that he is subservient to Cerridwen and must do her bidding. In light of the circumstances that arise, it is easy to empathise with Cerridwen's fury when one in her employment robs her of the miraculous potion. But, as with all things in the Celtic mysteries, there is complexity and various levels to the tale, more so than first meets the eye. As we have explored in the previous sections, this tale is more than just a folk tale and is beautifully described by professor Patrick Ford:

> ...the tales of Gwion Bach and Taliesin cannot be lightly dismissed as "folktale" or late developments. Perceptible in them and in their attendant poems, despite the layering of successive generations and external influences, lies the myth of the primeval poet, in whom resides all wisdom.[88]

---

88   Ford, *The Mabinogi and Other Medieval Welsh Tales*, 21.

The above quote reiterates the origins of the tale in the distant past and not as simply a product of medieval Wales. The tales' deep magic causes those who come into relationship with them to be transformed, and they do this, as we are exploring, by means of the archetypes that swim within them. As our journey brings us to the main protagonist of the tale, the one who is to undergo transformation, it is pertinent to explain his primary function above all others.

Our initial encounter with Gwion may cause us to feel a little sorry for him; after all, he had been minding his own business for a year and a day. To suddenly be burnt by boiling liquid was, again, not entirely his fault, and then all at once he is to be chastised or at worst killed by the wrath of Cerridwen. We would be somewhat hard and cold-hearted to not feel a dash of sympathy for poor Gwion and the incommodious situation he has got himself into. His innocence and the accidental nature of the calamity that befalls him draw us in; we feel for him, and on many levels we can identify with him. We have all been in situations where things have seemingly conspired against us, corners turned to be met by brick walls or, worse, hostility. Sometimes things just happen. And in this case, this lowly lad is at the sharp end of Cerridwen's wrath, when in all honesty he hasn't really done anything wrong.

The realms of mystery are difficult to enter; to begin with, they are invisible to human eyes. You may find clues that allude to them, but they are elusive and enveloped in mists of secrets. To access them we must find the keys that unlock the appropriate doors, and this entire tale is one of those. But even when we find the keys that match the mysteries, we must still find the locks into which they fit. The material may at first seem compelling yet incredibly baffling, leaving one scratching the head in confusion. This is a typical symptom for the majority of folks who approach the doors of the Celtic mysteries. But there is a significant key that allows all other keys to find their matching locks with ease. The riddled poems of Taliesin and other Celtic verse and mythologies cannot be explained unless one refers to a folk tale, which the scholar Ifor Williams identifies as being the tale of Cerridwen and Taliesin. He claims that the shapeshifting Gwion Bach, who is transformed by means of successive initiations and a triple birth, is the key to accessing the mysteries. The legendary and prophetic myths and poems, without exception, require this key to activate their power.[89] When activated, the mysteries begin to glow with a light that shines to the furthest recesses of the spirit. The process is quite simple once the key to mystery has been acknowledged, and Gwion Bach is only half the story—the rest of it is fulfilled by you.

For all that is to follow to make sense, a deep and profound acknowledgment must be accepted at this point. By all means, the study of Gwion Bach, the etymology and the interpretation of his part in the story, both visionary and scholarly, is a worthy exercise. But for the tale to be incorporated as experience, not simply a mental exercise, we must accept that the role of Gwion Bach is indicative of you, the hero on his or her own quest to inspiration and the divine receipt of Awen. This is achieved by seeing oneself in the role of Gwion Bach and accepting the tools that he provides along with his fellow archetypes to embark on the journey. This is a journey in the true sense of the word, for it involves a deep commitment to the study of mystery and immersion in the teachings of our ancestors. The quest becomes a source of knowledge and our heartfelt attempt to access the blissful rapture of connection to the mysteries and the gods of the Celtic continuum.

The most important aspect of the entire journey, as epitomised by the trials and initiations of Gwion, is the heroic journey into the self. This is achieved by being immersed in every single facet that makes up the self; to balance the otherworldly components of the spirit in harmony with the earthly aspect, not to antagonise or belittle the other but to create harmony. The Celtic systems are the opposite of the traditions of belief commonly found in the East, which encourage the transcending of the self and the acceptance of a universal truth that we have no other choice but to adhere to. The Celtic mysteries do not demand that we transcend or even seek enlightenment per se; they ask that we be of the world whilst simultaneously being aware of the otherworlds and the inexorable link to our primordial

---

89   Williams, *Chwedl Taliesin.*

origination. By being in the world we learn, we seek, we educate ourselves and expand the mind to be a child of this world and of all others. In Celtica the world is not perceived as an illusion that gets in the way of enlightenment; in fact, the experience of being here, now, is deeply illuminating.

This old, deep magic is one of being fully present and aware of our true purpose; the meaning of life is to live. To live is to live in all worlds, to sense the worlds beyond the veil and those that inhabit the furthest reaches of our galaxy. To live is to be here now without the desperate searching for another dimension that transcends the one we currently occupy. We are mortal, yet we are facets of the universe learning about itself; the more we learn and experience, the richer our contribution to the whole will be. As we encounter the words of Taliesin in subsequent verse and poetry, we realise that he speaks of being present in all places and as all things simultaneously. Taliesin describes being the universe experiencing itself through a plethora of lives and objects and elements. He also makes reference to his previous life as Gwion Bach, the yeoman's son who knew nothing of such magic until the blessed drops descended to scald his thumb. The Gwion that he speaks of is you—that is, if you are prepared to embark on this journey into lucidity and magic, where you walk side by side with those who inhabit the other realms. Into the cauldron you have cast aspects of your shadow, your stability, and your strengths; you have acknowledged aspects of yourself, which is necessary for the brew's productivity. You have identified your talents and skills, your flaws and your passions; you have sought out the witch goddess, lest you impudently approach her cauldron without consent. With all things in preparation, there is only one thing left: the acceptance of you as the vessel that is Gwion Bach.

It is easy at this point to become lost in gender identification, and it is not the intention of the mysteries to privilege one sex over the other. Gwion Bach may be presented to us as a boy, but in actuality he transcends gender. Gwion's position in the tale and subsequent transformation applies to both males and females. You are Gwion Bach regardless of your sex.

Now, as we will discover a little later, the actual realm that Gwion Bach occupies has always been a subject of contention. There is a school of thought that claims the entire tale is based in the otherworld. Eventually it interacts with our dimension with the passage of the babe in the coracle. This concept is worthy of exploration, for although we are told that the tale takes place in an actual, real location, the events that unfold are nothing other than supernatural in nature. Some versions of the tale suggest that it unfolded on an island in the middle of the lake—a physical impossibility, as the lake is a glacial cleft and is unfathomably deep. Now this may imply that aspects of the tale took place between the worlds, in a dimension that bridges this world and the ones that run parallel with it. This theme is a common one in Celtic mythology, particularly in reference to islands; consider the associations with Avalon. If this is the case, then we are provided with a scenario that explains the interconnection of the worlds and how they are blended or knitted closely together, hidden only by the doubting mind. This hints at the fact that the relationship with the otherworld is imperative to the understanding of the mysteries; they are so tightly interlinked that to dismiss the otherworld as mere fantasy is to dismiss the mysteries themselves, for they originate there. Regardless of where the tale takes place, what actually matters is your role in it. It is the search, the quest, famed in Celtic tradition as the quest for the grail. The search, as the term *quest* implies, reaches into all worlds and deep between them into the space occupied by the flowing spirit of Awen.

What's in a Name?

Gwion Bach literally translates as Gwion the Small, or Little Gwion. It is suggestive that he is either small in stature or demeanour, that his body is perhaps thin and wiry, and that he may not be as strong or robust as his siblings. The name Gwion is constructed from two specific components—*gwi* and *on*. If we take the suffix *on*, we are given a vast storehouse of information relating to the nature of Gwion Bach as something other than entirely human. This opens doors into the world of mystery that otherwise would have remained closed. Within the Welsh language, the suffix *on* denotes a creature or individual of supernatural erudition and quality; they seem human on the surface, but their identity places them in the realms of the otherworld or in having originated from there. The meaning of *on* is eloquently described by the scholar Eric Hamp:

> The segmentation Gwi-on is immediately natural since in the Taliesin material we are dealing with a mythical stratum of personages comparable to those whom we meet in the Mabinogi. Therefore we have the Celtic suffix "on" which characterized supernatural beings.[90]

This provides us with the notion of how we must commence our examination of this character; again, all is not as it seems. Without the keys of language this information would remain unknown, and we would be ignorant of a cauldron of knowledge that we would otherwise be unable to access. Gwion shares a name in line with other enigmatic supernatural characters of the Celtic mysteries—there is magic here, much more than initially suspected. Owing to the meaning of this suffix, Gwion Bach's position is similar to that of Rhiannon, who also shares the same "on" aspect. When we meet this creature of magic it is in the first branch of the Mabinogi—she rides upon a white horse and is unable to be stopped unless asked. Her origin is otherworldly, and she is commonly identified as heralding from the realm of Annwn, from the indigenous underworld of the Celts, the land of shadows and the Fair Folk. The implication here is that Gwion Bach may not have been entirely human to begin with, and that his innocent human aspect is a construct that allows us to access him prior to engaging the mysteries. This concept is articulated by John Matthews in his exploration of Taliesin:

> ...he is perhaps not human at all, but an Otherworld child whose first adventures take place in the Otherworld but who, once he has undergone a human birth, must go out into the world of men and become human.[91]

This is an interesting concept, for it is demonstrative of the complex levels that this tale is engaging with and expressing. On one hand, as we have seen

---

90   Hamp, "Varia II," 149–154.
91   Matthews, *Taliesin*, 21.

in previous sections, it is a tale set amidst the valleys and woods of Bala, a real place in the apparent world, yet the unfolding tale is nothing less than supernatural. It is easy to imagine that these people were flesh and blood and that they lived real lives among the villagers of the time. But we find that their names belie a deeper, mysterious aspect to them that seems to indicate they are of another origin. I believe that they exist on all levels; as we saw in the examination of Cerridwen, we approach her as a mother and we leave her in the guise of a Mother, yet her attributions betwixt are immensely magical. The same can be said for Gwion Bach; we are able to sympathise with this lowly creature from a humble background. We can sense the pressure of back-breaking work that he endured within Cerridwen's employment, and finally we empathise with him as the cauldron's contents accidentally imbue him with the knowledge of the universe. It wasn't his fault; his innocence draws us in, and this is a vital aspect of his song that is imperative for our own personal approaching of the mysteries.

The initial attributions of Gwion Bach are related to his innocence; he is a child. The Celtic myths are abundant with stories that tell of children who are born with magical powers or abilities, or who inherit these powers during their childhood. John Matthews refers to these individuals as "The Wondrous Children."[92] Something happens to them—they are changed or transformed or face terrible adversity, some are kidnapped or kept prisoner—but eventually they are rescued or found, and wondrous situations befall them and their kin. The main protagonist in the Four Branches of the Mabinogi is Pryderi, the son of Pwyll and Rhiannon. He is half human, half otherworldly. He is stolen by a supernatural force in his infancy and is subject to myriad magical adventures before being reunited with his parents. Similarly Gwion Bach is taken from his family, from the comforts of his home, and positioned in liminality; he is subsequently transformed and chased through an initiatory process before being reborn as the divine Prophetic Spirit. But vital to our understanding of the entire process is the acknowledgment of the initial quality of Gwion Bach: innocence. Without this incredible attribution we

---

92 Ibid.

may never find our way to the cauldron, for we must approach it with the innocence of a child. We may come prepared, but we also come trusting that the witch goddess will guide, protect, and ultimately initiate. A child can do nothing other than trust his or her mother; there is no alternative that is conducive to transformation. This is a further lesson of Gwion Bach—to abandon the doubting, cynical, overly analytical mind of an adult who may have succumbed to the apathy of modern society, and to throw caution to the wind and engage with the mysteries in a manner that encourages development and permits magic to enter and dance with the spirit.

To approach the mysteries with innocence does not imply that we do so uneducated. A child spends years immersed in the tasks of learning, and it would be wise for us to do the same. For we are approaching these mysteries and the teachings therein as children, in a way; we are in the process of learning, of becoming learned. In the same manner as Cerridwen was learned in her arts, so must we become learned in ours. To do this whilst retaining an innocent disposition is a part of the overall magic—to approach the task of learning, of building relationships with a heart and spirit that gasps in awe at magic, is a giant step towards transformation.

Gwion Bach sings numerous songs of mystery, just as Cerridwen, Morfran Afagddu, Creirfyw, and Morda do; each song is unique, each one a vital ingredient of the brew's making. The mysteries require us to listen—not just hear, but to listen intently with our spirits. Mystery can hide amidst the colour and drama of a tale, and the keys to accessing them may elude us until we are guided towards them. To begin to understand, we must first study and then commence relationship before eloping fully with the archetypes. In this instance, the name alone provides keys to the teachings of Gwion Bach. Having explored the meaning of the suffix *on*, we move on to the prefix *gwi*, where things become a little more interesting, if somewhat befuddling.

The Paradox of Poison

The first three letters of Gwion Bach's name belie another mystery, for they refer to something that at first glance may appear contradictory to the entire process of transformation. The element *gwi* is cognate with the Old Irish *fi*, meaning "poison, venom"; this has been extensively explored and researched by the scholar Eric Hamp, who refers to Gwion Bach as "the little proto-typic poison." Since this seminal work was published in the 1970s, it has been accepted that Gwion Bach's name in its entirety can be translated to mean "the little divine poison."[93] Now this may seem a strange and somewhat per-plexing piece of information that is in direct contrast to the nature of Gwion Bach within the tale. For him to be identified as poison or poisonous may seem a harsh blow to deal upon an innocent. But, as usual, there is more going on here. There is more to learn within the meaning of his name.

Consider the immediate consequences of the ingestion of the three blessed drops. We are informed that the contents of the cauldron are instantly turned to poison, which implies that everything within the brew's constituents, except for the three drops, were deadly toxic. We are informed:

> …the cauldron broke in two pieces, the water within was now poi-son except for the three blessed drops, the liquid poisoned the horses of Gwyddno Garanhir who drank from the estuary whose waters were contaminated by the cauldron, and because of that the estu-ary has forever been named *Gwenwynfeirch Gwyddno* (the estuary of Gwyddno's poisoned horses).[94]

It seems apparent that once the brew had reached critical mass and expelled the required drops, the contents thereafter were rendered useless. This is a clear indication that the brew is only meant for ingestion by one individual alone; it cannot be shared. Only the initiate must partake of the brew. To receive Awen secondhand is to be in receipt of something that is impure or corrupt, as only the true initiate for whom the brew is truly intended may be imbued with the Prophetic Spirit. Regardless of how much

---

93   Hamp, "Varia II," 153.
94   Peniarth MS 111, Hanes Taliesin.

we want it or how noble our intentions, unless we stir the cauldron and tend to it, it will serve only to poison us. There is a profound occult warning hidden within this theme. In order for us to be in receipt of the Prophetic Spirit and assimilate the mysteries, we must undergo the experience alone and with integrity. We cannot receive it by proxy of someone else's experience; we are not permitted to share. There are rules, as Cerridwen herself states in the poem "The Chair of Cerridwen": "This is my cauldron and these are my rules!"[95]

In order for us to approach the vessel and undergo assimilation of the mysteries, we must be fully prepared and do so of our own volition. We cannot hope to be in possession of the Prophetic Spirit unless we are prepared to work for it. The process requires commitment and devotion. Nothing less is acceptable or in line with Cerridwen's rules. "The Chair of Cerridwen" poem speaks of her appreciation and acknowledgment of learning; her admiration for Gwydion, the Son of Don, from the Fourth Branch of the Mabinogi, whom she refers to as having "the best learning." She refers to herself as being one of the most knowledgeable ones within the court of the goddess Don. Knowledge and learning are vastly important qualities that are essential to the brew, combined with innocence and trust. These attributes are the primary qualities we must possess before engaging with the mysteries. We approach them informed and educated, and trust that the archetypical forces will serve to guide and assist us. Cerridwen's demand that we be learned enforces the primary Druidic tenet of ages past that the skills of the mind and the intellect must be encouraged and developed. Learning is of immense importance, not only to the development of the mind and to enrich the storehouse of wisdom, but also to encourage relationship with the mythological material and the archetypes therein. It highlights a common condition of the twenty-first century and its inappropriateness to occult study: the "I want it now" mentality.

We are blessed to live in an age where we have access to information at the touch of a button; we have health care and medicines that would have

---

95   "Kadeir Kerritwen," The Book of Taliesin.

turned our ancestors green with envy. We have technologies to improve our lives and enable exploration of our planet and universe. But by proxy of this we have become used to the "instant society" we have created. Alas, this expectant attitude can also infiltrate the realms of the spirit and its exploration. We can buy courses, purchase the mysteries, and be awarded a title for a few hundred dollars—but, just as the remains of the cauldron were toxic, so can the "I can buy my spirituality" mentality poison and corrupt. The mysteries of any tradition require utmost devotion and commitment, and the Celtic mysteries are no exception. The subtle power of words informs us of how we must commence and what the gods require of us. The process of the brew becoming toxic is teaching us that collateral damage is a real and apparent risk. If we approach the mysteries without integrity and due attention, we may cause damage to ourselves and our environment. In an instantly gratifying world, the Celtic mysteries teach us the importance and value of patience, of absorption and commitment.

We are also informed by means of Gwion's name that he becomes the embodiment of poison. Whatever collateral damage has been enacted by the spilling of the cauldron's contents, it seems evident that Gwion is not only transformed into the Prophetic Spirit but is also an embodiment of poison. Gwion becomes the epitome of what nourishes but also poisons, a quality that we explored earlier within the cauldron fort of Caer Feddiwt. Gwion tells us a little of his nature after he is transformed in the Book of Taliesin poem "Prif Gyuarch Geluyd":

> *I am old, I am new, I am Gwion,*
> *I am universal, I am the sense of fine things.*
> *I am a bard, I do not disclose secrets to menials.*
> *I am leader, I am a sage in contest.*
> *Convoluted bards will come,*
> *To meet about the mead vessels,*
> *To sing wrongful verse,*
> *To secure rewards that they will not get.*[96]

---

96 "Prif Gyuarch Geluyd," the Book of Taliesin (my translation).

Here Taliesin speaks of his previous incarnation as Gwion Bach, and of the nature of his being, he claims a universal presence and that he is of superior sense. He also states that he will not (or cannot) disclose his secrets to menials. The term *menial* is taken to be representative of those who are not in possession of the Prophetic Spirit, and therefore not privy to receive them. To do so would be akin to being poisoned. He also condemns those who tarry about claiming great things and speaking in verse as if they are knowledgeable, and seems to be portraying the common "jack of all trades and master of none" persona. It is apparent that the Gwion Bach/Taliesin figure has very little patience for those who do not approach the mysteries with good intent and preparation. Gwion, as a vessel of poison, mirrors the poisonous virtues of the natural world; not all that is sweetness and light is necessarily good for us. The bees forage among flowers, gathering nectar; their honey is a rich source of carbohydrates, yet it can be immensely toxic to a child. The humble nut can provide protein and nourishment, and yet, to an unfortunate few, it can kill. Hidden within innocence and beauty is the risk of toxicity. The collateral damage that the natural world can cause is emulated in the occult mysteries. A little knowledge is a dangerous thing, particularly in the wrong hands. Cerridwen's rules are steadfast. We must embark alone to seek the wisdom and magic of the cauldron; anything else would be untrue and impure, a corruption of Awen, and, as we have seen, the remains serve only to poison. Gwion Bach's multilayered meaning serves to guide, to inspire, but also to warn.

There is a further teaching here that emulates the message of Morda: liminality. We are informed that the horses of Gwyddno Garanhir (whose weir Taliesin is later discovered in) were drinking at the estuary of Gwyddno Garanhir and consequently ingested the poisoned waters. Their deaths are eternalised in the name of the river and estuary to this day: *Afon Gwenwyn-feirch Gwyddno* means "the river of Gwyddno's poisoned horses." The horses are the only victims of the cauldron's toxicity, or at least the only ones that we are informed of. It would stand to reason that every creature within the river is also poisoned and subsequently dies. But there is a dichotomy here. To begin with, this is the river in which the watery aspect of the chase takes place; therefore, we must assume that somehow Cerridwen as an otter and Gwion as a salmon are immune to its effects. Secondly, the horses are drinking from an estuary, which is odd in that the water would be primarily salty. Also, an estuary epitomises liminal space: it is neither land nor sea but a combination of both; it is a place that is betwixt and between. However, a further complication to the significance of the horses' poisoning arises in relation to the fact that horses are indicative of the sovereignty of Britain. Their deaths seem to imply that something is being challenged; perhaps this something is identity, both national and individual.

What can be deduced is that liminal space is a key aspect to the entire transformational process. It does not happen in actual or apparent time. Regardless of whether the tale unfolds in the otherworld or not, what is significant is that the section immediately after the ingestion of Awen takes place in liminality. As mentioned previously, we are not informed of how long the chase sequence takes, but we are informed that the newborn child is set adrift for forty years after birth and then found by Gwyddno Garanhir's son, Elffin. A paradox is immediately apparent here, as the poisoned horses belong to him; now he must be incredibly old or another creature of supernatural erudition. All of this serves to demonstrate the complex nature and interconnection between the various characters or archetypes in Celtic myth. Whilst they all provide a meaning or teaching significant to them and their part in myth, there is a crossover point where certain attributes are mirrored or mimicked by others, perhaps as a process of reiteration. Therefore, to interpret the archetypes and explore their meanings as I am attempting to do here is fraught with difficulties, for they have a tenacity to share certain attributes and meaning.

Within the sequence that directly involves Gwion Bach, we can see the interchange between him and the other archetypical qualities that continue to interact throughout the chase and birth sequences. Therefore, although the character of Morda seems to have vanished from the tale, what he represents—i.e., the qualities that he brought to the cauldron—continue to be paramount to the unfolding of the initiatory events. All the archetypes are present; they are simply not referred to. If we take Morfran Afagddu and his qualities of shadow, we can see them at work in Cerridwen's wrath and in the fear that Gwion evokes. Creirfyw's influence remains in the sense of beauty and wonder and love that Cerridwen feels as the great Mother. This interaction is essential to the unfolding of transformation, reaffirming that the qualities we initially placed in the cauldron are never vanquished; rather, they are assimilated.

EXERCISE

So what *is* in a name? How important are names to you? We have seen what mystery lies in the name Gwion Bach. How about your name—what does that invoke? Stop for a minute and consider your given or chosen name; what does it describe, if anything? Does it express your qualities? Perhaps your name honours something, maybe an ancestor, or it may provide you with a sense of heritage and belonging. Names are incredibly powerful things, and although we may dismiss their power as simply an unimportant label, we cannot deny that we live in a world of labels. Our names may well be one of those badges, but how do we give them meaning? Meditate on the function of your name, and what it means to you, your loved ones, and your community.

For example, my own name is vitally important to my identity within my tribe. My surname honours the Celtic Hughes tribe; derived from *Hu* or *Huw*, meaning "fire" and "inspiration," by proxy of this name I sense my connection to centuries of Celtic history and heritage. My first name honours my parents and their choices in naming me.

The Sacred Chase

We now move on to the most magical aspect of the transformation process, the chase. In the section devoted to Cerridwen, we were introduced to her role within the chase sequence and the significant use of shapeshifting magic that she utilised. This section differs in its point of view, for we now explore the chase through the eyes of the hunted. As we previously saw, Cerridwen is the hunter; she forces the initiate ever forward. However, there is further magic to behold in the smallest details. On first glance, it may appear that the purpose of the chase is directly related to the wrath of Cerridwen, and that Gwion Bach is simply responding in a "fight or flight" fashion. The witch goddess may seem to be the aggressor intent on destroying what has, for all intents and purpose, been stolen from her, but by now we realise that there are deeper levels of meaning.

The transformational combat has a specific purpose and meaning and is perfectly adapted in a mythological sense to be of a dual nature. On one hand, it serves to entertain—to pass the dark nights sharing stories by candlelight—and on another level it speaks of a sequence of mysteries that addresses an audience of another nature, those of the schools of mystery. One can imagine the storytellers of old expertly articulating the tale, creating tension and drama, culminating in the thrill of the chase and the peril it contains. Without the latest Hollywood productions to capture the imagination, the old storytellers were the A-list celebrities of their day, each one capable of mesmerising his or her audience. Mouths would be gaping in anticipation, bottoms firmly rooted to the spot as myths and legends were brought expertly to life. And yet, in the gloom of a court or a gathering hall, sat other folk who simply smiled knowingly at the contents of the tales. The old storytellers and travelling bards were the teachers of the day. With no newspapers and no Internet, the only manner by which the students of mystery heard of the latest teachings and developments was through the mouths of the wandering orator.

If we leave aside the thrilling nature of the chase and descend below the depths of entertainment, we begin to find meaning in the transformational combat. This meaning is not a mental exercise but a template for our own initiation into the mysteries of the Celtic tradition. Caitlín Matthews suggests that the changes are in keeping with the various levels involved in the training of the initiate as he or she travels towards transformation. Each sequence of the tale provides the initiate with insights into the nature of things and eventually to a state of "all knowing." Matthews explains how the chase forces the querent through deeper levels of understanding until he reaches "the primary essence of life itself, here symbolised by a grain of wheat."[97]

This is interesting, for the implication is that we have, at some point in our lives, lost this meaning and connection to the primary essence. The individual elements of the chase sequence transmit the mysteries of being to the initiate as he or she is immersed within the experience. There is a relay of information happening whereby the initiate is in receipt of teachings by means of the natural world and its direct link to the source of all being. The aggressor, who appears in this case to be Cerridwen, is none other than the initiator; her role is to ensure that inertia does not occur and that the immersion in each component of the chase is in perpetual motion. Throughout the sequence the initiate is bombarded with information by proxy of the lucidity of Awen; an element of threat and danger is also present in the form of the hunter pushing the querent onwards. Eventually there is a period of rest and assimilation by which the initiate digests and makes sense of the teachings he or she has received. In the darkness of the womb, the teachings coalesce into meaning. Therefore, a function of the chase is the initial coalescence of wisdom and knowledge. The blessed drops have opened the doors to mystery, and the chase sequence is their entrance.

In order for the mysteries to be admitted unhindered, it is necessary for certain human functions to be temporarily suspended. Gwion Bach is suddenly in receipt of such a vast storehouse of wisdom that he is in danger of a mental breakdown; therefore, the functions of the human are briefly halted to allow unhindered ingestion of the mysteries. An animal acts in accordance to its nature; there is no other agenda. Humans, on the other hand, are riddled with agendas. Gwion's form is transformed, but his essence remains unchanged; therefore, a component of his humanity is retained whilst in animal form, but he is, in essence, acting according to the instincts of the animal shape he finds himself in. The primary instinct here is survival.

There is always an ordeal within transformational rites and initiations, and it is imperative that this element be present, for it causes us to act on

---

97   Matthews, *Mabon and the Guardians of Celtic Britain*, 141.

instinct. The ordeal causes the brain to be reset to factory settings, if you like, to reconnect with the primary essence of life. The conscious mind is temporarily suppressed to allow access to the higher states of being. Gwion's form is changed, and he goes forth through the elemental realms, receiving their wisdom as he travels whilst being free of the restraints of the critical mind. His spirit is open; he has surpassed the doubting, insecure, disbelieving aspects of himself and is immersed in the lucidity of mystery; he has been returned to the primary state of being.

At its heart, the purpose of the transformational combat is to return the mind to the default state. It bridges the canyon that forms between the mind and the spirit as we succumb to the programming of our societies. A powerful spell must have been cast over the minds of humans that caused them to believe that they are separate from the world. We are taught to strive to make our lives better by working hard and earning buckets of money—only then will we be truly happy! The spell is so powerful that it may cause us to believe that rather than being an aspect of nature, instead we can control it. Nature is something "out there," and all that matters is the here and now and the constant battle for gain. The spell also causes us to believe that a lost part of ourselves left and travelled elsewhere and that we must embark on a physical (and sometimes costly) journey to "find ourselves." And yet, the "self" was there all the while—within us. It never left, it didn't go anywhere; we simply were led to believe that such things hold no value and do not necessarily exist. The effects of this spell still grasp our human world in its clutches. The process of transformation by returning us to factory settings breaks this spell and causes us to see clearly the interconnection of all things and the primordial origination of the soul. Doreen Valiente, the mother of modern Wicca, captured this sentiment beautifully in her *Charge of the Goddess,* where she exclaimed that if we seek what we do not find inside us, we will never find it outside of us either.

But is all this worth it? Imagine all the study, the work, the devotion, the commitment that is needed to embark on a journey into the spirit. Surely it's just a huge waste of time, right? After all, it's not going to get you a bigger house or those designer shoes that you just have to have. It's not really going to put an awful lot of money in your purse either, nor will it cause your credit card debt to miraculously vanish. It won't get you a better job, nor will it cause that sexy guy who works at the coffee shop to fall madly in love with you and whisk you away to the Caribbean! But it will cause pieces of your spirit to float gently back into coalescence with your entire being, so you will be unable to accurately define where you end and the world begins. It will cause you to realise that there was nothing actually missing in your life in the first place. The process of transformation causes our lives to be enriched by the realisation that we are the world experiencing itself. This lucidity brings the spirit in line with the soul of the universe as it sings in praise of itself— aware, conscious, and blissfully swimming in the rapture of being.

Each culture, each tradition has its own unique set of keys that allow doors to open, that return us to factory settings. Our lives are not restricted by this action—nothing is impeded; in fact, the opposite is true. We learn to live by means of a positive morality whereby all life—all elements of the earth and its inhabitants—is an integral part of us. The act of initiation into the mysteries brings all dimensions of the universe into awareness and causes us to experience this world as integral aspects of it, not separate from it. We fall into meaningful relationship. What you hold in your hands is one of the keys of the Celtic tradition that fits neatly into the lock of a door that society has taught us is forever locked. The chase allows us to ingest this information before we assimilate it into meaning.

In the past, some of our greatest and perhaps most criticised authors have explored the meaning of the chase and its significance, and without exception they are all in agreement that a profoundly magical process is at work. Edward Davies claims that the swallowing of the initiate at the culmination of the chase is his symbolic placement in the sanctuary of the Goddess and implies that there is much more going on than initially is apparent. He believed that the aspirant is intended for the priesthood and that his imprisonment in the womb is the manner by which he assimilates the doctrines and rites of Cerridwen.[98] Robert Graves, on the other hand, presents us with

---

98 Davies, *Mythology and Rites of the British Druids*, 236.

an interesting correspondence that has some merit and can be incorporated into an exploration of the tale. He claims that the entire cycle runs in strict seasonal order, and that by breaking the sequence down we can attribute a particular season to each facet of the chase. He states that the hare is indicative of the autumn coursing season, the fish takes place in the rains of winter, the bird in the spring during the migrating season, and the grain of corn during the summer harvest.[99] These links may be somewhat tenuous, to say the least, but it would be foolhardy to dismiss them entirely, for the seasons are of great importance to Pagan practise.

These varying thoughts that span centuries of exploration teach us that there is an abundant source of inspiration and guidance out there where folk have made tentative steps to approach the cauldron. The interpretations of these authors permit us to freely explore meaning and significance that is appropriate for our journey into transformation. Although it is easy to academically dismiss attributions of this kind, they do have visionary merit and can be used by current practitioners of the mysteries. These seasonal correspondences can be utilised by means of ritual, used for meditation and developing relationship with each sequence of the chase. All explorations are worthy of investigation; they cause us to be further involved and strengthen our relationship with the material and its archetypes.

◆ ◆ ◆

Perhaps the first thing we notice when we look at the tale from an occult point of view is the obvious elemental correspondences; the chase takes place within earth, water, and air. This fact alone is immensely significant, and it is tempting to cause these components to fall in line with modern Pagan concepts, but as you will see our concepts can also be challenged. Within current Druidic practise there is the concept of land, sea, and sky, and this falls neatly into the elements described in the tale at hand:

---

99   Graves, *The White Goddess*, 400.

- Land/earth—the hare and greyhound sequence
- Sea/water—the fish and otter sequence
- Sky/air—the wren and hawk sequence

Pagan ritual consists of honouring four elements, each of which occupy a cardinal point within the circle, or sacred space; these "quarters" form meaningful correspondences that practitioners invoke and connect with during ritual. The use of the four elements in Pagan ritual is influenced by their usage as the four classical elements of ancient Greek philosophy and science. However, there is no evidence to suggest that the Celts honoured them in the same manner. In fact, there is some evidence to imply that only the three elements of earth, water, and air were acknowledged. This is not a discourse to negate the current practise of honouring four elements, but rather a challenge to the current assumption that all four are sequentially present within the tale, for as you will discover, they are not. It is somewhat tempting to assign all four classical elements to the chase sequence—understandably so, for three of the elements are sequentially present. The corresponding animals emulate the qualities of these elements, but the fourth is missing or not so obviously placed. The general school of thought has thus far dismissed the obvious sequential inconsistency and assumed that the element of fire is represented by the corn and hen sequence. Admittedly this is a tenuous link to say the least; fire is not mentioned, and the digestive fire or the metaphorical fire of conception is a further tenacity that simply hides a more magical meaning.

It is sometimes easier to make assumptions than go to great efforts to explore exactly what is going on, but as we have seen previously, the act of learning and of being learned is a sacred rite in itself. Within the Celtic mind, Fire is what brings about the transformation of the other elements; it instigates change and was present at the beginning of creation. "I was gleaming fire when I was caused to exist" said Taliesin in the Black Book of Carmarthen, reiterating the fact that fire underlies the other elements. If we explore the significance of fire and its interactions, we gain a deeper understanding of its nature and how it was perceived in the Celtic mind. The Celts conceptualised everything in a tripartite fashion. Just as our apparent space has only three dimensions, they believed that only three primary elements existed and that they arose and were transformed by means of fire. Now we are more than aware that our physical universe was created by an explosion; fire initiated its commencement and caused the other elements to spring into being. I quote the eloquent Jean Markale, who explains that

> when a solid burns, it becomes gaseous; earth becomes air thanks to fire. When a liquid burns, it becomes gaseous; water becomes air thanks to the activity of fire. When a gas burns, it becomes a different gas, whether it is a liquid, for example (the hydrogen and oxygen that create water), or a solid: air becomes air, earth, or fire through the activity of fire. For fire is the very principle of action.[100]

The Greek philosopher Heraclitus challenged the classical assumption of the existence of four equal elements by claiming that fire gave rise to the other three. He believed that fire was the fundamental element. Therefore, with this in mind, fire underpins all things in the physical universe; it is the primordial element that encapsulates all the energy contained within the other three. They are all changed by the action of fire.

Taliesin describes how he was gleaming fire before he was caused to exist, and his subsequent existences contain all aspects of the elemental world. He originated as fire, and those flames cause the subsequent transformation of the other elements. Interestingly, some of the manuscripts claim that Taliesin was found during Beltane, perhaps the greatest fire festival of the Celts. This is the feast of Bel, the shining one, or "he of fire." This festival is the celebration of light and heat and flame, and it is recorded that the druids built enormous pyres and would drive herds of animals between them for cleansing. The fact that it is either Beltane or Samhain when Taliesin is found is in itself demonstrative of the connection each author had to the subject matter. To one author, fire may have been of immense significance to the meaning of the tale, whereas to another it may have been the liminality of Samhain. When we examine the tale, we find the presence of fire throughout. Initially

---

100   Markale, *The Druids*, 152.

we encounter it as the flames lit beneath the great cauldron. This fire causes the transformation of the water within to boil into steam, and water becomes air because of the action of fire. Earth dissolves into water as the ingredients are transformed by the action of fire. A metaphorical fire is present in the searing heat of the three drops that alight on Gwion's thumb. Subsequently the fire of all knowing and its sheer power to transform is imbued within the innocent. The simple yeoman's son travels through land, water, and air because of the action of fire. Fire underpins the entire process.

The subject of the elements is an interesting discourse, for it challenges our own concepts of the elements and how we honour them, but not in a manner that negates their usage. To further explore this idea serves to deepen our relationship with the very real components of Pagan practise. After all, we are not dealing with mere concepts when we call each cardinal power; we are dealing with forces that are awesome and present. To explore them in a manner that challenges our current working practise serves to further our understanding of them and why they are included in our rites to begin with.

Prior to exploring the remaining three elements involved in the chase sequence, it is pertinent to contemplate what has been said concerning fire. This concept may well be new to you; you may find it an interesting discourse that differs from the normal elemental functions in modern Paganism. You may, on the other hand, completely disagree with it. However, take some time to meditate on the ability of fire to cause the transformation of the other three elements.

EXERCISE

"With seven created beings I was placed for purification; I was gleaming fire before I was caused to exist." These words by Taliesin sing of the mysteries of fire. How do you perceive fire and how do you relate to it? Look to the ball of fire in the sky and feel its heat upon your skin; what causes such a thing to perpetually burn? What understanding do you have of the physical properties of fire? Fire can be a metaphor—it may represent your passion, your vigour and zestfulness. Identify the fire aspects of yourself and how they are presented to the world at large. In Celtic traditions, the "fire in the head" is a common theme whereby the light of spirit shines from the radiant brow to inspire and transform. What is the nature of your own "fire in the head"? How brightly does it shine? Chant the words of Taliesin over and over until the mind is lost in the rapture of fire: "I was gleaming fire before I was caused to exist!"

Earth/Land

Immediately after Gwion ingests Awen and awareness descends upon him, he senses the wrath of Cerridwen and goes forth in the shape of a hare. Cerridwen wilfully changes her form and pursues him. The subsequent chase takes place in the realm of earth, or land. It is within this sequence that the teachings of earth are transmitted to the initiate. He goes forth as one of the Britain's most enigmatic and symbolic of animals: the hare. The moon gazer (as the hare is lovingly referred to) is the epitome of the divine feminine by means of her association with our satellite.

Traditionally the element of earth is placed in the northern quarter of the Pagan ritual circle and is the embodiment of security, hardness, coldness, darkness, and stability. It is the reign of the Earth Mother and the metaphorical location of the gods and the ancestors. Gwion's initiation into the mysteries of earth is not restricted to this planet alone but expresses the meaning and teaching of all matter in the entire universe. There is a temptation to consider that this reference to land is related only to our planet and her qualities of nurture and security. But there is a vast universe out there with an infinite amount of planets that also sing of the universe's secrets. We may not be able to physically see or visit them, but they are there, and their gravitational pull affects our homeworld just as we affect them. Therefore, the message of earth/land during the chase encapsulates the mystery and meaning of the entire physical universe. Gwion Bach eventually transforms into Taliesin, who further elaborates that he has been all things, even the light of distant stars. It is by means of the mystery of earth/land that he receives this omnipresent quality.

When we look to the stars, we are looking at our point of origin; every single molecule of carbon in our bodies was forged in the searing, incomprehensible heat of stars. Nothing is entirely new but rather in a constant state of recycling. Our corporeal forms, our earthly components, are made of the stuff of stars in precisely the same manner as the substance of our planet; we all come from the same place. It is only the arrangement of molecules that causes us to appear different. With this in mind, we are inexorably connected to the earth beneath our feet, for we share the same birth; we have never been separate from it. It is this knowing that deepens our relationship with the globe which we inhabit and causes us to appreciate and understand the significance of origin. We are the impeccable dance of molecules and atoms, forever locked in a galactic embrace until the moment our sun implodes upon itself. Even then, the dance will begin again—a new star will be born, a new stage will spring into being. Nothing is ever lost; it is simply recycled. As each molecule sprang forth and coalesced, life arose from the primordial soup, and we are now its sum totality.

Our relationship with the world can be as superficial or as profound as we choose. For many, it is sufficient to skim the surface and dash through life without even a glance at the magic that surrounds them. To others it is not enough, and to hear the song of spirit compels one to observe through different eyes. The mystery of earth/land and the chase in animal form serves to teach us all these mysteries, the whys and whatnots; it causes new eyes to open to a universe of mystery. Our relationship to this element is complex, for it has two distinct aspects to it. On one hand, we have the universality of earth/land and its presence throughout physicality. On the other, we have the apparent aspect that relates to the element as it directly affects our lives. We move constantly through earth/land, interacting with it, changing it, and being transformed by it. It holds our communities and our homes. Where we are located on the earth serves to identify who we are and the history of our people. Earth/land serves to display the cycle of moon and sun and the unfolding faces of the season; it is the element that causes us to connect to the natural world.

Ponder on this aspect of the chase: visualise the pursuit of the hare by the hound. What does the landscape look like? How does it appear in your vision? Is it indicative of the landscape you inhabit? What is the song of your land? Consider the aspect of the hare. They differ in relation to rabbits in that they do not burrow beneath the ground, they are fully present in the light of the sun, and they gaze towards the moon at night. What does it mean to be in the form of a hare; what teachings does she relay? Be imaginatively immersed in the chase—feel the pounding of your hind legs against the land, the hot breath of the greyhound behind you. Sense the fear and trepidation and the coursing of survival hormones that flood the bloodstream. Write your experience in your journal.

Consider the land upon which you live. Choose an appropriate day for this walking meditation, then gather your journal and thoughts and embark on a journey into earth. When you move from one location to another, how do you do it? More often than not, you will move by means of an internal automatic pilot. Our lives are busy; we are constantly moving from one place to another, performing chores, our minds preoccupied by duty and purpose. Today, walk consciously. Make every step matter; sense it and the ground upon which you move. How does it appear, and what is its nature? Perhaps you are moving through the suburbs or the countryside, or perhaps you are near water. Are there tall buildings around you? Is your view of the sky impeded?

Sense the ground beneath you and the facets of earth that surround you. Everything that you look at originated from the same place that you did. Listen to the sounds of your landscape as it sings the songs of being. What are their lyrics? What do they tell you of their nature and their interaction with one another? Nothing is truly inanimate; everything is in a constant state of flux and movement. Can you sense this? Do not be a passive observer of your environment; instead, question your relationship with it and how you interact with it. Sense the people who share the landscape with you and how they are the sum totality of the people who went before them.

Challenge your knowledge of your landscape. Jot down the following questions into your journal and attempt to answer them by reflecting on the properties of the land you inhabit:

- How many generations of your family have occupied this land?
- Where do your blood relatives originate from?
- Who are the native peoples of your landscape? What is their history?
- Are there monuments to people long past? What is their nature and meaning?
- When was this place initially colonised? What structures exist that sing of its history?
- What do the given place-names of your locale mean?
- How do the seasons affect it? How does it change with the cycle of the year?
- What are the most striking features of your landscape? How did they arise?
- How did the land evolve? Was it by glacial action or volcano?

All these things serve to deepen our relationship; our eyes open to the meaning of earth/land and our connection to it. The chase initiates this perception and the sense of being at one with the element that sustains our physical forms.

Water/Sea

At the culmination of the teachings of earth/land, the initiate becomes weary; the legs leaden and the claws of the hound draw ever closer, the snapping of its powerful jaws like a chill wind against the hind legs. The hare sights a river ahead and is forced towards it. With a final pounding leap, the furred creature takes momentarily to the air before diving into the crystal-clear water. As the surface breaks, the fur vanishes, to be replaced by scales; the initiate goes forth in the form of a fish. Its gills open to hasten the absorption of oxygen from the surrounding water, its heart beats to a different tune, and its auditory senses no longer operate in the same manner. But its heartbeat quickens as it senses the crashing of the hound against water, then the sleek form of an otter appears beneath the river's surface, its claws ever deadly and its jaws poised in readiness. The chase continues through the realm of water.

It is believed that it is the presence of water that provides the stage for life to develop. To discover water on another planet would indicate the possibility of alien life. Our blue planet is awash with this magical, life-giving element; it causes our skies to be filled with fluid-soaked clouds. It causes the greening of the earth and the nurture of vegetation. Without water, no life would be possible. Within earth we explored the physical molecules that make up the hardness of our bodies, our bones and flesh, yet they constitute only a small percentage of our entirety; water makes up the rest. We are indeed creatures of water. The Celts believed that water affected both the spiritual and physical dimensions, and it is perhaps this belief that gave rise to the numerous healing springs and wells of Britain and Ireland. It was believed that water contained elements of the spirit and hid other worlds beneath its surface. Not only was water an element that encouraged or facilitated healing, it was believed that it could also heal the spirit. Hence shrines and temples were erected near significant stretches of water or at the bending of a river or where fresh and salt water mixed.

The river Severn in the British Isles is perhaps one of the most famous rivers in the islands and is known for being sacred to the goddess Sabrina. Temples to her were built along its course, from its origin in the west of Wales to the current monuments in the Shropshire town of Shrewsbury. In Gloucestershire Sabrina meets the sea, and twice a day the Severn Boar, a gigantic wave of tidal water, courses its way inland, affecting everything in its path. Tutelary deities of rivers and springs are recorded in the current names of many of Britain's rivers and springs. Where thermal waters erupted from the ground, ornate temples and baths were constructed to benefit from their healing properties and to honour the deities of that place. Every spring, every brook, every stream and river, pond and lake was believed to be the habitat of divine creatures. Our ancestors noted these places to be immensely sacred, especially banks and estuaries where land and water collide. But these rivers were more than simply sites devoted to local deities; they epitomised the well-being of the land and of its tribe. Primarily fertile, the waters were sacred on many levels; they sustained the land and also provided a link to the unseen worlds.

When Gwion Bach enters water, he is admitted into an almost alien world, a place not often explored by man, or at least not for very long. Life down here is incredibly different to that of the land, and the creatures that inhabit it are equally as mysterious and enigmatic. In Celtic tradition, the salmon is traditionally associated with wisdom, which implies that water is a conduit for the transmission of wisdom. In Irish traditions the Salmon of Wisdom is eaten, and it is the act of consuming its flesh that imparts wisdom; however, the British system differs significantly, for it is not a salmon that is found in the weir but a human being. The salmon is the carrier of wisdom, whereas Gwion Bach, who later becomes Taliesin, is the actual personification of wisdom. (More on this in the section devoted to Taliesin.) Water is perceived as a conduit for the transmission and assimilation of wisdom, but this is fraught with another of its attributes: emotion.

In the esoteric arts, water is seen as what represents the emotions; the ebb and flow of our hormones' impact upon our emotional stability. The waters of our oceans are pulled by the gravitational attraction of the moon, which in turn is believed to influence human emotions. Considering that we are primarily made of water, it stands to reason, esoterically, that we are affected by our satellite. Our emotions mimic the nature of water; they both arise from an unknown, invisible place and they must run their course or risk breaking their banks or, worse, being dammed. The relationship that we have with this invisible world within us teaches us a great deal about the nature of our selves and the nature of the realm of water. Not everything in life is visible or in plain sight, and as students of the mysteries, we gain this teaching from the wisdom of water. Throughout the tale, its presence is constant—the initial components take place on the edge of a vast, deep lake. The cauldron requires water to contain the ingredients for the brewing of Awen. The mysteries are transmitted via water, the drops, into the body of Gwion Bach. The salmon and otter interact with a sacred river before Gwion

Bach swims in the amniotic waters of the witch goddess. The newborn child is placed on a river and set adrift for forty years before being discovered in a weir. The waters of our tale are symbolic of the interaction between the land and the element that sustains it and its riches. It is a constant that holds the initiate and causes him to be moved from one experience to another; it facilitates assimilation. The teachings that it transmits are suggestive of the hidden worlds and the effect they have on the apparent world. It is the conduit for the transmission of wisdom and the assimilation of it before its utilisation in the visible world.

EXERCISE

Meditate on the quality of water within your own body. Your blood emulates the action of rivers, irrigating and bringing nourishment to what surrounds it. It holds within it a life force that no microscope can detect, no scientist eviscerate. The ebb and flow of your hormones floods the bloodstream, the rivers and streams of your being, and causes you to affect yourself and the world around you. The water within you acts in the same manner as every other body of water on the face of the earth. Therefore, the elements of mystery contained within it are, by their very nature, contained within you.

The Celts were renowned for their riddles and for their tendency to answer a question with a question. On the surface of things, this can appear a little annoying, but there is much that can be learnt from this process. Contemplation is a vital skill of any student of the mysteries. With this in mind, I ask that you contemplate the following statements made by Gwion Bach after his transformation:

> *Awen I sing,*
> *From the deep I bring it,*
> *It is a connected river that flows.*
> *I know its might,*
> *I know how it ebbs,*
> *And I know how it flows,*

I know of its course,

I know when it will retreat,

I know what creatures there are beneath the sea.[101]

Taliesin is describing the knowledge of these things; his immersion in water has enabled this knowing. What do you know of the nature of water? Do you go with the flow, or is it only dead fish that go with the flow?

It is one thing to be observant of water and indeed to be immersed within it, but how different is it to "be" water? Taliesin elaborates:

I have been a drop in the air,

I have been a bridge over sixty estuaries,

I have been a coracle on the sea,

I have been the sparkling bubbles in drink,

I have been a raindrop in a shower

And foam in water.

From the ninth wave's water was I made.[102]

Repeat the verses above; if possible, memorise them and chant them in a mantralike fashion. If you are able, contemplate the nature of water whilst reciting the verse near a body of water—allow the mind to drift, letting the words flow like rivers from your lips.

The ninth wave is a common motif in Celtic mythology; although its meaning is lost to the mists of time, it carries a certain enigmatic quality that inspires awe to this day. The ninth wave contains within it the magic of the Celts' most sacred number, three. The number nine—three times three or the square of three—was perceived to be immensely sacred. The ninth wave can be perceived as the mystical border between the worlds; it is the wave that carries the mystery of the sea to the land.

Record your experience in your journal.

---

101   Extract from the poem "Angar Kyfundawt" in the Book of Taliesin (my translation).

102   Adapted from the poem "Kad Godeu" in the Book of Taliesin (my translation).

Air/Sky

The teachings of water are transmitted and the salmon grows weary; the waters become murky and the brine of the sea stings the gills as it nears the estuary. The otter is relentless, merciless; she continues her pursuit, pushing the initiate ever onwards. As the waters shallow, the salmon is forced upwards, and as its head appears above the surface, a beak takes its place. Feathers appear where once scales were, and a tiny wren emerges from the water's broken surface. Its small form ascends into the sky; its pure, bright voice calling to the element that holds it. The otter breaks the surface tension of the river and she emerges as a hawk; her cry shatters the air with its piercing call, pushing the little wren onwards and upwards. Cerridwen senses the resentment rising within her yet again, but it is subdued by the mysteries. This is her task: to force the wren onwards into the mystery of air.

The realm of air/sky is perhaps the most ambiguous of the elements, for we are so accustomed to it that we barely pay it any attention. Unlike water, we do not seek to consciously replenish ourselves with air; the process happens naturally. When we need water, we thirst, thereby responding to the call of water within us; it is not often that we encounter situations of suffocation that would make us gasp for air. Our need to breathe is obviously vital, but we tend to give it little thought. Yet the breath has long been associated with the spirit, and this can be seen in the etymology of the word *spirit,* which is derived from the Latin *spiritus,* meaning "breath," which in turn is related to *spirare,* meaning "to breathe."[103] The breath carries the voice and the voice carries the power of words; magic exists within breath, within the element of air.

Air is the realm of winged creatures, both physical and mystical. Inhabited by birds and insects, the world of air is also believed to be the domain of other elemental creatures and spirits, in particular the Fair Folk. On the physical plane, many birds and insects have long been associated with divinity or as vessels for gods and goddesses. Several archetypes of the British Celtic system are identified with the crow family or with the wren. In the

---

103 *Chambers Dictionary of Etymology.*

insect world, the bee is particularly associated with the dead for its ability to carry the spirits of the dead across the border into the next world. It is believed that aspects of the spirit are held within the breath and that at the last breath it is set free to continue its journey into mystery.

Air has long been associated with magic, and the raising of the winds was a particularly special skill of the witch. In Britain, the "tying up the wind" spell is as ancient as man's ability to build sailing vessels. This spell involved the tying of three knots into a piece of string, rope, or cloth. The witch would summon the winds as she tied each knot and use her breath to invoke their powers into the material used. This would then be sold to a sailor who in turn would release the wind tied into the knots, if and when needed. For a moderate wind, one knot would be untied. Two knots untied would summon half a gale, whereas all three would surely call a hurricane. This spell is still used to this day in coastal regions of Britain.

As Gwion Bach, in the form of a wren, takes to the skies, he is immersed in the teachings of that element. As he flies through it, it also courses through him, his heart thumping as it takes the vital gas and sends it to his organs, powering him away from the claws of the hawk. As you course through air, stop and meditate on its qualities. As each breath enters your mouth and descends into your lungs, its encounters the bronchial tree. Incredibly, within our bodies we have a representation of a tree, the most sacred symbol of the British Celts. Albeit upside down, the tree mimics the nature of trees in its processing and exchange of gas. The magical quality of air happens within our bodies every single second of our lives. Each red blood cell holds a molecule of gas in its concavity and sends it to the tissues and organs of your body, thus ensuring your well-being. The powers of air are entirely invisible, yet their effects are more than apparent. A gentle breeze can be a welcome relief on a warm, sunny day. A hurricane may mercilessly kill thousands of innocent lives. Like all the other elements discussed, air acts only according to its nature; it is amoral, it simply serves to be itself.

EXERCISE

Consider the following riddle from the Book of Taliesin. It speaks of something indicative of the element discussed, yet I shall not offer the answer. Meditate on the statements and the message and teaching that it relays.

Guess who it is.
Created before the flood,
A creature strong,
Without flesh, without bone,
No veins, and no blood,
Without head and without feet.
It is not older, nor younger
Than it was in the beginning,
It will not stray from its mission
Through fear nor death.
It has not the needs
That created beings have.
It is in the field, it is in the wood,
With neither hand nor foot,
Without old age or illness.
It is not troubled by affliction.
It is as wide as the face of the earth,
And it was not born,
And cannot be seen,
It is on the sea and on the land,
It sees but is not seen.
It is bad, it is good,
It is there, it is here,
It unarranges and apologises not.
It makes no amends for what it does.
For it is blameless.[104]

---

104   Adapted from the poem "Kanu y Gwynt" from the Book of Taliesin (my
       translation).

Meditate on the riddle above, but do so in the knowledge that what you read connects you to countless centuries of wisdom and magic. These are not words that have been plucked from air; instead they speak of it in a manner that is as old as the standing stones that decorate the fields.

Record your encounters with air in your journal.

◆ ◆ ◆

At the culmination of the chase, Gwion Bach is forced by the relentless hawk to descend into a farmer's yard and assume the form of a grain of wheat. Here he becomes, in essence, the symbol of life itself: the humble seed. Cerridwen, in her form as the hen, maintains her role as initiator; sensing the journey's end, she pecks at the grain until she consumes the initiate. Instead of certain death, Gwion Bach is mysteriously transferred from the belly of the hen into the womb of the witch goddess, whose fury returns upon the assumption of her human form. Within the form of various animals, it seems that Cerridwen is able to temporarily switch off her vengeance and accept that the chase is part of a mystery that even she may not entirely understand. Yet within her human form, her anger returns to the forefront of her mind: within her womb is the subject of her wrath, and she is still intent on killing him.

Gwion Bach now finds himself in different waters, the womb waters of the mother. This process is necessary for the assimilation of the previous experience. For it to be fully incorporated into the mind and spirit, a period of isolation and absorption must take place. The initiate must retreat in order to make sense of what has happened and to become one with the knowledge and wisdom that he or she has received. With any course of study there must always follow a period of reflection and revision, but there are obvious questions that warrant asking. Primarily: if Gwion is in possession of the Prophetic Spirit and is indeed the vessel for all the knowledge and wisdom of the universe, why does he not prevent the chase from ever taking place? Surely he has the ability to transport himself to the furthest reaches of the galaxy or to another realm entirely? With his newfound abilities and powers, Cerridwen would surely be unable to follow him. With a similar question in mind, one would imagine that for a witch as learned and skilled as Cerridwen, she could prevent the transfer of the grain into her womb. With her magical prowess, one would imagine this task to be easily achievable. There must be a reason why these alternatives do not take place. It seems that Gwion must pass through a triple birth to be in effective possession of the Prophetic Spirit and be reborn as Taliesin. First he is born of his ordinary mother in a small Welsh village, secondly he is born to the witch goddess Cerridwen, and finally he is birthed, almost by means of a caesarean section, from the coracle, or skin-belly. On some level both the initiate, Gwion, and the initiator, Cerridwen, are aware of this. The old life of Gwion Bach, including his features and personality, is destroyed in the womb of the great mother; for all intents and purposes, he is killed. It is his spirit that is transferred into the foetus that Cerridwen carries. It is at this point that our exploration of Gwion Bach comes to its natural end, but we have explored much. We have established that Gwion has a supernatural element to him, that his birth and life are not as clean-cut and transparent as we may have initially thought. We discovered the nature of what nourishes and also poisons, and that learning and assimilation are imperative to transformation. We have also established that Gwion Bach, in essence, represents you—you are the hero of your quest, and Gwion's tale serves as a template that guides you into the understanding of mystery.

EXERCISE

Gwion's initiation is silent; he does not protest nor raise his voice in objection. For the duration of the chase he is silenced by being in animal form. He is silent in the womb, and only when he is reborn does he begin to speak. But one could argue that this is no longer Gwion Bach. An exercise into the nature of Gwion Bach is, in a manner, counterproductive, for the act of immersion in the tale and assuming Gwion is the exercise. But there are methods that our ancestors used to prepare themselves to be in receipt of Awen.

It was common for the Celts to retreat into dark cells for long periods of contemplation, where light was not permitted entry. Within the darkness they would meditate on questions that required answers or clarity. After several hours or days, they would emerge into the sunlight, at which point Awen would fill them with wisdom and the answers would spill forth. In a similar fashion, take yourself to a room or space that can be entirely darkened to prevent any admission of light. Ensure that you will not be disturbed, and remain there for a lengthy duration of time. Watch your thoughts as your mind projects images onto the walls of darkness. Immerse yourself in the nothingness, and relish in the sheer potential of the unmanifest.

Memorise and meditate on the following questions:

- What is silence?
- How important is it in your life to have periods of silence and reflection?
- Do you set aside times to reflect? Do you retreat periodically?
- What is the nature of retreating?
- When you last studied a subject, how did you assimilate the information?
- Why do you seek mystery?
- Why do you seek transformation?
- What is your most innocent quality?
- What is your most poisonous quality?

The goal here is to lose the restraints of your mind by being deprived of the sense of sight; this, in turn, will affect your other senses. Some may be heightened, others dampened. Remain in the darkness until you feel it is time to leave. Walk out into light and record your experience in your journal.

Taliesin
THE PROPHETIC SPIRIT

◆ ◆ ◆

And it is not known if my flesh is meat or fish,
And I was for nearly nine months
In the womb of Cerridwen the Witch.
Formerly I was Gwion Bach,
But now I am Taliesin.

Taliesin

Inadvertently, our exploration of Taliesin commenced at the beginning of this book; the babe in the weir is the culmination of our experience with all components of the tale. The true meaning of the Taliesin spirit is conveyed within the Gwion Bach sequence and the subsequent assimilation process. Everything leads to this moment. But it is pertinent here to explore a little more deeply the nature of this being of radiance.

Our knowledge of Taliesin is compounded by the very fact that he spans an impossible amount of centuries; the rational human mind strives to make sense of this by attempting to locate him as an actual historical figure. This is no easy task, for the information that we discover is conflicting, contradictory, and indicative of something other than ordinary history. To begin with, our knowledge of Taliesin as a historical figure stems from the ninth century, when Nennius, in his Historia Brittonum, mentions him as one of the five poets famed among the Welsh during the sixth century. Elis Gruffudd, in his Chronicle of the History of the World, also places the birth tale of

Taliesin within the same century. It is tempting to accept Nennius's writings and accept that Taliesin was a mortal poet who was alive and well and living in sixth-century Wales, and for centuries scholars have been attempting to convince us of this. However, academia itself has had to be rather creative in its attempt to pinpoint the time and place of the physical embodiment of wisdom. Their attempts to convince us of the existence of Taliesin have served to simultaneously enlighten and confuse.

There can be no doubt that some of the works attributed to Taliesin are in direct relation to prominent figures in history; the satirical nature of the material further demonstrates that they were indeed composed by a skilled, courtly bard. We also find incredible poetry that is clearly synonymous with supernatural events and omnipotence. Academia has strived to make sense of or separate the contrasting nature of the poetry for centuries, and as a consequence the material can be split into two groups. On one hand, we have poems that allude to being composed by an actual sixth-century bard who may have been called Taliesin or adopted the title for reasons lost to us. The other is that several poems belong to a body of work of mystical and legendary origin that surpasses the life span of a single individual. The Taliesin material identifies the poet with historical figures who are separated by centuries; this impossible feat indicates that the persona of Taliesin is something other than the ordinary. Marged Haycock states:

> [T]he poems of the present collection are clearly dealing with a legendary and extraordinary being—a figure who claims to have been created at the world's beginning, not born of mortal father and mother, who has been in the company of the divine family of Don and has lived many different forms.[105]

We are unable to realistically accept beyond any doubt the singular presence of a historical Taliesin, for there is so much of the material that is far from human or in accordance with history. Although there may well have been a Taliesin working as a bard in the sixth century and singing in praise of historical figures, he may have been one in a succession of Taliesins spanning

---

105   Haycock, *Legendary Poems from the Book of Taliesin*, 9–10.

a mind-boggling array of years. Therefore we can assume that the figure of Taliesin is something that transcends time and its limitations; it is suggestive of a spirit that inhabits various poets throughout time, who themselves act as mouthpieces for the Celtic material. We may never discover the names and identities of the individuals who composed most of the poetry, but it is more than possible that they were written and disseminated by people who identified themselves as possessors of the Prophetic Spirit and by proxy were of "radiant brows" themselves—they were Taliesin. It is my belief that the name Taliesin is, in fact, a rank that may be bestowed on any individual who subscribes and is an initiate of the Celtic mysteries. It simply refers to the shining light of Awen that beams from the forehead, the third eye region, and is the fire in the head that burns from the wisdom of ages. It is this mythologized Taliesin that this section is concerned with, as well as the exploration of the spirit of Taliesin as an experiential component of spiritual practise.

There can be no doubt that the historical poems that speak of Urien Rheged and Maelgwn Gwynedd—actual historical figures—are of immense value. They do not, however, form a major discussion within this current body of work; to do so, I fear, would steer the material into another realm of exploration beyond my capabilities. For the purpose of this book it is sufficient to explore Taliesin from a mystical point of view, a notion that is not without standing, as confirmed by the scholar Ifor Williams. In his *Chwedl Taliesin,* he comments that there is no difference between Taliesin and the old gods, and that he took his place with Lleu and Dylan, with Gwydion and Manawydan, with Math and Don and Arianrhod—in fact, with the entire pantheon of the British Celts.[106] Therefore, Taliesin's standing as a creature of supernatural erudition forms the basis of this examination, as it is pertinent to the exploration of the mystery of transformation contained within the tale of his birth. But in order to understand the nature of the transformed Gwion Bach who is found as the newborn Taliesin, we must consult various bodies of work that substantiate the significance of the embodied wisdom found at the salmon weir.

---

106   Williams, *Chwedl Taliesin,* 24.

Other than the tale at hand and the various manuscripts that contain it, Taliesin appears in several other ancient manuscripts of Wales. There is the vast body of work that you will have noted has been utilised throughout this work called the Book of Taliesin. He appears in the works of the Mabinogi, notably the Second Branch, and also within the Black Book of Carmarthen, the elements of which were explored previously in relation to Cerridwen. He is also mentioned within the *Triads of the Island of Britain* and within a body of work known as *The Life of Merlin: Vita Merlini*. All these sources are important and worthy of study and will initiate further relations with the figure of Taliesin. However, to begin with, we must look at some of the sources that are suggestive of the state of Taliesin's being.

His persona undoubtedly supersedes his mortal birthing, first in the guise of Gwion Bach, secondly in the womb of the witch goddess, and finally in his gestation and subsequent birthing from the skin-belly. To identify Taliesin as a single historical figure in this sense would be foolhardy, for we would be attempting to identify with a personage of such incredible supernatural knowledge, we would find it almost impossible to connect with it. Instead we must look at the birthing and nature of Taliesin within the context of the tale. It is indicative of the post-initiated state; it is demonstrative of the universal occult wisdom having been assimilated into the spirit in a manner that can be expressed. To accept Taliesin as a mere historical figure would be to miss out on the vast storehouse of wisdom that he is attempting to teach us. For the language and concepts that Taliesin transmits to sing to the spirit, we must first understand the nature of rebirth—but not simply by cerebral methods. The mysteries of Taliesin and his omnipresent, omnipotent state of being cannot be understood by the mind alone; it must be incorporated into the spirit as experience, and it is this tale that teaches us how that is achieved. It is by process of assimilation in the womb of the witch goddess and within the confines of the skin-belly that the mysteries coalesce into meaning. It is only by means of these actions that we are able to compre-hend how Taliesin's poems recounting various states of being and the nature of his birth are, in fact, relating directly to his spirit, not simply his mortal coil. To understand these facets of the spirit as concepts is all very well—

they are pretty, poetic, and full of profound meaning—but for the spirit to be moved into *knowing* what they speak of, we must also be transformed as Taliesin, in the tale, demonstrates by example.

When we left the reborn figure of Gwion Bach in the previous section, it was by means of the coracle, or skin-belly. We are not informed of the reasons why Cerridwen stitched the babe into this device and set him adrift on a river for an impossible length of time, but we can safely assume that this is necessary for the transformation process to be complete. Part of the process of assimilation, we can deduce, took place within the womb of the witch goddess, but the Welsh word for skin-belly is *bol croen*, and the first word, *bol*, is synonymous with belly, bag, and womb.[107] Therefore, this is suggestive that the womb of the witch goddess served only as part of the assimilation process. For Taliesin to be fully transformed and in possession of the Prophetic Spirit, the babe had to undergo another sequence of assimilation, this time by means of device rather than person. This is not unusual; as Celtic scholar Angela Grant notes, the babe Lleu Llaw Gyffes in the Fourth Branch of the Mabinogi also undergoes transformation by device through being placed in a magical chest for a gestational period, in addition to his embryonic stage in the womb of Arianrhod. This subsequent gestation by a nonanthropomorphic device is a recurring theme in Celtic mythology and is explained by Grant as acting "as a sort of suspended animation device, protecting the infant Taliesin until it arrives in Gwyddno's weir up to forty years later."[108]

Upon discovery of the skin-belly in the weir of Gwyddno Garanhir by his son, Elffin, Taliesin is seemingly birthed by caesarean section when the bag is sliced open with a knife. The characters that are involved in this discovery are human figures that belong to a specific time and place. This episode seems indicative of the possessor of the Prophetic Spirit coming into the world and interacting with it, which is in stark contrast to the Irish material, which makes no account of the life of he who is imbued by the Salmon of Wisdom. In the British material we are told of his adventures in the court of Elffin and treated to poetry that is suggestive of the time and also of the

---

107   Bevan, *Geiriadur Prifysgol Cymru*, 296.

108   Grant, *Magical Transformations in Pedeir Keinc y Mabinogi and Hanes Taliesin*, 23.

Prophetic Spirit. But at the point of his birthing at the weir, one can sense the dismay of Elffin, who is expecting a hoard of fish to line his pockets with silver; instead he finds a battered old bag of skin, a coracle. However, the gift it contains is worth more than all the salmon in the river. It is at this point that we are introduced to the name of Taliesin and how it came about.

Upon slicing open the coracle, Elffin notes the forehead of a human baby and says, *"Wele dal iesin* (behold, a radiant forehead)!"

To which the babe within replies, *"Taliesin bid* (I am Taliesin)."

From this point onwards the child is able to converse as an adult, even though we are told that he is merely a baby. However, his name, as you can see, consists of two words compounded together; the first term used by Elffin is *dal*, a mutation of the word *tal*, meaning "brow" or "forehead"; interestingly, it is also synonymous with a catch of fish.[109] The latter term, *iesin*, can be taken to mean "bright" or "radiant." The text of the tale further elaborates that the people accepted this to be the spirit of Gwion Bach, who had been in the womb of Cerridwen; after she delivered him into fresh water, he was reborn as Taliesin. It does not inform us of how or why the people were familiar with the original tale—which, according to the story, happened forty years previously. We are not informed of the reaction of the people at the weir; surely to discover a babe that is fully conversant is not an everyday occurrence, yet they seemingly accept this without question. This implies that although we are dealing with actual historical figures here, they are obviously accustomed to events of a supernatural quality. At every twist and turn we are met with mystery and paradox, and no adequate explanation is provided within the text itself. We are not informed of the reason for Taliesin's shining brow; that this is synonymous with the region of the third eye and the concept of the fire in the head cannot be disputed, but no obvious explanation is given. Further mystery only pertinent to the initiate must be present in the birthing sequence.

Taliesin's transformation by device takes him on a journey through the land by means of water, yet he is not actually *in* water, he rides upon it. In

---

109   Ford, *The Celtic Poets*, 14.

perpetual darkness he is carried by the veins of the land through the landscape of Wales until he arrives at the salmon weir. He claims that it cannot be known if his flesh be that of meat or fish, indicating that his time in the coracle took him through the mysteries of nature and culminated in his being able to fathom and sense the nature and existence of all things, naturally including the animal kingdom. This can be seen mirrored in yet another poem where Taliesin speaks of having been in the form of animals and fish:

> *I was a blue salmon,*
> *I was a dog, I was a stag,*
> *I was a roebuck on the mountain.*[110]

He may appear in human form, but his spirit is able to conceive any form or shape, and this causes his physical being to be an expression of mystery. It cannot be known if he is meat or fish, for he is all these things at all times—he is the Prophetic Spirit, not an actual individual. He speaks of the connectedness of the spirit that applies to all life; we just don't hear the message as clearly as we should. Life gets in the way.

The Book of Taliesin provides further clues to the nature of the Prophetic Spirit. This book should be essential reading for any student of the Celtic mysteries, and its spirit is captured dramatically in the following words by one of Wales's greatest Celtic scholars:

> Delphi is deserted and Taliesin is jettisoned, and no lecture room open that names the name of Taliesin. The learned who write in encyclopaedias are like the bards at the court of Deganwy—who in the presence of Taliesin became mute mutterers of nonsense.[111]

These words were written by the remarkable and groundbreaking Celtic scholar J. Gwenogvryn Evans, who expressed his disbelief that the works of our Celtic ancestors were not being utilised within our society. He took it upon himself to change this and faithfully copied, translated, and interpreted

---

110   "Angar Kyfundawt" in the Book of Taliesin (my translation).
111   Adapted from J. Gwenogvryn Evans's introduction to his *Facsimile and Text of the Book of Taliesin*.

dozens of ancient Welsh manuscripts. Among them was the legendary Book of Taliesin. Evans belies a mystery here, perhaps one that he himself did not fully understand, for the mysteries of Taliesin have captured the heart of a nation for centuries. It was the Narrative Spirit and the efforts of the bards and scriptoriums that ensured the survival of the material, but without the Prophetic Spirit that is embodied as Taliesin, the present would be devoid of the magic that the Celtic culture has retained. The spirit of Taliesin is more than its connection to mystery and the subtle realms; it is more than the initiatory journey into the cauldron of transformation. This spirit is alive as the beating heart of a nation and a culture, a culture that has spread its wings and flown to distant shores and lands to inspire a new people. The current identity of Wales is proudly held in the emblem of the Welsh dragon, a mythical creature that symbolises power, strength, and the determination of a people, and yet within it there swims something else. It is the collective spirit of a nation and its culture; it is the spirit of Taliesin. One does not need to be a practitioner of the Celtic mysteries to appreciate and connect with this energy, for it exists as a sympathetic link that people have with their identity as Welsh Celts.

If we look to other countries, we may encounter emblems that capture the spirit of a people; for example, the bald eagle of the Americans. It sings of something ethereal and powerful; it is the collective spirit of the people. Taliesin embodies these qualities, for throughout the passage of time and the many obstacles that it has cast in the roads of Celtic culture, the spirit of Taliesin is alive and well. It is celebrated annually in the National Eisteddfod of Wales; periodicals that express the beauty and value of poetry and the arts bear the title of its name. Within the landscape of Wales and the tongue of the people, one can sense the whispers of the Prophetic Spirit. Something mysterious and unique happened to this figure. As the people became transformed by the mystery Taliesin represents, his wings opened and he soared to become the beating heart of a new tradition: Celtic Paganism and Druidry. The spirit of Taliesin is now inexorably woven into the very fabric and traditions of modern Paganism, and we, the practitioners of the twenty-first century, ensure its applicability.

When J. Gwenogvryn Evans wrote those words nearly one hundred years ago, I doubt he had any idea that you would be reading about Taliesin—or about him, for that matter. I imagine that his essence smiles from beyond the misty veils in pleasure that lecture rooms do name the name of Taliesin. That these rooms also consist of Pagan teaching groups, circles, and orders may bemuse him further, but they also serve to perpetuate and ensure the continuation of the spirit of Taliesin as something other than a historical poet. The figure of Taliesin has been taken to represent Wales and its literary jewels long before its adoption by modern Paganism, a fact which continues to bemuse many modern-day Welsh speakers. The identity of the Prophetic Spirit as a tool to access mystery in a Pagan sense means little to the majority of the native Welsh, and this may serve to dishearten—but, in fact, the opposite is true. This totem of mystery and culture has a dual aspect that may be appropriated by Pagans and non-Pagans alike; its power refuses to be compartmentalised or restricted to one form of expression; its brow shines too brightly. Taliesin is totemic of the magic of transformation and also of a nation and its pride in securing the past for future generations, and it does this through the act of celebration. As Pagans, we can share the best of both worlds!

J. Gwenogvryn Evans captures the spirit of Taliesin, and he devoted his life to the preservation of its poetry. The Book of Taliesin is perhaps the most magical and pertinent of that collection. Within this book we encounter the epic poem "Kat Godeu," meaning "Battle of the Trees," where we are offered a snapshot into Taliesin's birth:

> *It was not of a mother and a father*
> *That I was created;*
> *My creation was created for me*
> *From nine forms of consistency*
> *From fruit of fruits*
> *From the fruits of the first god*
> *From primroses and from flowers*
> *From the flowers of trees and shrubs.*

From earth, from the soil
Was I made.
From the flowers of nettle
From the water of the ninth wave.[112]

There has been speculation and erroneous conclusions that the above is referring exclusively to the creation of Blodeuedd, the magical woman created from flowers in the Fourth Branch of the Mabinogi. But eminent Celtic academics have concluded that this is indeed in reference to Taliesin's spiritual origin, and that Blodeuedd and everyone else on this planet have been spiritually created in the same manner. It claims that the Prophetic Spirit, although inhabiting the form of a human being, in fact has no active parent, for it is a vital aspect of the universe. This is in stark contrast to the revealed religions, who claim that our spirits are born of an uber-being who controls our destiny and punishment or reward. This is anathema in Celtica, where the spirit is perceived as an inherent aspect of the universe in its totality; it was not born of it and is not subservient to it; it *is* it. The universe serves only as soul, which in turn is the house of the spirit, not its parent. The poem explores the nature of the body's physical creation—that it comes from the natural world and that it is formed, nurtured, and sustained by the forces of nature. This animistic view is beautifully Pagan in spirit and sings of our oneness with the entity that we live upon, Earth.

The poem also raises an interesting question that thus far has not been explored in these pages. Following the impregnation of Cerridwen and the subsequent birthing of the babe, there is a liminal period wherein the baby is set adrift in the care of nature; it is forty years later that the babe is identified as Taliesin. Therefore, the implication is that the intermediate babe is of no identity—he is neither Gwion Bach nor Taliesin; he is someone who exists between. It takes a prolonged period of gestation for the brow to shine and for the Prophetic Spirit to be fully assimilated, so this begs the question, what is the nature of the babe in the between times? He floats on a river; he does not require food or water to sustain him; he lies in darkness

---

112   "Kat Godeu" from the Book of Taliesin (my translation).

within a coracle, seemingly abandoned and suspended in time and space for four decades. The journey downriver from Cerridwen's home in any direction would be three days at most; why would it take him forty years? This liminal, Morda-like quality is present within the tale, as are the attributes of Creirfyw that can be seen expressed in the immense beauty of the babe and in Cerridwen's failure to kill him. It is my perception that the babe is the true innocent, a child of the mystery who swims the waterways of spirit. This portion of the tale acts as an allegory for the true nature of the spirit as an energy that is fully immersed in the flow of Awen. Within this portion of the tale we are provided a glimpse into the mystery of our permanent identity. The babe in the bag is the epitome of the true nature of the spirit, an energy in perpetual motion floating through the connective fabric of the universe, represented by the river, lost in the blissful rapture of being. If we consider for a moment the possibility that the entire cauldron, chase, and birthing sequence takes place in the otherworld, then this sequence is indicative of the transition from the realm of the spirit to the physical dimension. The journey causes the spirit to concentrate into the denseness of matter; it is born into this world so that body and spirit may dance together. It is only during the times when we return to the state of nonbeing that we are truly at one with the universe, and every day we get the opportunity to sense this, to recharge and be reminded of our permanent identities.

> *Do you know what you are when you are sleeping?*
> *Are you a body or soul, or an occult and mysterious thing?*[113]

The above lines, taken from the Book of Taliesin, belie a secret that we partake of each and every day. Recall the last time that you were incredibly tired and simply longed for your bed more than anything else in the world. The chances are your head touched the pillow and the lights of your eyes went out; sleep took you into the laps of the gods. Now recall the sensation upon waking after a luxurious, undisturbed night of restful sleep. What can you recall? It is a difficult question to answer, for it is impossible to assign any

---

113   "Mabgyfreu Taliesin" from the Book of Taliesin (my translation).

actual emotion to the state of sleep. Taliesin specifically asks if you know what you are when you are sleeping, but why does he ask? The answer is perhaps one of the most revealing and profound messages that swim within the Celtic mysteries.

There is perhaps one human sensation that can be assigned to the state of sleep: bliss. One cannot say we are happy whilst asleep, and neither can we say we are contented either; they are too specific for such an ethereal state of being. Bliss, however, seems to capture the feeling of being in the void, of being back in the lap of the universal battery charger. During our nightly sojourn into the realm of nothingness we become "occult and mysterious things," and Taliesin in his wisdom attempts to tell us this, to teach us the nature of the spirit. Marged Haycock translates the second line of the verse as "a pale and mysterious thing,"[114] which is suggestive of something deeply energetic or spiritual. The permanent facet of our being is a constant, and this ever-changing apparent identity, a product of our environments, is a mere fleeting second in the grand scheme of time, yet it is essential and deeply valued. We do not need to climb a far-flung mountain to meet a wise man who will show us the way to find ourselves; we discover who we are every night whilst asleep. We have no need to abandon the world and all pursuits within it for the delusional concept that we may become so spiritually advanced we will no longer need the functions of our bodies—that we may vanish into a spectrum of light and ascend to some higher level of existence. The message of Taliesin teaches us that such a quest is unnecessary and that all we require is to listen, and in that listening we will hear the whispers of our eternal aspects singing from the primordial origination of the universe.

Taliesin is able to express his nature as all things, having been in a multitude of existences before attaining his current form, simply because his spirit and body are in tune, one with the other. When we study the works of our Celtic ancestors, we find subtle clues pertaining to the human condition; it seems that our forefathers understood that a symptom of human density is the deafening of the spiritual ears. But this is only a temporary

---

114   Haycock, *Legendary Poems from the Book of Taliesin*, 243.

quandary, for we are able to experientially connect the lucidity of the spirit with the wakefulness of the body and allow both songs to raise their voices in pure harmony. We do this by listening to the songs of the spirit that our ancestors provided us; locked into the language and symbolism of culture and heritage, they allow us to access the mysteries. We do this to enable the denseness of the body to become receptive to the ethereal quality of the spirit—not for enlightenment per se, but for lucidity. Our eyes open wider to the magic that surrounds us; the secrets that we could not fathom before become clear as the spirit and body combine consciously.

The dense nature of our human bodies and the material components that make up our vital organs are not antagonistic to the spirit, they are simply constructed of different material. But they cannot be separated; to do so would remove the life source from the physical, and it would fall out of the stream of energy and decompose, as our bodies do upon death. Celtic Paganism, being a life-affirming tradition, does not concern itself much with death, but I offer this as food for thought. The simple question that Taliesin asks is indicative of the "little death" that we partake of every day of our lives—that in order to thrive and live we must succumb to a state of nothingness every twenty-four-hour cycle. We are not given the opportunity to opt out of this state; to survive, we must sleep. It is during this time that we return to the state we occupied prior to the condensing of our spirits in the field of our physical forms. The ability to carry the lucidity of this state into wakefulness is dependent on the human mind's ability to acknowledge the spirit and respond. Julius Caeser, in *De Bello Gallico*, recorded that the ancient druids had no fear of death, for they believed in the immortality of the human spirit and of its continuous existence after bodily death has occurred. The Celtic mysteries teach that upon death, the spirit does not leave the body, it is the body that leaves the spirit—it simply falls from the stream of energy that maintained its life force. The spirit does not move or go anywhere; it is in the same position today as it was at the beginning of time. Sleep serves to reminds of us our true state, where consciousness is a more fluid affair than it is in the denseness of our skulls. Celtica empowers people to hear the whispers of the spirit for themselves; they are not reliant

upon gurus or self-confessed masters to bring the spirit and body into har-
monious lucidity. There is no sense of denial or abstention; we need not turn
our backs on the magic of physicality in order to partake of the mysteries,
for they are inescapably woven together. This message is further reiterated
by material that alludes to another spirit in human form that shares parallels
with Taliesin. In the poetry of the *Ystoria Taliesin*, we are introduced to the
following verse:

> *Johannes the prophet called me Merlin,*
> *But now all kings call me Taliesin.*

Within the same manuscript that our tale appears, NLW 5276D, there is
an account of the death of Merlin in the hand of Elis Gruffudd. This immediately precedes the tale of Cerridwen and Taliesin. It is important here not
to confuse this material in relation to the fictionalised Merlin popularised
in the later Arthurian romances, which are not directly related to the Celtic
chronicles. They exist as works of fiction inspired by the Celtic material. In
his "The Death of Merlin," Elis records that

> Some hold the thought that Merlin, who was a spirit in human form,
> was in that shape from the time of Vortigern until the beginning of
> King Arthur's time when he vanished. After that this spirit appeared
> again in the time of Maelgwn Gwynedd at which time he is known
> as Taliesin...

It seems that the Prophetic Spirit was the same spirit within Merlin and
Taliesin, and that both were present in human form during various times.[115]
It can be deduced that the human individuals they represent were, in fact,
initiates of the mysteries and in possession of the Prophetic Spirit, which
enabled them to be of immense poetic skill and also adepts of the magical
arts. Both Merlin and Taliesin identify themselves as poets and magicians; it
seems that both skills are derived from the same place and cause the magi-
cian/poet to make manifest what was previously unmanifest. However, there
is an implication here that may cause concern, which requires examination.

---

115   Ford, *The Death of Merlin in the Chronicle of Elis Gruffudd*, 379.

We noted that Cerridwen is "learned" in the magical arts, and yet Taliesin and Merlin, who are both adept practitioners of magic, seemingly did not derive their skills by means of learning alone. They are in possession of an inherited skill that comes to them by proxy of their connection to the Prophetic Spirit. This does not imply that one form of magical attainment and knowledge is superior to the other; I believe the implication is that both are a requirement for the effective practise of the magical arts. Within human form we must learn the arts of magic and the mysteries by proxy of those who inspire and teach us; they, in turn, disseminate that teaching effectively because of their connection to the Prophetic Spirit. It sings of the essential connection of the body and spirit. The process of learning itself is devoid of power or ability if is not in contact with the "force" that gives it animation and motion. A spell or act of conjuration would simply be a recitation of words without reaction; for the magic to be effective, we must access what gives it essence and power: the Prophetic Spirit. To call upon it without connection would be akin to shouting at someone across a dance floor—your voice may rise and move through space and time but not reach its destination, as there is too much dense material in the way. Even if the words arrive by some means at their target, they will be illegible and nonsensical; their impact and intention would be ineffective. Our magic is effective when the voice transcends the denseness of matter and connects directly with what it aims to affect, change, or transform.

The message is clear: Cerridwen epitomises aspects of the physical art of learning, of study, of knowing our Craft. Taliesin acts as the bridge that connects us to the universal flow of Awen by means of the Prophetic Spirit. For us to move lucidly through life we must be in possession of both facets, the structure of learning and the ethereal quality of the Prophetic Spirit. Both are essential aspects of the adept.

The ability to swim between the two is perfectly articulated in the discourse of *The Life of Merlin: Vita Merlini*:

I was taken out of myself and I was as spirit, and I knew the acts of peoples past and could predict the future of things. Since then I know the secrets of things and the flights of birds and the wandering motions of the stars and the gliding of fish.[116]

The above serves to demonstrate the power and ability of the Prophetic Spirit. It is all-knowing, it has the ability to predict the future of things, and is simultaneously aware of the existence of all things by means of the omnipresent spirit. By proxy of this connection, Taliesin is able to fully assert his powers over time, space, objects, and the shape of things. He does this by means of the combined magical transformation that occurs throughout the tale; the sequence is teaching us how to access the mysteries and provides us with every single tool that is required. In other words, reading the book is not enough; we must also get out there and do it by putting the information into action and being transformed as a consequence. It is the resulting lucidity of mind, body, and spirit that is expressed by means of the Prophetic Spirit in our earthly lives.

Taliesin continuously sings the praise of the human body and its function and senses; it is a vital aspect of the combined elements of mind, body, and spirit. The body is never denied or denounced as it is in some Eastern philosophies. In the Book of Taliesin we are offered the following verse, which sings the praise of the bodily senses:

I give praise to my sustainer,
Who added through my head
A spirit into my design.
Happily it is made for me,
My seven consistencies
Of fire and earth
And water and air
And mist and flowers
And sweet southerly winds.

---

116   Geoffrey of Monmouth, *The Life of Merlin: Vita Merlini*, 33.

My senses were designed
One with which I exhale,
And two with which I breathe,
And three by which I have voice,
And four with which I taste,
And five with which I see,
And six with which I hear,
And seven by which I smell.[117]

The above demonstrates the vitality and value placed on the senses, where they are experienced as essential elements that connect us to the experience of living. Taliesin expresses himself as an extension of nature, where components of it are imbued into the body and spirit; they are inseparable until the point at which we die. This deeply animistic viewpoint values the earth and earthly life, for it is an essential expression of the universe's creative force. The Prophetic Spirit is therefore the epitome of the mind, body, and spirit in unison; its outward expression is that of creativity and magic. The importance of poetry and the arts in expressing Awen is a recurring theme in the Celtic material, for realistically we are only able to articulate this connection by means of our creativity. We have seen how the Prophetic Spirit is also able to prophesy the future and divine the nature of things, a task which Taliesin performs in several prophetic poems contained within the Book of Taliesin. We find teachings of deep, old magic in this sequence of verses, for the body is a pathway to the spirit; before we can ascend into the subtle realms, we must live, we must complete the descent into matter. The keys to the spiritual are tied into the land and the bodies of the physical world; every tree and plant, plankton and mountain, child and woman sings of the origin and meaning of the universe. Our brows are literally alight with the magic of it; we need only shift our awareness in order to perceive it. Taliesin and the spirit he represents is one method of attaining this lucid state of being.

◆ ◆ ◆

117   "Kanu Y Byt Mawr" from the Book of Taliesin (my translation).

Taliesin speaks of talents and gifts that seem to directly emulate the abilities of Cerridwen as a witch. He also claims to be a magician and says, *"Wyf dryw, wyf syw* (I am a wizard, I am a sage).["118]

Marged Haycock translates the term *dryw* to mean "wizard," and this effectively captures the spirit of the word, which may also be translated as "magician." However, it also means "wren" and is cognate with the Old Irish *drui*, which can be taken to mean "druid." Therefore, one could argue that the term *dryw* may have been the actual indigenous British word for "druid." The term *syw*, meaning "sage," is also indicative of the wisdom required by the magician in the pursuits of his arts. He is learned, wise, and clearly in possession of the Prophetic Spirit. Through the words of Taliesin it is apparent that magic, poetry, and wisdom are expressive components of the mysteries; they provide us with a notion as to the nature of the initiate and the skills that he or she possesses. These facts surmise that the Celtic mystery traditions are indeed magical traditions, not simply facets of celebration and philosophy. Magical transformation and the practise of the subtle arts are byproducts of immersion in the Celtic mysteries.

The poems of Taliesin have been noted and explored throughout the course of this book. Indeed, the actual qualities of Taliesin can be seen swimming within every other archetype and component of the tale; everything is leading up to this point of being. Becoming Taliesin is the true nature and secret of the mystery. Taliesin may be identified as a demigod or other creature of supernatural origin, but this is not the point of the tale. Everything we have encountered thus far serves to guide us to become Taliesin.

Gwion Bach is imbued with Awen, and the creature that he becomes in not of a mother or a father, for the creature that is Taliesin is, in fact, a spirit; little Gwion is still in there somewhere. The babe that is found in the weir is indicative of our coming into the lucidity of the spirit, where we experience the wonders of the universe in this life without the need to transcend it.

In essence, Taliesin acts as the catalyst who creates a lucid experience of the spirit and the spiritual realms; too often these dimensions are mere con-

---

118   Haycock, *Legendary Poems from the Book of Taliesin*, 79 and 83.

cepts. The figure of Taliesin breaks down the barriers that may prevent us from encountering the spiritual, and it does this by providing keys to unlock the doors of transformation. What good are concepts if all they are are rationalisations of ethereal ideas? Concepts are all very well, but for us to experientially connect with them, we must identify them as real, not simply fantastical ideas that may be perceived as delusional by the world at large. The commitment involved in attaining the radiant brow immerses us in a spiritual and cultural continuum that has sung the songs of these lands for endless generations. That alone is worthy of devotion to the Celtic mysteries.

So how do we connect to this spirit? How do we become Taliesin? You will note that there is no exercise of connection at the conclusion of this section, and for good reason. The tale is the exercise. Becoming Taliesin is not something that should be conceptualised as mere ideas from a book, which is why this section is naturally concluding. The experience of assuming the radiant brow is too magical to be denigrated as mere conceptualised ideas. But becoming radiant with Awen is not an impossibility; it is as real as the land upon which you walk. It provides a depth of spirit that may be missing from your practise and spirituality, and its attainment is possible. It is by process of devotion and commitment that we journey towards the salmon weir. Our encounter with the cauldron and the witch goddess catapults us forwards, towards the lucidity of mind, body, and spirit in unison. But the journey is far from easy. It requires effort and gumption, but the rewards are incredibly profound and illuminating. The initiate of the Celtic mysteries becomes, in essence, the embodiment of what Taliesin represents. He or she becomes possessed with the Prophetic Spirit and is the expression of profound knowledge and wisdom; this state is the imitation of the divine energy of the universe. Flowing as the ever-coursing river of Awen, the transformed initiate literally becomes the conscious universe singing in the rapture of being. To quote Taliesin, "There is nothing in which I have not been."

Conclusion
A TEMPLATE FOR TRANSFORMATION

So what do we have here? There is no doubt that the tale we have explored presents a powerful mystery, one that is an allegorical tale of initiation and transformation. The sequences it describes are vital processes by which we gain the insight that is required to experientially understand the mysteries, whereby they are incorporated by the mind, body, and spirit into lucidity.

You have read the tale and discovered its origin and history; you have met the characters, archetypes, and spirits contained therein and have, by proxy, initiated a relationship with them. As you read each account, you connected to powerful figures totemic of the magic of Celtica. These figures are very much alive and, as you have discovered, aspects of yourself swim within them. To have accessed this information is one thing; what to do with the information is a whole other matter. This book is not intended as a source of information alone; after all, the mysteries must be utilised and experienced in order for them to be assimilated. We must be in possession of a template that allows us to practically access the mysteries in a manner that instigates the ingestion of the drops, the subsequent chase, and the process of transformation.

The key elements of the tale must be incorporated into your life in order for it to cross the barrier that separates fantasy from reality. Without the practical application of the mysteries, the material remains a relic of linguistics and the written word, but it is infinitely more than this. The magic within the Celtic material is applicable, but no amount of studying will bring about that realisation unless the mind is engaged in a visionary sense. We must balance our relationship with it so that we swing harmoniously between the skills of the intellect and the skills of magic. The various exercises at each section's conclusion have already served to move you closer to the realisation of the journey into the cauldron. How you progress from here can take on various forms.

For a template to become experiential, you need a format that is applicable to you, which must include and consider your own unique personality and set of circumstances. One must also consider the reasons for wanting to seek the cauldron in the first place. So, logically, your template must commence by asking yourself a set of questions that pertains to your intentions. It may be that you are naturally drawn to the Celtic mysteries and its gods and you seek to deepen your connection, explore these concepts, and note them in your journal. Your template will differ in accordance to the form of study you have partaken; it be that your descent into mystery is a solitary task, but you may well be studying as part of a group. Either way, your template must be applicable and appropriate.

The mysteries can be entirely experienced as a mental exercise, or you can incorporate aspects of physical ritual into your template. Your entry into the cauldron may well be in the form of a deep meditation spanning a period of weeks or a pathworking course that you share with a group. It may take the form of contemplation and physical interaction—do what feels right, find the templates that suit you and your lifestyle, and employ the most effective manner by which you access your subtle senses. There is no right or wrong way of accessing the subtle realms; what is imperative are your actions and intentions. Another vital aspect of transformation must also be considered: that of service. Whatever your intentions, they must be balanced by a sense of service. This material should not be kept and neither is it a secret; we serve the mysteries and our gods through serving them and our communities. Therefore, contemplate on your contribution to the material—what do you give it in return? How does your service perpetuate the myths of the Celts and disseminate that wisdom? This tale forms a template for your personal transformation, but you are also able to impart that magic onto the world at large. Go forth and inspire.

The following section contains rites that incorporate contemplation and interaction with the physical plane in a ritualised format.

PART 4

Stirring the Cauldron
RITUAL AND PRACTISE

◆ ◆ ◆

Unrestrained is my tongue, a repository of
inspiration—my inspiration of poetry,
oblated by offerings of milk and dew and acorns.

Adapted from "Golychaf i Gulwyd" in the Book of Taliesin

◆ ◆ ◆

It is appropriate here to share with you some rituals and practises that have been tried and tested. The following offerings range in complexity and construction, and they have been utilised by many people over the years. However, ritual is a complex subject, with some individuals preferring to construct their own without influence whilst others seek inspiration from the pages of a book. I hope that the following may be useful to you, even if only as ideas or accompaniments to your own ceremonies.

Cerridwen's Cauldron

A YEAR-LONG RITUAL MEDITATION

Two words adequately sum up this ritual: "brace yourself"! This is pretty hard going, and there is a tremendous amount of information ahead. But bear in mind that the information here is intended for a year-long ritual, which you will easily incorporate into your ordinary practise and devotions. Please do not be daunted by the sheer volume of information and practise; in bite-size pieces they are easily digestible.

We live in a "want it, have it now!" society—everything is readily available and at our disposal, and to a degree even spirituality has become a victim of this attitude. The legend at the heart of this book is not immune to this condition. The purpose of the following year-long rite is to immerse one-self totally in an experience that is connected to the tale and that involves a journey of concentration, devotion, and commitment, mirroring what Cerridwen herself undertook for the love of her son.

Rituals enable us to stop, step out of the humdrum noise and distractions of the modern world, and move into that most exalted of states, liminality. With this in mind, the following rite provides liminal space each and every month for a year and a day, culminating in a powerful ritual of honour and reverence to the archetypes of this tale and its transformational qualities. However, like any true traveller, one should not be intent only on arriving, for it is the journey that matters; it is the treading of the wheel that connects one to the sublime.

This ritual has been tried and tested over several years, and it comes with a hearty dash of commendation from folks who have performed it and been totally immersed in the experience for an entire year of their lives. Not only does it cause the mind to focus on certain tasks that are required each month, but it also trains the mind to the act of devotion and commitment, as one must think of what is happening, what is going on, why this is being done, who the archetypes/creatures/spirits are and what they stand for, etc. Questions of relevance and applicability will filter into the mind during this ritual; a relationship will develop with the allegories and ultimately with the archetypes. This is a pretty mammoth ritual; it isn't something you should take lightly. Prepare well, knowing that it won't interfere with your life but should instead fit seamlessly into your everyday activities. Rituals should never be in the way; if they become a burden or a worry, then the intention is not well-founded and a rethink is likely in need. So grab your journal, roll your sleeves up, and let's get to work!

Intent

The intention of the rite is to connect via the powers of nature and meditation to the archetypes and themes of the tale, and to be immersed in a practical application of the allegories contained therein. The rite enables you to question, ponder, and conclude the importance of transformation, initiation, and the relevance and usage of inspiration in a manner that actually affects the world and your place in it. By means of foraging, the rite requires us to spend time in nature, wandering the leafy lanes or bountiful woodlands of our locale; certain ingredients must be harvested, and these too require us to develop a relationship with them, to understand their qualities, and to sense the natural world as kin, not as something to be exploited or taken for granted.

The list of ingredients has not been randomly selected; they have been chosen for their qualities in relation to the tale itself. If you do not have access to some of them or they are not indigenous to your part of the world, fear not; this rite is not written in blood nor carved onto stone. If something cannot be located or just doesn't sit right with you, change it. But do not change it on a whim, for much energy and devotion has gone into the making of this rite. Do so with integrity; if you cannot find wild garlic bulb, then consider what else shares the qualities of underworld, healing, purification, and detoxification...the answer should come out of research and connection; always remember that the "C" word is vital! Connection, connection, connection!

This ritual will require you to collect a range of ingredients; each month the ingredients will be brewed in a cauldron and heated over low heat. This liquid will be retained and added to each month until the conclusion of the rite. Instructions for this aspect of the ritual can be found immediately preceding the full list of ingredients.

Equipment

I suggest that you find a suitable box or shelf or cupboard to store these items in; after all, you are going to be using them for a year and a day, so make it special, make it something unique, and be as elaborate or as simple as you want. You will need the following:

- harvesting or foraging basket
- cast-iron cauldron or saucepan (minimum of 1.5-litre capacity)
- journal
- handbook of local plants and trees
- selection of bottles, jars, and pots
- wooden spoon
- pipette

Ingredients

I have chosen to begin the list of ingredients during November because of its liminal position betwixt Samhain and the winter solstice. I am not suggesting you must wait until November to begin the rite; by all means, begin it at any point during the wheel of the year. I offer November simply because I had to start somewhere!

The amount of each ingredient will be entirely dependent on the size of your vessel; it would be pointless for me to instruct you to add 150 acorns when your cauldron barely holds half a pint of liquid. On the other hand, your vessel may hold five gallons or all the variables between. Do not assume that you need vast quantities; less is more. You must calculate the amount of ingredients needed in direct relation to the volume of liquid your cauldron will hold.

You will also note that some ingredients are a little, well, let's just say unsavoury. However, their attributes and qualities are of immense value and power. If you cannot justify placing these substances directly into the brew, consider using their essence instead. Place the ingredient on a piece of glass above a small bowl of water. Allow natural sunlight or moonlight to shine upon the item for at least three hours, thus sympathetically transferring its essence to the water below. Add this water to the brew.

The ingredients are essential to the brewing of Awen. They must be collected consciously and with awareness of the properties and qualities of the tree, plant, or organism from which they stem. I suggest that prior to collection you study the item required and learn a little about its life. Consider the following points as part of the immersion process:

- What are the ingredient's movements and moods through the turning year?
- How does it live, and where does it thrive?
- How does it contribute to its surroundings?
- How does it ensure its continuation and survival?

- Does it bear fruit? If so, who else may benefit from its bounty? What can you make or prepare with it?
- What does the ingredient and its host smell like?
- Does it have a taste?
- Is it baneful or poisonous?
- What ground does it grow upon? Who are its neighbours and why?
- Does it have divinatory qualities?

The above are just a fraction of the questions one could ask. Ask them all and more; note them in your journal, and engross yourself in a deep connection with the ingredients required each month. Let them become your friends, allies, and cousins in nature.

INGREDIENTS AT A GLANCE

November: Spring, lake, or river water; pine resin; moon water

December: Holly berries, mistletoe, frost water

January: Yew leaves, pine needles, snow water

February: Snowdrop flowers, a liminal object

March: Wild garlic, primrose flowers

April: Bluebell, dandelion

May: Hawthorn blossoms, elder flowers

June: Clover, valerian

July: Oak leaves, gorse flowers

August: Wheat, blood

September: Acorns, rowan berries

October: Wormwood; semen, menstrual blood, or breast milk

And so we begin…

November

Contemplation and Study

Meditate on the lands from which the myths arose. Contemplate the people who created them. What is your connection to the lands of the Celts? What do you know of the indigenous language of the British Celts? Research it—the Internet is a vast resource of linguistic information, and there are simple introductory books on the Welsh language.

Practical

Natural Spring, Lake, or River Water: This is the base ingredient, and you will need significantly more than you anticipate; store any excess in a glass jar in a cool, dark place. Your initial ingredients will be cast into this water. Try your best to collect it from a source as close to your home as possible. Perhaps there is a spring, well, or sacred river close by that you often visit or a place that is a focus of your devotional practises or rituals. Leave an offering for the spirits of that place once you have collected your water.

Pine Resin (*Pinus* spp.): Any coniferous forest will have plentiful amounts of pine resin that you can discreetly and honourably harvest, or perhaps you have a pine tree or trees growing on your land. If the tree has been damaged by the elements or been struck by something, it will attempt to heal itself by secreting a thick, sticky substance known as resin. Initially the resin is white and creamy or almost translucent, but it eventually turns black and crystalline in nature. It is this final stage that you should collect to prevent further damage to the tree.

Pine imbues the ritual with cleansing, healing properties; the resin is useful in banishing unwanted influences or negativity. It can also promote financial stability and assist in keeping illness at bay. Its smooth, fresh fragrance clears the nose, breaks down congestion, and instils a sense of general well-being. In the Celtic Ogham system, the pine is known as *ailm* (pronounced *aye-UM*).

Moon Water: Take some water from a source that is special to you or has some other significance—it may be a holy well, a river sacred to a specific deity, or a lake that has myth or legend attached to it. Perhaps you live by the sea and are drawn to the qualities of briny water. Whatever source you choose, collect the water in a glass vessel and place it on a windowsill or ledge during the gibbous phase of the moon (i.e., the three or so nights prior to the full moon). Here we collect the properties of the divine feminine and the wisdom that entails; we connect to the power of the moon, to beauty and serenity. Honour her movements and her pulling of the earth's oceans and the water in our own bodies. She waxes and wanes and shares the cycle of menstruation. She is the essence of beauty and feminine wisdom that the brew requires.

December

Contemplation and Study

Reread part 3's section on Divine Intoxication, dedicated to Awen. If you can, find further references to it and immerse yourself in its study. *The Barddas of Iolo Morganwg* is recommended as a historical and influential study of Awen as a symbol and philosophy. Study the origin of Awen and what it means in your life. How do you creatively express it?

Practical

Holly Berries (*Ilex* spp.): In Welsh Celtic lore this tree is known as *celynnen* (*kel-un-en*); in the Ogham system of divination it is *tinne* (*TEEN*). The holly is the blood of winter, the promise of life amidst the darkness and cold of the dead time of year. Holly thrives in shadow; it is bold and powerful, and its thick leaves ensure its survival and ability to absorb sunlight even when very little of it filters through the canopy. Our Celtic ancestors believed nature spirits resided in the evergreens and as a gesture of goodwill would bring boughs of them into the home during the festive season, adorning the mantle with green and reds, which continue to be the traditional colours of Yuletide.

There is a steadfast quality to holly, and it is a powerful aid in seeking balance; it is also traditionally associated with anti-lightning protection and was sacred to the Celtic god Taranis. Crushed holly berries bring to our potion the qualities of balance, good fortune, resilience, tenacity, and defence.

Mistletoe (*Viscum album*): Use the entire plant: leaves, stalk, and berries. This is the all-heal, traditionally sacred to the ancient druids of Britain and Gaul. Due to its position between heaven and earth and the fact that it never touched the ground, it was believed to prevent epilepsy. Mistletoe is perhaps one of the most mystical plants revered by our ancestors. The perfectly formed berries that hang between paired leaves are filled with a sticky semen-like substance. For countless centuries fertility rites have been conducted beneath its green and white stare, and these continue in the Yuletide tradition of kissing beneath the mistletoe. The plant brings the gifts of symbiosis and magic to the potion; it is a powerful protector and the epitome of fertility and love. Reverence and humility are imbued into the liquid by this most magical of plants.

Frost Water: December is the month when we frequently awake to be greeted by the serenity and stillness of frost. This enchanting quality of nature descends from clear skies, transforming the landscape upon which it settles. The whole world seems hushed into silence when it opens its eyes to frost-covered countryside. Observe the patterns on leaves and bark; you will note the most remarkable shapes, from brittle spikes to swirls and whorls of coldness. Frost exists between ice and snow; it is neither yet similar to each, its effect is different, its magic lies in its subtlety to amaze and bewitch. Awake early, and venture into the world with a small, clean vessel. Perhaps you have a sacred collecting vessel at hand; if not, use anything from a glass to an old yogurt pot. Gently skim the vessel over frost-covered grass until a sufficient amount has filled it. Remain outdoors and enjoy the qualities of frost. Remove your shoes and socks: feel the shocking cold of it, sense its caress upon your body as well as the land.

Allow the frost to melt into water, then add it to the cauldron or store it in a dark glass vessel until ready to use.

January

Contemplation and Study

Reread the section devoted to the cauldron. Research and study the importance of cauldrons in Celtic culture and their associations with the divine feminine. What does the cauldron mean in your current Pagan practise?

Practical

Yew Leaves (*Taxus baccata*): The majestic yew, its beauty tinged by the perilous nature of its poisonous qualities, adorns our landscape with a timeless presence. Its roots reach deep into the underworld; it sings of ancestors, of heritage, and of connection to place, time, blood, and breath. It teaches us that in the midst of life there is death, and that death is essential to the continuation of life. Its berries entice with their blood-red, attractive lustre, yet within its seeds hides the gift of death, for it takes only a few to ensure the rapid deterioration and ultimate expiration of the hapless consumer. Cemeteries and churchyards lay claim to some of the most ancient yews in the British Isles, some believed to be over 2,000 years old, whilst others claim that the yew is a true immortal, able to dampen its life force indefinitely and then reawaken at will.

The mighty yew brings immensely powerful and transformative qualities to our brew; it harbours the true message of death and rebirth, and it teaches us the nature of immortality. It brings the qualities of fear, authority, and experience to our potion. In the Celtic Ogham system this is the last tree and is called *ioho* (*eye-OH-HO*). WARNING: The leaves of the yew are toxic. One single yew leaf is enough to imbue its qualities to the brew and will pose no threat to the well-being of an average adult. As an alternative, create an essence by allowing sunlight or moonlight to radiate a few leaves placed on a plane of glass above a small bowl of water. Add this water to the brew.

Pine Needles (*Pinus* spp.): The qualities and attributes of pine needles, although of the same tree as the resin we used during November, have a slightly different gift. Its power and ability to heal is more apparent in that it can be digested by the human body with ease. A tea made from pine needles not only tickles the senses through its exquisite aroma but also calms the system and encourage a general sense of well-being. The needles are symbolic of good health and sovereignty and bring to our potion the quality of movement from weakness to strength.

Snow Water: Yet again we take something directly from the elements themselves, this time from the divinely complex and magical substance that is snow. Its ability to utterly transform the landscape and thus our perception and sense of place is immense; it is beautiful yet destructive, and it epitomises the merciless power of nature. Snow has the uncanny ability to dampen sound; the world sounds different when blanketed in snow. This particular ingredient of our potion reminds us of the sometimes hostile conditions that the plant world endures whilst we retreat to the fireside. To find snow you may need to journey elsewhere, to venture into high mountains. Yet again, sense it in its entirety—step out of your comfort zone, feel its power, and greet it naked if you can. Collect sufficient snow for your brew to imbue it with the qualities of transformation, illusion, subtlety, and severity.

February

Contemplation and Study
Reread the section devoted to Morfran Afagddu. What is the nature of your shadow? What do you understand of human psychology and mental health? What is the nature of mind in relation to the brain; are they inexorably interconnected? Study the functions of the brain and the mind. Read the second branch of the Mabinogi and meet the other shadow, Efnysien.

Practical
Snowdrop Flowers (*Galanthus nivalis*): The humble snowdrop serves to amaze and enchant with its simple beauty and yet is awe inspiring in its hardiness and strength. This tiny flower, indigenous to lands that have mild to cold winters, heralds the beginning of spring. Entire woodlands may be blanketed in these little flowers, whose heads bow almost in reverence to the powers of winter from which they sprang. Inadvertently trample a snowdrop, and it will spring back—they are resilient, powerful little creatures who

serve to demonstrate that good things come in small packages. They are the true heralds of spring; they are the great song that is sung prior to the full blooming radiance of summer; they serve as the alarm clock for nature, for once the snowdrop arrives we can be assured that the whole of nature is yawning awake from its winter bed.

The snowdrop imbues our rite with humility, innocence, hope, and new beginnings. It also epitomises resilience and the ability to survive hardship and severity with humble beauty and grace.

A Liminal Object: February's intercalary day resets the limitations of our calendar every four years, and with her short days and cold, dark nights she is the epitome of magic and liminality. For your second object of the month, find a natural object that grows in a liminal place. This item can be anything that catches your attention. It may grow between the bank and its river; it may occupy wasteland or common land or another liminal location. Seaweed trapped between the lines of the tide may add significant liminal qualities to the brew. The item may be something that you pluck during a liminal time or something that catches your attention within the circle of ritual, perhaps a flower or blade of grass that sings to you. Use your imagination, and cast the item into the cauldron's belly.

March

Contemplation and Study
Reread the section devoted to Creirfyw. By means of study, introduce yourself to the various goddesses of Celtic mythology. What are their attributions? What are their tales? What are *your* most beautiful qualities, and how are they imparted to the world?

Practical
Wild Garlic Bulb, Leaves, and Flowers (*Allium ursinum*): A carpet of wide green leaves adorns woodlands and hedges as the wild garlic, or hedge garlic, erupts from the dark soil. The breath of spring summons this delectable creature from the realm of darkness; soon its fragrant white flowers will burst forth to adorn the woodland air with a heady, pungent aroma. The

dark March leaves with their deep green colouration bring warmth and hope to the undergrowth. They herald the coming of the spring and the wakening powers of the sun as he strengthens on his journey ever higher towards his zenith. Deep beneath the soil the small bulbs, infused with volatile healing oils, sing in praise of the coming warmth. Traditionally used as a protective charm, garlic has an established folkloric association and has long been used as a device to defend, protect, and heal.

The garlic bulb and leaves—and perhaps the flowers, if open—bring to the rite the gifts of protection and deep healing. The volatile oils of the plant provide a powerful remedy that soothes the spirit of damage and heals aspects of the self that have become compromised. It brings to the brew qualities of the underworld and the realms of the ancestors and the Fey.

Primrose Flowers (*Primula vulgaris*): Perhaps these are the true sentinels of springtime. Their flowers erupt in a display of sheer abundance and determination; many have been flowering since the snow initially retreated. Others are yawning into life, bursting forth from the sanctuary of their roots to raise their glorious heads in praise of the sun. The common primrose (*Vulgaris*), with its short stems and dense foliage, expresses sheer feminine beauty and vitality, whilst its long-legged counterpart the cowslip (*Primula veris*) stands tall and proud, demanding attention and adoration.

Their properties are as varied as they are abundant, but primarily they bring to the rite the gifts of femininity and love. They also bring a subtle sedateness to the brew and the ability to invoke restful sleep and relaxation. Medicinally they are powerful antioxidants and provide effective pain relief.

April

Contemplation and Study

Reread the section dedicated to Tegid Foel. Contemplate your physical location and its qualities; find places you have never visited before in your own locale. How psychically healthy and defended is your home? What rites do you partake of to protect your property and the well-being of your family?

Practical

Bluebell (*Hyacinthoides non-scripta*): These incredible, stunningly beautiful plants are indigenous creatures of deciduous woodlands. They may abound in millions, their delicate blue, bejewelled heads bowing in reverence to the sun. Woodlands can appear to be filled with a blue-tinged smoke when bluebells are viewed from a distance. Their heady hyacinth-like scent demands attention. In the islands of Britain they are the symbol of summer's arrival. They abound wherever woodlands stand, and to lie amidst them, breathing in their heady aroma, is to lie in the lap of the spring goddess in all her vibrant glory.

In the United Kingdom, the Wildlife and Countryside Act of 1981 deemed the bluebell a protected species, and their removal or harvesting is strictly prohibited by law and punishable in a British court of law. Bear this in mind. It may not have been something that Cerridwen would have worried about, but in the twenty-first century we must be mindful of the law, which is there to protect this wonderful species. British folklore continues to perpetuate the idea that it is bad luck to bring bluebells into the home, which thankfully prevents idle picking of the plant. A meditative walk in a bluebell wood will connect you to this magical plant, which brings to our brew the qualities of adoration, truth, and good fortune. Find a plant that has been naturally damaged by wind or animal, or one that is nearing the end of its cycle of display. From a damaged stem pick three bells of flowers; do so gently, and sing your praise to its spirit and speak of your intention. Do not pick flowers from a healthy plant.

Dandelion (*Taraxacum officinale*): The dazzling yellow flowering head of the dandelion reflects the radiant light of the sun, and regardless of them being the blight of many a gardener, they are undeniably beautiful. A bed of deep green leaves forms an oval mattress from which springs a tall, slender stem, upon which the flowers burst into song. The "Pee the Bed," as it is often called, has a bitter aroma and taste but can make a glorious tea and its leaves an adornment to any salad. Its folklore is widespread and is in direct relation to its diuretic properties. It was commonly believed that a child who would pick a dandelion would wet the bed that very evening. The vibrant flowers eventually give way to a circular head of fluffy seeds; typically the blowing of the seed heads predicts the future in relation to love, longevity, or simply to tell the time of day.

Their diuretic and laxative properties make them excellent candidates for healing; crushed, they provide anti-inflammatory qualities and also act as a digestive aid. It is said the milky substance within the stem will cure warts. Dandelion brings to our brew the gift of divination, wishes, and banishing. Use all parts of the plant.

May

Contemplation and Study

Reread the section on Morda. Dedicate the month to studying the magic of liminality and its usage in the magical arts. Record your senses during liminal times or when visiting liminal places.

Practical

Hawthorn Blossoms (*Crataegus* spp.): "Ne'er not a clout till May be out," this typical English proverb advises not to remove any winter clothing until the arrival of the May flowers. In the Pagan traditions the May flowers herald the arrival of Beltane and the true beginning of summer. In the Ogham system it heads the second tribe, or *aicme,* of trees and is called *huath (WHO-ath).* Branches of May flowers would adorn the wreath atop the May pole, a fertility ritual in its own right. The staggering white flowers boldly stand against the green leaves of the hawthorn bush, but use caution: the flowers draw one in, but be mindful of her thorns that may pierce and infect their victims. It is still considered bad luck to bring May flowers into the home, and there has been some speculation that this is due to their direct association with the pre-Christian traditions and the crowning of the May Queen. Other suggestions refer to the chemical trimethylamine, present in the flowers and also in rotting animal tissue, being indicative of the pungent aroma of a decaying corpse as it lay awaiting burial. To bring the flowers into the home was to imbue it with the smell of death.

Collect the flowers of May and cast them into the cauldron to infuse it with powers of fertility and magic. Their medicinal properties include powerful cardiac diuretics that can sympathetically be utilised to alleviate heartbreak, grief, and melancholy.

Elder Flowers (*Sambucus nigra*): Perhaps the most enigmatic tree of British and American plant lore, essentially identified as divinely feminine, elder's folkloric associations are as numerous as the flowers she bears on a single stem. Elder's folkloric attributions are indicative of locality-specific associations, and each region may have completely contrasting lore and traditions in relation to her. Often identified with witches, it was considered acceptable to harvest her flowers and berries but never to cut or burn the wood and certainly not to bring the wood indoors for fear of being cursed by the witches. The Wiccan Rede states that "elder be the lady's tree, burn it not or cursed ye'll be," further implying its sacred nature and traditional associations. Traditions in the south of Wales prevented the building of anything next to or near an elder tree, whilst in other parts of the country elder was actively planted near outdoor toilets due to the insect-repellent properties of the flowers.

The elder's flowers are highly fragrant, giving way in the autumn to a dazzling array of deep-purple berries. Both flower and berry are edible, yet paradoxically they are surrounded by toxic leaves that contain cyanogenic glycosides. To our potion they bring the gifts of the Goddess and the wisdom of Witchcraft, as well as prosperity, exorcism, and protection. The alluring powers of adoration and enchantment seep from the flowers to imbue the liquid with immense power. In the Ogham she is known as *ruis* (ROO-SH).

June

Contemplation and Study

Reread the section dedicated to Cerridwen. There is much value in reading some of the old accounts of the witch goddess, therefore obtain a copy of *The White Goddess* by Robert Graves and read it, consult other written interpretations of Cerridwen, and compare them to your own experience. What does Cerridwen look like? Dedicate a portion of the month to creatively portraying her.

Practical

Clover (*Trifolium* spp.): A favourite symbol among the Irish and one steeped in mythology and tradition, this small, unassuming plant is prevalent throughout northern Europe and the United States. Nestled amidst the grass, the small leaves, normally found in groups of three, adorn the base of flowers that spring from tiny stems in well-drained soil. It is said that the discovery of a four-leaf clover will bestow luck and good fortune upon one who picks it. This feminine plant contains flavonoids that are oestrogenic, and as a consequence clover has long been connected with the ovaries, the breasts, and the female reproductive system. This tiny plant has a long list of medicinal qualities that bring significant properties to the brew and also imbue it with sympathetic associations regarding success, fruition, fidelity, and love.

Valerian (*Valeriana officinalis*): Standing tall and proud in wild hedgerows, white or pinkish flowering heads sway in the summer breeze; country lanes abound with the pungent aroma of this dreamy creature. Enchanted sleep threatens to subdue the hardiest warrior or mischief maker, for no matter how tough a person deems themselves to be, nobody is immune from the mighty powers of valerian. She can heal and cure a number of ailments, but she can also be used to enchant or bewitch. This versatile plant has a history as long as civilisation itself. Long before Cerridwen walked the banks of Lake Tegid, the folk of the Mediterranean utilised its powers. Commonly referred to as "all-heal," the name may well be derived from the Latin valere, meaning "to be well." She was allegedly used by Hippocrates in the fourth century BC, and she also appears in Anglo-Saxon herbals and the English healing tradition known as leechcraft.

The mighty ability of valerian to heal was extensively used during both world wars as a tincture to relieve the psychological damage caused by shell shock, implying that even modern medicine was aware of valerian's underlying, sympathetic properties. She brings to our brew the powers of sedation, sleep, purification, relaxation, anaesthetics, and the ability to guard the mind against damage caused in the darkness of trauma.

July

Contemplation and Study

Reread the section devoted to Gwion Bach. Spend the month contemplating your own spiritual journey since your spirit sensed the subtle. What brought you to the practise of Paganism? How different is your knowledge now compared to what it was a few years ago?

Practical

Oak Leaves (*Quercus* spp.): The king of the forest, the mighty oak stands proud, tall, and majestic; lowlier trees and shrubs bow in his presence, whilst within his branches creatures seek shelter. His strong, capable arms shelter and comfort the weary, and his deep-green canopy offers respite from the searing heat of summer. The oak needs little introduction. Long associated with the druid priest caste and a revered tree of northern European ship builders, his reputation as a tree of power, potency, protection, and abundance has been long established. The oak has presence; one can feel him before coming across him. Fancifully imagine the witch goddess approaching a glade where little grows; at its centre is the mighty trunk of an aged oak. She bows at the edge of the oak's canopy's range and whispers a greeting. She sings the songs of his leaves as she approaches his trunk, her hand caressing the rough bark. Her heart leaps in joyful connection with the king of the forest.

Let yourself be guided to the mighty oak and there become lost in the rapture of his presence; touch him, sing songs of praise to him. Wrap your arms about his trunk in loving embrace, sleep beneath his canopy and dream of the woodlands' tale. Gently ask and take a few leaves for the potion to imbue it with a deep sense of majesty or sovereignty. Oak's powers of protection shall instill the brew with the ability to soothe the weary spirit and offer solace and comfort. Think of potency and vitality as you cast the leaves into the simmering cauldron's belly. In the Ogham system the oak is called *duir* (DOO-ur).

Gorse Flowers (*Ulex europaeus*): Also known as the whin bush or furze, these fantastic yellow flowers emit the most delicious aroma, evocative of a distant coconut smell. He is a bush that demands attention. On moorland or in hedges and scrubland, the gorse makes use of the poorest soil and will thrive against most odds. He is a plant attributed the qualities of fire and is traditionally associated with the heathen god Thor. In the Ogham tree system he is called *onn* (ON). The yellow blossoms can be added to boiling water and simmered for an hour, into which wool or cotton may be cast for dyeing. Perhaps Cerridwen herself wandered the woodland banks of the Tegid dressed in gorse-dyed robes, her basket swinging in the crook of her arm. Take an old robe and dye it deep yellow by use of the furze blossom to use in summer rituals and ceremonies. An old English phrase states that "when gorse is out of blossom, kissing is out of fashion"; thankfully, owing to the large number of gorse species, it can be found flowering at almost any time of year.

Think of sunlight captured in a flower as you cast a handful of gorse flowers into the simmering cauldron. As the steam rises, see within it the powers of longevity and sustenance.

August

Contemplation and Study

Reread the section dedicated to Taliesin. Study the poetry of Taliesin; translations can be easily found on the Internet or by means of books listed in the bibliography. Attempt to recite some of the verses in the original language by means of the pronunciation guide included in this book. Discover how much impact the metered nature of the poetry has on the mind. Contemplate the nature of transformation. What is its purpose in a spiritual context?

Practical

Wheat (*Triticum aestivum*): The feast of Lughnassadh—*Gwyl Awst* in Wales—is the first baking of the earth, the initial harvest. It is the time of sacrifice, when John Barleycorn must be slaughtered by the harvest queen and his blood spilt upon the blessed earth. The fields transform in colour from the darkest greens to the golden ripeness of wheat, whose heads bob in the warm breeze of late summer. Crop circles magically appear amidst fields of gold; whether by hand of man or fairy, these enchanting symbols tickle the mind and senses, alerting people to the coming sacrifice. The spilling of the harvest blood results in fields of wheat sheaves that stand as sentinels to the coming change of seasons. By crushing and milling and subsequent baking, they transform into bread, the stuff of life.

Watch the wheat heads dance on the surface of the brew before they are consumed to imbue it with nourishment, strength, and the true nature of sacrifice.

Blood: The life force within every living being. In animals it is the red liquid that connects us to the realm of water; in the plant world it is the sap that rises in spring to course through branch and leaf. Blood is one of the most sacred components of the brew, for it imbues it with your quality, with the very spark of life from your own body. Previous ingredients have been from external sources. The cauldron bubbles with the essence of nature, and now you add to it the element of human nature.

The manner by which you do this can only be decided by you. The brew does not demand a pint of the blood, but it does require a good dash of the red stuff. This aspect is a true sacrifice, for it will involve the act of cutting, slicing, or sticking and some pain. Whatever method you choose, use your common sense and be responsible; ensure that any tool is extremely clean and sharp, to create a smooth cut that will heal well. If sticking, be cautious not to jab the centre of a finger, which is rich in nerves; instead, aim for the side. The resulting blood flow should be directed into an offering receptacle, held up before the gods, and then cast into the cauldron. If in any doubt, exclude it or create an essence by allowing light to shine through blood placed on a sheet of glass above a bowl of water.

September

Contemplation and Study

What is the nature of your relationship with the seasons and the phases of the moon? What do you know of the science behind the movements of our heavenly bodies? Study the passage of the sun and moon and how and why they affect the wheel of the year. How has the dance of the seasons affected the various sites you have used for the foraging of ingredients?

Practical

Acorns: The fruits of the mighty oak bring the same quality as oak into the brew, with the additional quality of nourishment and magic. Gather the acorns and crush them with a mortar and pestle before casting them into the cauldron.

Rowan Berries (*Sorbus aucuparia*): This is the mountain ash. It is the second tree of the Ogham tree alphabet and is known as *luis (loo-SH)*. It is a hardy, small tree that can grow in rather inhospitable environments. Woodlands bedecked with rowan become adorned with a profusion of blood-red berries during late summer and autumn as bunches of berries hang gracefully from branches that bend under their weight. What were previously cream flowers that sang to the bees have now been transformed into berries that sustain the birds. Witches and hedgerow pickers gather in their kitchens over simmering pots of steaming rowan-berry jellies and preserves. She is a tree of magic. Sometimes called the witching tree, she is renowned for her ability to heighten psychic abilities and visions; a branch worn about the neck will prevent enchantment by the fair folk. A loop made of her branches and hung above doors and windows will ward off negativity and unwanted spirits. Always plant a rowan near your house, in the garden or in a pot, to protect the dwelling and all who reside there.

A single bunch of rowan berries should suffice for any amount of brew prepared. Remove each berry from its stalk and lightly crush with a pestle in a mortar. Take them into your hand and feel their energy pulsing through your skin; as you cast them into the cauldron, think of the subtle powers essential for any Pagan in his or her work. The rowan brings these gifts to the brew.

October

Contemplation and Study

How does your Paganism and dedication to the gods serve your tribe and community? How do you disseminate your wisdom and skills of the magical arts? Do you teach? What is the nature of a teacher, and what responsibilities accompany this role?

Practical

Wormwood (*Artemisia absinthium*): This is artemisia; she is alluring yet deadly, and in high doses she is extremely poisonous. Her qualities are peculiar and diverse. Traditionally wormwood was used to ease digestive discomfort and stomach ache. The highly addictive liquor absinthe was created from a tincture of the plant and caused significant social problems during the nineteenth century. Common wormwood, or mugwort, has long been an important herb in Druidic and Saxon spirituality and was considered one of the most powerful herbs to repel evil spirits and counter poisons. Wormwood is highly fragrant and attractive and can be infused with boiling water and administered as a tonic after illness.

Wormwood walks the path between beneficial and baneful; she must be handled with caution and deep respect. To our brew she brings the gift of caution, warning, psychic powers, and divination. She also brings the threat of addiction and death.

Semen, Menstrual Fluid, Breast Milk: These embody the high mystery of creation and the powerful dance of sexual energy and prowess. They represent our passion, our lust and carnality; they are how we renew our species and feed our infants; they are the substances that come from the secret, powerful place in the core of our being. They embody the magic that we are inherently and inexorably attached to; they connect us to the singularity of the universe and the origin of our soul. Unlike the offering of blood, this ingredient need not be from your own body. It could be donated by a partner, or perhaps a member of your grove, coven, or group is lactating.Wherever it comes from, be sure to honour its significance and the person who donates it.

Be sensible and safe. No instructions for their extraction are needed here! Honour yourself and our species as you cast the material into the cauldron.

If you find these particular components abhorrent or wish to exclude them, by all means do so—simply subsititue the energy they embody with something of equal value. If you would rather not include them in the brew but still wish to have their potency present, create an essence by placing the substance on a piece of clear glass above a small bowl of water, then allow sunlight or moonlight to transfer the essence into the water, which you may then add to the brew.

A note for menopausal women: I would suggest that you use your own blood for this ingredient. Your blood carries the memory of your sexual potency and virility and is a beneficial addition to the brew. Rather than repeat what was performed in August, you may wish to find an alternative to blood for the August selection. I suggest a kernel of corn or that you fashion a miniature grass doll in the guise of the great mother. You may also wish to bake a loaf of bread as an offering to the spirits of the first harvest, and place some of that into the brew.

Ritual Instructions

Preferably choose either the night of the full moon or the dark of the moon to perform your monthly ritual.

You will have previously spent time meditating and connecting to the ingredients prior to and during their collection. On your chosen night pour your spring/river/lake water into your cauldron until half full, and set your cauldron above a flame to simmer.

A reality check is needed at this point! In an ideal world your cauldron will be set in the middle of your own stone circle, hung from a tripod by blackened chains above a fire of sacred woods. We don't all have such privileged ritual locations—you may have better—but the chances are you may also live in a town or a city or in the dizzying heights of a block of flats. Either way, this ritual can still be performed effectively. As previously stated, the size of your cauldron must realistically fit your location, the number of people in your group, etc. The location itself will affect the logistics of the ritual. Just remember there is no right or wrong way—it can be as elaborate or as simple as you want it to be. A cauldron big enough to accommodate a small child is equally as effective as a small cooking pot placed over a flame on your kitchen stove. The ultimate point is to connect.

Once a month, set your cauldron above a flame to warm it. Do this gently, never boil the concoction, and accompany the act with flickering candlelight and incense that pleases the spirits. As the cauldron begins to simmer and vapour rises from its surface, cast your newly gathered ingredients into it. Perform this task with vigour, with ecstatic energy; evoke the memories you have of connecting to the ingredients you offer. Summon that emotional connectivity and cast it, too, into the bubbling brew.

Take a spoon that has been specifically acquired for this act and stir the cauldron well; a good tip is to do this in multiples of three minutes, depending on the ritual you have created; i.e., stir in multiples of three minutes (three, six, nine, etc.), retain the intention, chant the verse, and so forth. Keep the mind alive and burning with intention, sing to the Goddess whose actions you mimic, call to her, see her hand upon yours, and feel her breath about your neck. Chant the following or similar:

> Stir the root, stir the flower
> Into this brew release your power!

Remove the cauldron from the heat and allow it to cool naturally. Place a lid over the vessel and ensure it is safely stored until the following month. Thank the spirits and the archetypes you have invoked during your rite.

Ritual Climax

If you began the ritual in November, the natural conclusion would be to bring it to its climax on the nearest full or dark moon a year later. Gather in some secret place and bring the cauldron to a simmer. This is the climax of your rite; you will hopefully have spent the previous year planning this night. Throw every ounce of your being into it. Ensure that the location for the final ritual is bursting at the seams with candle lights and incense smoke, with ritual attire and tools. Go crazy; launch yourself into the biggest, most dramatic ritual you can conceive. Invoke the Goddess and the prophet and summon Awen; sing until your heart is near bursting.

> *Yr Awen a ganaf, o dwfyn y dygaf*
> *(Urr Ah-when a GAN-av, ohr DOO-vn uh DUG-av)*

At a pivotal point remove some of the liquid from the belly of the cauldron, either by spoon, pipette, or what have you. If this is a solitary rite, quickly place three drops of the burning liquid onto the side of your left thumb; do this at its base where the flesh meets your hand and the skin is thicker. In a group scenario ensure that each participant has a suitable receptacle by which to perform this task; effectively time it so that each member experiences the climax simultaneously.

The brew will scald your skin. The accompanying pain is conducive to the ritual. At once, thrust the burning skin into your mouth and suck the brew away. It is at this point that the burning rays of Awen sear your very spirit; it is the culmination of all that you have done previously. Stand tall, cast your arms to your sides and out, palms forward, your body mimicking the pattern of Awen. Raise your voice in chant to invoke Awen. Become Awen. Chant until near bursting:

> *Awen, Awen, Awen!*

The ritual is complete.

What must naturally follow is the chase sequence through the elements; this can be achieved by meditation over the coming days. A process of quiet reflection and assimilation should also be planned whereby you ensure that you have time alone to digest the ritual and its effect upon you.

A Note on Inspiration

Central to the theme of the tale is the imbibing of Awen, a facet of which is inspiration. With that in mind, a major aspect of this ritual must be led by inspiration. The ritual format presented here acts only as a framework, a loose skeleton that you clothe by means of your own connection. It would be pointless for you to follow a rigorous set ritual without incorporating the primary tenet of its function: inspiration.

I can imagine that you have begun to format the manner by which this rite will be put to practise; perhaps it will serve to deepen your connection to the prophet or the Goddess. It may serve your tribe, grove, or coven as an intense, year-long working practise. Whatever the intent or idea, do make room for inspiration. As previously stated, none of the suggestions presented here are written in stone; they are as fluid as Awen itself.

Over the years, I have received several reports from groups and individuals who have practised the rite, and they all differ. Some of them retain a beautiful simplicity whilst others are elegantly dramatic. Some groups developed chants and mantras taken from the Book of Taliesin to utilise whilst casting their ingredients into the cauldron, and others developed meditative journeys to accompany the acts. Take your inspiration from this; sing to the items that are cast into the potion, and be a part of the process as much as is humanly possible. The ritual climax should reflect the dedication, devotion, and commitment you have put into this rite during the previous twelve months. You bring to this ritual your progress and myriad beings and spirits that will have followed your course. Your journal will be crammed with intricate details of plants and landscape. These are your allies; these are the friends that impart their wisdom and magic into the sacred brew. Acknowledge them as such.

Be aware of yourself and what you bring to the rite; after all, a great proportion of the brew and the magic it contains are derived from your efforts and commitment. Imagine the sheer vitality of power and inspiration the brew holds in a group setting, where several people have been immersed in a single, collective experience to achieve a singular goal.

Be inspired, be led by the spirits of your locality, and sing in praise of the gods. Enjoy the experience as a ritual of growth and transformation that will heighten and enrich your spiritual development. Ritual should be fun. It should be an enjoyable process that not only offers heart-filled connection but brings a smile to your spirit as it swims in the sense of familiarity. When we are immersed in ecstatic ritual, the subtle messages we receive from the invisible realms are like hearing news from home—they are the gossip of the gods, and they call to the part of us that is ageless.

A final word on safety and issues of health: in a group setting it may seem vulgar if not totally disgusting to ingest a fluid that contains blood, semen, etc. In a solitary rite this should not be a problem; however, in a group setting it may raise issues of concern. Practically, however, the heat of the brew will render most microbes and bacteria inactive, and the ingestion of three drops will cause no harm. Preparing the substances as an essence is a viable option that will remove this concern from the equation. Everyone is different.Be sensible and considerate of others. If the issue is too great for some, then simply substitute the items concerned.

And finally, do not keep any of the remaining fluid—remember what happened to the horses? It is symbolically toxic; therefore, pour it down the toilet.

Pagan Pilgrimage
ENCOUNTERS WITH THE LAND

The concept of pilgrimage tends to evoke images of Lourdes or the Camino to Santiago. Pilgrimage is of immense value to any tradition and serves to connect the individual with the spirits of a place and its ancestral associations. It calls for a degree of sacrifice and commitment, whether these are by means of time, effort, or finance. Taking time out of our busy lives and embarking on a physical journey to meet with the archetypes of tradition is an immensely powerful and transformative process. It causes the mind to focus on the journey; anticipating the destination but not wholly intent on arrival, the getting there is equally as important. The intention of pilgrimage is to intensify our relationship to a place and what it embodies or represents. To our forefathers, this ritual journey would have been conducted entirely on foot and may have taken days if not weeks to complete. The act of walking all or part of a pilgrimage is important, but realistically one cannot walk across the Atlantic Ocean!

The suggestion here is that a physical journey is contemplated and perhaps planned in order to visit the actual location of the tale and the home of the archetypes contained therein. The region of Bala in North Wales is incredibly beautiful, and the quiet banks of the lake are the perfect location for a ritual. However, there is no suggestion of where Cerridwen and her family may have lived, no ruin to wander amidst, no monument or altar dedicated to her and to the tale that made this place famous. It is the landscape alone that connects one to the source of the story and the mystery it contains. If the archetypes of this tale connect with you deeply and you are moved to travel to their lands, consider the following:

- How do I get there? What means of transport do I require?
- How much will it cost me?
- How much time do I need?
- Do I plan to walk some of the journey?
  If so, what plans are needed?
- Where do I stay when I arrive?
- What do I do when I arrive?

Use the Internet for advice on pilgrimage and travel planning. If you decide on a physical pilgrimage to Bala, I suggest that you ritualise your preparations. Begin by repeating the exercises given for each component of the tale; take a natural object to represent that connection, then paint or draw upon it a symbol or glyph that expresses your relationship with it. Place these objects on your altar until you depart. As part of your ritual in Bala, incorporate the connections you have forged into the ceremony and leave the objects near the lakeshore as offerings to the energies they represent.

The Book of Pheryllt

Cerridwen consulted the Book of Pheryllt for instruction in the brewing of Awen. We know very little of the actual function or role of the Pheryllt, but the name can be translated to mean "chemist" or "alchemist." Academia links the Pheryllt as a euphemism for the magician Virgil, but in local lore and legend they are proclaimed as supernatural beings who watch the affairs of humanity. This exercise encourages you to connect to them and to glean from that connection information to create your own Book of Pheryllt.

It is believed that the Pheryllt occupied a city in North Wales, perpetuated by Edward Davies as *Dinas Affaraon*, meaning "the ambrosial city." Gather your thoughts of the Pheryllt and their location, extinguish all artificial lights, and bathe yourself in the subtle glow of candlelight. Create sacred space according to your own practise, but rather than call on the four elements, focus instead on the Celtic powers of land, water, and air. Acknowledge each one by means of your connection to them. Light the three candles on your altar and call to Cerridwen, Taliesin, and Awen. Now imagine the following:

A closed curtain appears before you, and for a moment you contemplate it; you cause the material to part. Before you is a mountainside, green and lush. With the bleating of sheep breaking the stillness, it is raining. Dark grey clouds pummel the sky above you, and the raindrops fall to bleed against your skin. Ahead of you rises a city that seems to erupt from the very fabric of the earth; its surfaces are encrusted in gems and crystals of the earth. Approach the city.

An arched gateway leads you beyond the walls of the city. In the centre of the courtyard stands a tall, square building set apart from the others. Its doors are open and lights flicker within; from its interior the sweet scent of burning pine reaches your nostrils. You venture closer and enter the dry warmth of the building.

It is a single hall, its floors polished black as night. In the centre stands a fire bowl in which burn flames of green and blue. Beyond it there stands an androgynous individual dressed in a black robe. Its hair is pure white and drapes gracefully about its shoulders; it nods and smiles at you. This is one of the Pheryllt.

You approach the fire bowl and take your place opposite the creature. Reach out with your mind and ask that it share some of its wisdom and magic with you. If in agreement, observe as the Pheryllt reaches forward, its hand moving directly through the flame; in its hands it holds a book. Feel the heat of the flames prickle your skin as you reach forward and accept the book from it. Allow the subtle powers of your imagination to accept symbols and messages from this hall and your interaction with the Pheryllt. When you sense it is time to depart, allow your body to float backwards and away from this place.

As the curtains close, sense yourself returning to your physical location.

Now create your own Book of Pheryllt, a book of magic. There was a time that every witch and druid would have one of these, but I fear the practise is waning. And yet a Book of Magic is essential for the continuation of our legacy. Be creative: what did you see with your encounter with the Pheryllt? What did the book look like? Can you re-create it? Find, buy, or make a book that will be used exclusively to collect your spells, incantations, and conjurations. Begin by transferring the details of the ingredients needed in the primary ritual into your book, and record any chants or mantras that you may have employed during the ritual. This book should not be confused with your journal; rather, it should reflect the practical aspects of your Craft and the recording of your magical practise.

Keep the book in a safe place and ensure that it will be bequeathed to someone worthy of its knowledge upon your death.

Afterword

Where do you go from here? What happens now?

The cauldron has brewed its magic, and the searing heat of Awen has scalded your thumb and caused your spirit to burn brighter. The journey into mystery continues—it does not end with the spilling of the cauldron's content. The end of this tale is merely the beginning of your adventure into the heart of the Celtic mysteries.

Consider the components of the tale—Morfran Afagddu, Creirfyw, Morda, Tegid Foel; what of them? Have they simply vanished into some Celtic otherworld of redundant archetypes? On the contrary, they continue to exist in you; you carry their qualities with you. Having acknowledged them as facets of your own spirit, humanity, and personality and offered them to the cauldron, they remain aspects of you that continue into your future; they are an essential aspect of your unique song. They have not been vanquished, they are not individual beings who lived in a distant era, and they rise anew from the spirit of every initiate that treads the damp grass to the cauldron's rim.

Having faced the cauldron and your own magical transformation, you also face the responsibility of using that experience for the benefit of yourself and others. You are in prime position to tease the qualities essential for the brew—as seen in the archetypes—from the spirits of those who are called to the cauldron. One responds by disseminating the wisdom of the Celts to those of good intention, and by doing so you strive to maintain a mystery tradition that has been thousands of years in the making.

Do not lose your connection to the cauldron and its guardian; continue to serve the witch goddess in your endeavours, in your Craft and magical practise. You are transformed and inspired by the rays of Awen that shine from the darkness of potentiality; powerful spirits and gods walk with you, allies in your quest of mystery and magic. Other secrets await you; seek them out, find them in hidden pages of wisdom, and listen to them in the whispers of trees.

The burning fire of the Celtic spirit gleams within you, its light radiant and awe inspiring, for you are from the cauldron born.

Glossary

Please note that the Welsh letters "ll," "ch," "dd," and "rh" remain in their current form with no phonetic equivalent provided. Refer to the pronunciation guide for guidance.

Annwfn (*ANN-oo-vn*), **also Annwn** (*ANN-oon*)—A Welsh term for the indigenous underworld of the Celts, accessible via liminal locations. Its inhabitants are free to wander into our dimension and interbreed.

Arianrhod (*Ar-ee-ANN-rod*)—Goddess, daughter of the mother goddess Don, and figure in the Fourth Branch of the Mabinogi.

Awen (*AH-when*)—The flowing, unifying spirit of Celtic Paganism.

Ayrwen (*AER-wen*)—One of the Celtic goddesses of war and battle; a tutelary deity of the river Dee.

Bala (*BA-laa*)—The town in the county of Gwynedd in North Wales where the tale takes place.

Bard (*BARRED*)—A Celtic poet or magician.

Beli Mawr (*BELL-ee MA-oor*)—An ancestor deity of the British pantheon. Literally means "big fire or light."

Bendigeidfran (*Ben-dee-GAYD-vran*)—A giant, one of the rulers of the islands of Britain, and a character in the Second Branch of the Mabinogi. His head is said to be buried beneath the Tower of London and protects the islands from attack.

Blodeuedd *(Blod-AYE-edd)*—A woman created from flowers in the Fourth Branch of the Mabinogi. Her name changes from Blodeuedd in her human form to Blodeuwedd *(Blod-AYE-wedd)* when she is in owl form.

Bol Croen *(BOL KRR-oyn)*—Literally translated as "skin-belly" and synonymous with womb; the coracle, or vessel, into which the newborn Taliesin is placed.

Branwen *(BRAN-wen)*—Goddess and sister of Bendigeidfran in the Second Branch of the Mabinogi.

Bryn Y Carnau *(BR-in Uh KARNN-eye)*—A sacred cliff near the lake of Llyn Cerrig Bach on the island of Anglesey.

Caer *(KA-eer)*—Welsh term for "fort."

Caergyfylchi *(KA-eer-GUV-ul-Chi)*—The city reputed to be the location of a temple dedicated to Cerridwen.

Calan Gaeaf *(Kal-ANN Gay-av)*—The Welsh term for the feast of Samhain/Halloween. Literally translates as "the calends of winter."

Calan Mai *(Kal-ANN My)*—The Welsh term for Beltane/May Day. Literally translates as "the calends of May."

Celtica *(KELTEE-KA)*—The name given to the combined cultures of the six Celtic nations and the spirit of Celticness that unites them.

Cerridwen *(Kerr-ID-wen)*—The witch goddess and primary initiator.

Creiddylad *(Kray-DD-Ulad)*—One of the fairest maidens to have lived; two male deities fight for her hand in marriage every May Day until the end of time. She appears in the epic tale of how Culhwch won Olwen.

Creirfyw *(Kray-Rh-view)*—One of the fairest maidens to have lived; the daughter of Tegid and Cerridwen, sister of Morfran Afagddu.

Crochen *(Kraw-CH-en)*—Welsh term meaning "cauldron."

Culhwch ac Olwen *(KILL-Hoo-ch ak OL-wen)*—One of the oldest native tales of Wales in which appear characters from the tale of Taliesin.

Cyfarwydd *(Kuv-ARR-with)*—Literally means "to be familiar," a term used for magician.

Cynfyd *(KIN-Vid)*—The "before" world, or the old world.

Dall *(DA-ll)*—Welsh term meaning "blind."

Dallmor Dallme *(da-LL-more da-LL-mare)*—One of the names attributed to Morda, which can be taken to mean "blind sea, blind stone."

Daroganwr *(Darr-oh-GAN-oor)*—Welsh term for "prophet."

Deganwy *(Deg-ANN-wee)*—A coastal north Wales town reputed to be the home of Maelgwn Gwynedd.

Don *(DONN)*—Primary Celtic mother goddess whose offspring are the primary characters of many of the Mabinogi tales.

Dryw *(DREW)*—Alleged old Welsh name for druid/magician.

Duwies *(DEEW-yes)*—Welsh term meaning "goddess."

Dwygyfylchi *(Dwee-GUV-ul-chi)*—The modern-day location of Caergyfylchi.

Dyfrdwy *(DUV-rr-dooee)*—The modern Welsh name for the river Ayrwen; literally means "the river of the Goddess."

Efnysien *(Ev-NIS-ee-en)*—A counterpart to Morfran Afagddu and representation of the shadow aspect found in the Second Branch of the Mabinogi.

Elffin *(EL-phin)*—The son of Gwyddno Garanhir who discovers Taliesin in the salmon weir.

Feddwit *(FEDD-wit)*—A fortification in the poem "The Spoils of Annwn."

Gellilyfdy *(Gell-ee-LUV-dee)*—The location where John Jones compiled Peniarth MS 111.

Goludd *(GOL-eedd)*—A fortification in the poem "The Spoils of Annwn."

Gorsedd *(GORE-Seth)*—A seating or a collection of bards.

Gwion Bach *(GWEE-on BA-ch)*—The main protagonist and metaphor for the student of the Celtic mysteries.

Gwyddno Garanhir *(GWEEth-No GAR-ann-Heer)*—The owner of the weir in which Taliesin is discovered. *Garanhir* translates as "long shanks."

Gwydion *(GWEED-eeon)*—A magician renowned for his skills in magic who appears in the Fourth Branch of the Mabinogi and is mentioned by name in several of the Taliesin poems.

Gwyn ap Nudd *(GWIN ap NEE-th)*—A Celtic deity. Reputedly the king of the fairies, he leads the Wild Hunt on Samhain Eve to gather the spirits of the dead. He fights with Gwythyr every May Day for the hand of Creiddylad.

Gwyniad *(GWIN-iad)*—Small white fish. A remnant from the Ice Age, they inhabit the lake at Bala and are unique to that location—they aren't found anywhere else on the planet.

Gwythyr ap Greidol *(GWEE-thr ap GRAY-dol)*—A Celtic deity who fights Gwyn ap Nudd for the hand of Creiddylad.

Iolo Morganwg *(YOLO More-GAN-oog)*—Poet genius and recorder of Druidic wisdom and theology, some of which is believed to be forged.

Llanfair Caereinion *(LL-ann Vai-rr Kare-EIN-eeon)*—The village reputed to be the birthplace of Gwion Bach.

Llanuwchllyn *(Llann-EWWch-ll-in)*—The village on the western shores of Lake Tegid.

Lleu Llaw Gyffes *(LL-ay LL-aw GUFF-ess)*—Abandoned son of Arian-rhod, a central figure in the Fourth Branch of the Mabinogi. His name literally means "light, of skilful hand."

Llyn Cerrig Bach *(LL-in KERR-eeg BA-ch)*—Sacred lake on the island of Anglesey. A site of significant Druidic offerings discovered during the Second World War.

Llyn Tegid *(LL-in TEG-id)*—The Welsh name for the lake famed in the tale.

Llyr *(LL-ir)*—Celtic god of the sea whose offspring play significant roles in the Mabinogi tales. He was one of the three exalted prisoners of the islands of Britain.

Mabinogi *(Mab-INN-Og-ee)*—Small tales, or tales of youth, the collective name given to a series of native Welsh tales, the most famed being the Four Branches of the Mabinogi. Mabinogion is an Anglicisation assumed to have been coined by Lady Charlotte Guest; the correct form—Mabinogi—appears in the original manuscripts.

Maelgwn Gwynedd *(MA-eel-Goon GWIN-eth)*—King of Gwynedd in the sixth century.

Manawydan *(Man-ah-WID-ann)*—Primary character in the Third Branch of the Mabinogi.

Mona *(Moan-Ah)*—The Celto-Romano name for the island of Mon/Anglesey, chief seat of the British druids.

Mor *(More)*—Welsh word meaning "sea."

Morda *(MORE-da)*—The blind man employed to stoke the fires beneath the cauldron.

Morfran Afagddu *(More-VRA-nn Av-AG-thee)*—The ugly son of Tegid and Cerridwen, the brother of Creirfyw.

Ochren *(OCH-wren)*—A fortification in the poem "The Spoils of Annwn."

Ogyrwen *(OGRE-wen)*—Of unknown origin, believed to be a spirit of personification or a goddess of great antiquity.

Pair *(PA-eer)*—Welsh term meaning "cauldron." Used interchangeably with *crochen.*

Pedryfan *(Ped-RUV-ann)*—The four-walled enclosure synonymous with the island of Britain. A fortification in the poem "The Spoils of Annwn."

Pharaon *(FAR-Ah-on)*—Legendary priesthood of magicians perpetuated by Edward Davies.

Pheryllt *(FAIR-ee-llt)*—The unknown caste of magicians that Cerridwen consulted, also synonymous with the magician Virgil.

Pryderi *(PRUD-erry)*—The kidnapped son of Rhiannon who is the main protagonist in the First, Third, and Fourth Branches of the Mabinogi.

Prydwen *(PRUD-wen)*—The divine feminine figure in the poem "The Spoils of Annwn," she is represented as a ship that carries Arthur, Taliesin, and their explorers on a quest in search of the cauldron.

Pwca *(POO-ka)*—A mischievous Welsh nature spirit.

Pwyll *(PWEE-ll)*—The main character of the First Branch of the Mabinogi who trades places with the King of Annwn. He is Rhiannon's husband.

Rhiannon *(Rhee-ANN-onn)*—A goddess, also known as Epona in Celto-Romano culture, and a main character in the First and Third Branches of the Mabinogi. She is the otherworldly wife of Pwyll and the mother of Pryderi.

Rigor *(REE-gor)*—A fortification in the poem "The Spoils of Annwn."

Siddi *(SIDD-ee)*—A fortification in the poem "The Spoils of Annwn."

Syw *(SEE-OO)*—Alleged old Welsh name for "sage" or "sorcerer."

Taliesin *(Tal-YES-inn)*—The Prophetic Spirit, poet, he with the radiant brow; Gwion Bach becomes Taliesin.

Tegid Foel *(TEG-id Vo-yal)*—Cerridwen's husband, the tutelary deity of Lake Tegid in Bala.

Vandwy *(VAN-doo-ee)*—A fortification in the poem "The Spoils of Annwn."

Wydr *(WID-hr)*—A fortification in the poem "The Spoils of Annwn."

Ynys Y Kedeirn *(UN-is Ugh KED-airn)*—A Welsh term meaning "Island of the Mighty," an old name for the island of Britain.

A Guide to Welsh Pronunciation
THE LANGUAGE OF THE GODS

The Welsh language is one of the oldest indigenous languages in Europe; by connecting to it you are being linked to thousands of years of history. The language may appear to serve only to twist the tongue and demand guttural utterances from unfamiliar parts of your vocal range. Your lips may tremble in effort and your tongue collapse from the confines of your mouth whilst spittle spatters anyone in close proximity. But fear not: it is not necessary to engage the spitfire operations of your mouth. Welsh, whatever you have been led to believe, is not as difficult as you would imagine. All that is required is the complete surrender of your normal vocal programming and the ability to embrace something new yet ancient.

There are tricks, the most significant being your ability to enunciate. The English tongue and palate is firm, precise; the Welsh tongue is loose, the palate free, the mouth fully engaged. Let your mouth *move* when pronouncing the Welsh language—set free the muscles of your face and throw yourself into this most musical of languages. The English mouth can be a rather lazy mouth—words fall limply from the cavity—whereas Welsh is similar in nature to Italian, where the mouth is flung open to enunciate each letter and word with utmost passion and flair; whilst you're at it, throw in your arms! Our language is colourful, rhythmic, and dances from the whole body. Let loose the English stiff upper lip and go for it!

The key to effective pronunciation is in the phonetic nature of the language; i.e., every single letter is utilised, every sound is important to the whole word. If you can pronounce the letters, you can pronounce the words.

The World Wide Web has video and audio tutorials that can be consulted free of charge for sound comparison. So, with all that said, here follows a list of the letters and sounds.

The stress of any word almost exclusively stands on the penultimate, or next to last, syllable.

The Welsh Alphabet

a, b, c, ch, d, dd, e, f, ff, g, ng, h, i, l, ll, m, n, o, p, ph, r, rh, s, t, th, u, w, y

Welsh Vowels

a -	Short as in *mat*	long as in *farmer*
e-	Short as in *let*	long as in *bear*
i-	Short as in *pit*	long as in *meet*
o-	Short as in *lot*	long as in *lore*
u-	Short as in *ill*	long as in *limb*
w-	Short as in *look*	long as in *fool*
y-	Short as in *up*	long as in *under*

Welsh Consonants

Some may be similar in sound to their English counterparts but with emphasis on heavy aspiration of sound.

b-	as in *bin*
c-	as in *cat*
ch-	as in *loch*, never as in *chin*
d-	as in *dad*
dd-	as in *them*, never as in *thin*
e-	as in *elephant*
f-	as in *van*
ff-	as in *off*
g-	as in *gate*, never as in *gem*
ng-	as in *song*, never as in *linger*
h-	as in *hit*; it is never silent

l-   as in *lit*

ll-   no counterpart; voice by placing tip of tongue in *L* position and exhaling voicelessly through the sides of the mouth

m-   as in *mat*

n-   as in *nit*

p-   as in *part*

ph-   as in *phrase*

r-   trilled by the tip of the tongue, as *ravioli* in Italian

rh-   no counterpart; voice by placing tongue in *R* position and exhaling quickly and harshly but voicelessly through the narrow gap the lips form

s-   as in *sit*, never as in *kiss*

t-   as in *tap*

th-   as in *thick*, never as in *them*

Bibliography

Manuscripts Consulted

NLW MS 5276D. Chroncile of the History of the World. Elis Gruffudd. ca. 1552. National Library of Wales.

Peniarth MS 111. Hanes Taliesin. John Jones. 1607. National Library of Wales.

Peniarth MS 2. Llyfr Taliesin (Book of Taliesin). Fourteenth Century. National Library of Wales.

These manuscripts can be viewed by means of the National Library of Wales website, which can be found at www.llgc.org.uk; follow the links to "Digital Mirror."

◆ ◆ ◆

Ab Ithel, Williams J., trans. *The Barddas of Iolo Morganwg*. Boston: Weiser Books, 2004 (original 1862).

Anwyl, E. *The Poetry of the Gogynfeirdd*. Denbigh: Gee and Son, MDCCCCIX [sic].

Bevan, Gareth, and Patrick Donovan, eds. *Geiriadur Prifysgol Cymru (A Dictionary of the Welsh Language)*. Cardiff: University of Wales Press, 2004.

Blake, Steve, and Scott Lloyd. *The Keys to Avalon*. Shaftesbury: Element, 2000.

Bown, Deni. *The Royal Horticultural Society New Encyclopaedia of Herbs and Their Uses*. London: Dorling Kindersley, 1995.

Breeze, Andrew. *Medieval Welsh Literature*. Dublin: Four Courts Press, 1997.

Brickell, Christopher, ed. *The Royal Horticultural Society Gardeners' Encyclopaedia of Plants and Flowers*. London: Dorling Kindersley, 1989.

Bromwich, Rachel, and Simon D. Evans. *Culhwch ac Olwen*. Cardiff: Gwasg Prifysgol Cymru, 1997.

Bromwich, Rachel, ed. *Trioedd Ynys Prydein: The Triads of the Island of Britain*. Cardiff: University of Wales Press, 2006.

Caldecott, Moyra. *Taliesin and Avagddu*. Somerset: Bran's Head, 1983.

Campbell, Joseph. *The Inner Reaches of Outer Space*. Novato, CA: New World Library, 2002.

Carr-Gomm, Philip. *Druid Mysteries*. London: Random House, 2002.

Chopra, Deepak. *Life After Death*. London: Rider Books, 2006.

Cullum, Elizabeth. *A Cottage Herbal*. London: David & Charles, 1975.

Cunningham, Scott. *Encyclopedia of Magical Herbs*. St. Paul, MN: Llewellyn, 2000.

Daniel, Iestyn R. *A Medieval Welsh Mystical Treatise*. Aberystwyth: University of Wales Centre for Advanced Welsh and Celtic Studies, 1997.

Davies, Edward. *The Mythology and Rites of the British Druids*. London: J. Booth, 1809.

Davies, Sioned. *The Mabinogion*. Oxford: Oxford University Press, 2007.

Edwards, J. G., ed. *An Inventory of the Ancient Monuments in Anglesey*. London: The Royal Commission on Ancient & Historical Monuments in Wales, 1937.

Evans, J. Gwenogvryn. *The Black Book of Carmarthen*. Pwllheli: Evans, 1910.

———. *Facsimile and Text of the Book of Taliesin*. Llanbedrog: Evans, 1910.

———. *The Text of the Book of Aneirin*. Pwllheli: Evans, 1922.

———. *The White Book of Mabinogion (Llyfr Gwyn Rhydderch)*. Pwllheli: Evans, 1909.

Evans, William. *The Bards of the Isle of Britain*. Red Wharf Bay: Evans, 1915.

Flowers, Betty Sue, ed. *Joseph Campbell: The Power of Myth*. New York: Doubleday, 1988.

Ford, Patrick K. *The Celtic Poets*. Belmont: Ford & Bailie, 1999.

———. *The Death of Merlin in the Chronicle of Elis Gruffudd*. Los Angeles, CA: University of California Press, 1976.

———. *A Fragment of the Hanes Taliesin by Llywelyn Sion*. Paris: Etudes Celtiques, 1975.

———. *Ystoria Taliesin*. Cardiff: University of Wales Press, 1992.

———, ed. *Math uab Mathonwy*. Belmont: Ford & Bailie, 1999.

———, trans. *The Mabinogi and Other Medieval Welsh Tales*. Los Angeles, CA: University of California Press, 1977.

Fox, Cyril. *A Find of the Early Iron Age from Llyn Cerrig Bach, Anglesey*. Cardiff: National Museum of Wales, 1946.

Frazer, Sir James. *The Golden Bough*. Ware: Wordsworth Reference, 1993.

French, Claire. *The Celtic Goddess*. Edinburgh: Floris Books, 2001.

Fries, Jan. *Cauldron of the Gods: A Manual of Celtic Magick*. Oxford: Mandrake Press, 2003.

Geoffrey of Monmouth. *The History of the Kings of Britain*. London: Penguin Classics, 1966.

———. *The Life of Merlin: Vita Merlini*. Marston Gate: Forgotten Books, 2008.

Grant, Angela. *Magical Transformations in Pedeir Keinc y Mabinogi and Hanes Taliesin*. University of Oxford Mphil Thesis (unpublished), 2010.

Graves, Robert. *The White Goddess*. London: Faber and Faber, 1961.

Green, Miranda Aldhouse. *Dying for the Gods*. Stroud, Gloucestershire: Tempus Publishing, 2002.

———. *The Quest for the Shaman*. London: Thames & Hudson, 2005.

———. *Seeing the Woods for the Trees: The Symbolism of Trees and Wood in Ancient Gaul and Britain*. Aberystwyth: University of Wales Centre for Advanced Welsh and Celtic Studies, 2000.

Green, Miranda J. *Exploring the World of the Druids*. London: Thames & Hudson, 1997.

———. *The Gods of the Celts*. Gloucester: Allan Sutton, 1986.

Griggs, Barbara. *The Green Witch*. London: Vermilion, 1993.

Guest, Lady Charlotte, trans. *Mabinogion, the Four Branches*. Felin Fach: Llannerch Publications, 1990.

Gwyndaf, Robin. *Welsh Folk Tales*. Cardiff: National Museums and Galleries of Wales, 1999.

Hallam, Tudur. *Croesholi Tystoliaeth y Llyfrau Cyfraith: Pencerdd a Bardd Teulu*. Cardiff: Llen Cymru, Gwasg Prifysgol Cymru, 1999.

Hamp, Eric. "Varia II." *Ériu*, vol 29. Dublin: Royal Irish Academy, 1978.

Haycock, Marged, ed. and trans. *Legendary Poems from the Book of Taliesin*. Aberystwyth: CMCS, 2007.

———. *Llyfr Taliesin, Cylchgrawn Llyfrgell Genedlaethol Cymru Cyf XXV*. Aberystwyth: Rhif 4, 1988.

———. "Preiddeu Annwn and the Figure of Taliesin." *Studia Celtica*, vol. XVIII/XIX. Cardiff: University of Wales Press, 1983/84.

Hughes, H. Brython. *Tlysau Ynys Prydein*. Wrexham: Hughes a'i fab, 1902.

Hughes, Kristoffer. *Natural Druidry*. Loughborough: Thoth Publications, 2007.

Hume, Rob. *RSPB Complete Birds of Britain & Europe*. London: Dorling Kindersley, 2003.

Hutton, Ronald. *Blood and Mistletoe*. New Haven: Yale University Press, 2009.

———. *The Druids*. London: Hambledon Continuum, 2007.

Ifans, Rhiannon. *Gwerthfawrogi'r Chwedlau*. Aberystwyth: Y Ganolfan Astudiaethau Addysg, 1999.

Isaac, Evan. *Coelion Cymru*. Aberystwyth: Y Clwb Llyfrau Cymreig, 1938.

Jarman, A. O. H. *Chwedlau Cymraeg Canol*. Cardiff: Gwasg Prifysgol Cymru, 1979.

Jenkins, Gareth H. *Fact, Fantasy and Fiction: The Historical Vision of Iolo Morganwg*. Aberystwyth: University of Wales Centre for Advanced Welsh and Celtic Studies, 1997.

Jones, Gwyn, and Thomas Jones, trans. *The Mabinogion*. London: Everyman's Library, 1949.

Jones, Tho. *The Welsh-English Dictionary of 1688*. Llanwrda: Black Pig Press, 1977.

Jung, C. G. *Memories, Dreams, Reflections*. New York: Vintage, 1989.

Koch, John T., ed. *The Celtic Heroic Age*. Aberystwyth: Celtic Studies Publications, 2000.

László, Ervin. *Science and the Akashic Field*. Rochester, NY: Inner Traditions, 2004, 2007.

Lewis, Ceri W. *Iolo Morganwg*. Caernarfon: Gwasg Pantycelyn, 1995.

Lynch, Frances. *Prehistoric Anglesey*. Llangefni: The Anglesey Antiquarian Society, 1970.

MacCulloch, J. A. *The Religion of the Ancient Celts*. London: Constable, 1911.

Markale, Jean. *The Druids*. Rochester, NY: Inner Traditions, 1999.

Matthews, Caitlín. *Mabon and the Guardians of Celtic Britain*. Rochester, NY: Inner Traditions, 2002.

Matthews, John. *Taliesin: The Last Celtic Shaman*. Rochester, NY: Inner Traditions, 2002.

Morris, Jan. *Wales: Epic Views of a Small Country*. London: Penguin, 2000.

Morris-Jones, John. *Taliesin*. Cardiff: Y Cymrodor, 1918.

Morton, H. V. *In Search of Wales*. London: Methuen & Co., 1932.

Nash, D. W. *Taliesin or Bards and Druids of Britain*. London: John Russell Smith, 1858.

Neumann, Erich. *The Great Mother*. London: Routledge & Kegan Paul, 1963.

Osbon, Diane, K. *A Joseph Campbell Companion*. New York: Harper Collins, 1991.

Owen, Elias. *Welsh Folklore* (facsimile). Felinfach: Llanerch Publishers, 1996.

Parker, Will. *The Four Branches of the Mabinogi.* California: Bardic Press, 2005.

Pennar, Meirion, trans.*The Black Book of Carmarthen.* Felinfach: Llanerch Publishers, 1989.

———. *Taliesin Poems.* Felinfach: Llanerch Publishers, 1988.

Rees, Alwyn, and Brinley Rees. *Celtic Heritage.* London: Thames & Hudson, 1961.

Ross, Anne. *Druids: Preachers of Immortality.* Stroud: Tempus, 1999.

———. *Pagan Celtic Britain.* London: Constable, 1967.

Rowlands, Henry. *Mona Antiqua Restaurata.* Dublin: Robert Owen, 1723.

Skene, W. F. *The Four Ancient Books of Wales.* Edinburgh: Edmonston & Douglas, 1868.

Spence, Lewis. *The History and Origins of Druidism.* Van Nuys: Newcastle Publishing, 1995.

Taylor, Timothy. *The Buried Soul: How Humans Invented Death.* London: Fourth Estate, 2002.

Thomas, Gwyn. *Duwiau'r Celtiaid.* Llanrwst: Gwasg Carreg Gwalch, 1992.

Thomson, Derick S. *Branwen Uerch Lyr.* Dublin: The Dublin Institute for Advanced Studies, 1986.

Tolstoy, Nikolai. *The Quest for Merlin.* London: Hamish Hamilton, 1985.

Trevelyan, Marie. *Welsh Witchcraft, Charms and Spells.* Weston-Super-Mare: Oakmagic, 1999.

Vickery, Roy. *Oxford Dictionary of Plant-Lore.* Oxford: Oxford University Press, 1995.

Wade-Evans, A. G., ed. *Vitae Sanctorum Britanniae et Genealogiae.* Cardiff: Board of Celtic Studies, 1944.

Williams, R. *A Dictionary of Eminent Welshmen.* LLandovery: W. Rees, 1852.

Williams, Sir Ifor. *Canu Aneirin*. Cardiff: Gwasg Prifysgol Cymru, 1938.

————, ed., trans. *The Poems of Taliesin*. Dublin: The Dublin Institute for Advanced Studies, 1987.

————. *Chwedl Taliesin*. Cardiff: Gwasg Prifysgol Cymru, 1957.

Williams, Taliesin. *Iolo Manuscripts*. Liverpool: The Welsh Manuscripts Society, 1848.

Index

GET MORE AT LLEWELLYN.COM

Visit us online to browse hundreds of our books and decks, plus sign up to receive our e-newsletters and exclusive online offers.

- **Free tarot readings • Spell-a-Day • Moon phases**
- **Recipes, spells, and tips • Blogs • Encyclopedia**
- **Author interviews, articles, and upcoming events**

GET SOCIAL WITH LLEWELLYN

Find us on **Facebook**

www.Facebook.com/LlewellynBooks

Follow us on

www.Twitter.com/Llewellynbooks

GET BOOKS AT LLEWELLYN

LLEWELLYN ORDERING INFORMATION

 Order online: Visit our website at www.llewellyn.com to select your books and place an order on our secure server.

 Order by phone:
- Call toll free within the U.S. at 1-877-NEW-WRLD (1-877-639-9753)
- Call toll free within Canada at 1-866-NEW-WRLD (1-866-639-9753)
- We accept VISA, MasterCard, and American Express

 Order by mail:
Send the full price of your order (MN residents add 6.875% sales tax) in U.S. funds, plus postage and handling to: Llewellyn Worldwide, 2143 Wooddale Drive Woodbury, MN 55125-2989

POSTAGE AND HANDLING

STANDARD (U.S. & Canada):
(Please allow 12 business days)
$25.00 and under, add $4.00.
$25.01 and over, FREE SHIPPING.

INTERNATIONAL ORDERS (airmail only):
$16.00 for one book, plus $3.00 for each additional book.

Visit us online for more shipping options. Prices subject to change.

FREE CATALOG!

To order, call
1-877-NEW-WRLD
ext. 8236
or visit our
website

"Respectful to tradition and relevant to the present . . .
An engaging and readable introduction to Druidry for today."
—JOHN MICHAEL GREER,
Grand Archdruid of the Ancient Order of Druids in America and the author of *The Druidry Handbook*

Penny Billington

THE PATH
of
DRUIDRY

Walking the Ancient Green Way

The Path of Druidry
Walking the Ancient Green Way

Penny Billington

Druidry is very much alive and relevant in today's world. Discover how to embark on this green and magical path—and enrich your life with its ancient wisdom.

British Druid Penny Billington offers a clear and structured course of study that highlights the mysteries, magic, and modern practice of this nature-based tradition. Each chapter begins with a captivating Welsh mythic tale that introduces lessons and key concepts. Practical exercises will help you internalize these truths, develop a spiritual awareness rooted in nature, connect to the multi-dimensional world, and ultimately adopt a druidic worldview to guide you in everyday life.

From joining a druidic community to beginning a solitary path, this unique spiritual guide offers advice on everything you need to know about practicing Druidry today.

978-0-7387-2346-4

7½ x 9⅛

360 pp.

To Order, Call 1-877-NEW-WRLD

Prices subject to change without notice

ORDER AT LLEWELLYN.COM 24 HOURS A DAY, 7 DAYS A WEEK!

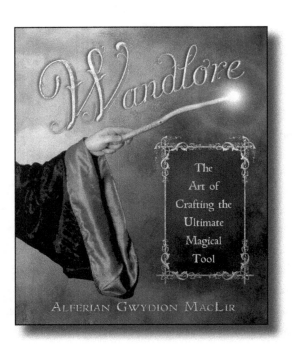

Wandlore

The
Art of
Crafting the
Ultimate
Magical
Tool

ALFERIAN GWYDION MacLIR

Wandlore
The Art of Crafting the Ultimate Magical Tool

Alferian Gwydion MacLir

This enchanting, one-of-a-kind guidebook is for anyone who's ever wanted to know how magic wands work or longed to have a real magic wand of his or her own. Written by the foremost authority on the making of wands, this book is the first devoted solely to the art of wandmaking and its mysteries. It approaches the craft from its theoretical foundations, through the selection of wood and the art of carving, to the enchantment and dedication that charge a wand for magical use. Readers will discover how a tree branch is transformed into a wand of magic, gain an understanding of the tree spirits, or dryads, and learn about stones and their powers. This book reveals the true use of phoenix feathers and unicorn hair as wand cores. No magician, Witch, or Druid should be without this groundbreaking work.

978-0-7387-2002-9

7½ x 9⅛

288 pp.

To Order, Call 1-877-NEW-WRLD

Prices subject to change without notice

ORDER AT LLEWELLYN.COM 24 HOURS A DAY, 7 DAYS A WEEK!

ELLEN EVERT HOPMAN

PRIESTESS
OF THE FIRE TEMPLE
— A DRUID'S TALE —